A Psychological Understanding of Criticism and Mental Health

A Psychological Understanding of Criticism and Mental Health examines how criticism impacts mental health, relationships and communication across diverse contexts, offering evidence-based strategies for mental health practitioners seeking to foster resilience and support healthier interactions in their clients.

Readers will gain a comprehensive understanding of how criticism is expressed, perceived and managed in various situations, including families, schools and diverse cultural contexts. Chapters explore topics including, but not limited to, the neuroscientific basis of responses to criticism, the role of caregiver burden in critical communication, the effectiveness of family interventions as it is tailored to cultural needs and Depict VR—a virtual reality intervention. Practical guidance is highlighted throughout to show how practitioners may support constructive conversations and promote positive communication.

This book is essential reading for mental health practitioners, educators, caregivers and individuals seeking to improve communication skills and navigate criticism in personal, professional and cultural contexts. It also serves as a valuable resource for practitioners aiming to strengthen therapeutic relationships with patients and those that support them.

Preethi Premkumar is a psychologist, neuroscientist and expert in anxiety in family relationships and other social contexts. She also designs digital mental health applications to improve relationships.

'We are all more sensitive to negativity than the positives in life, and this is more likely at times of stress and mental ill health. This book on criticism looks in detail at the research on how we can be affected by negative comments from others, particularly when there are ongoing serious mental health problems, and explains clearly what we know and the mechanisms that underlie our emotional and neurological responses. Helpfully, the chapters are threaded with suggestions about how these might be mitigated, and how negativity might be managed and reduced to improve our relationships.'

Professor Elizabeth Kuipers, *OBE, NIHR Senior Investigator Emerita, leading clinical psychologist and expert in family intervention and cognitive behavioural therapy for psychosis*

'Criticism is central to the mental health of us all. We know that helping families approach their loved ones without criticism can protect people from breaking down, including those with severe mental ill health such as schizophrenia. This excellent book explores the role of criticism in relationships and the social, cultural, educational, biological and behavioural explanations of the response to criticism – an outstanding contribution to the importance of criticism in mental health, with a ton of research to back it up. The book also gives really useful suggestions on how to handle criticism and be more constructive in our daily communication. A really valuable contribution, useful for academics and practitioners alike.'

Professor Tim Kendall, *CBE DUniv MD (Hons) FRCPsyc, national clinical lead for new models of mental health care within NHS England*

A Psychological Understanding of Criticism and Mental Health

From Theory to Practice

Edited by Preethi Premkumar

Routledge
Taylor & Francis Group
LONDON AND NEW YORK

Designed cover image: Kerry Annett via Getty Images

First published 2027
by Routledge
4 Park Square, Milton Park, Abingdon, Oxon OX14 4RN

and by Routledge
605 Third Avenue, New York, NY 10158

Routledge is an imprint of the Taylor & Francis Group, an informa business

British Library Cataloguing-in-Publication Data
A catalogue record for this book is available from the British Library

ISBN: 978-1-032-48259-0 (hbk)
ISBN: 978-1-032-48258-3 (pbk)
ISBN: 978-1-003-38815-9 (ebk)

DOI: 10.4324/9781003388159

Typeset in Times New Roman
by SPi Technologies India Pvt Ltd (Straive)

I thank my dear parents for their unconditional love and for helping me to see this journey through. I thank them for nurturing grace, humility, quiet obedience and acceptance in me. Their unwavering compassion and firm support have steered me through the still waters. I also thank my dearest friends and colleagues who have all stood by me, have rejoiced in my successes, shared in my struggles, been a shoulder to lean on and helped me to endure. You have all been an inspiration to me. I also thank my PhD supervisors who have encouraged me all along the way in my career, introduced me to this field of research on expressed emotion, guided me in my innovations and been resolute symbols of courage.

I am deeply indebted to the contributors of this book. It has been enriching to be on this journey with each author and to see their wonderful contributions come to fruition. I am truly grateful for their expertise, enthusiasm, patience and sincere devotion. I thank them for giving their time and effort in producing the evidence and sharing their insights on the subject of criticism.

Contents

Notes on Contributors

Alice Betteridge completed her BSc in Psychology (Mental Health) at Nottingham Trent University, where her final-year project examined sensitivity to criticism and its relationship to mental health, including depression, anxiety and stress. She went on to complete an MSc in Psychological Wellbeing and Mental Health before beginning her PhD at Nottingham Trent University. Her doctoral research explores how schizotypy interacts with the psychological portrayals of familial interactions, with particular attention to exploring the ways individuals interpret criticisms and praises.

Denise S. Chung-Zou, BS, is a pre-doctoral psychology trainee at the University of Miami. Her research focuses on isolation, loneliness and social dysfunction among persons with serious mental illness (SMI). She is also interested in barriers to care experienced by people with SMI who are members of multiple marginalised groups.

Mark Hayward is an experienced clinical psychologist with expertise in the treatment of distressing voice-hearing experiences across diagnoses and the lifespan. He has pioneered the exploration of voice hearing within a relational framework, acknowledging the voice as an interpersonal 'other' and researching differing aspects of the relationships that people can develop with their voices. These relationships have been central to the development and evaluation of new forms of individual and group therapy that can facilitate acceptance of self and voices through the use of assertiveness and mindfulness training. With over 150 publications, his work is highly cited. His roles combine clinical (Lead for the Sussex Voices Clinic – https://www.sussexpartnership.nhs.uk/sussex-voices-clinic), research (Director of Research for Sussex Partnership NHS Foundation Trust) and teaching (Honorary Professor at the University of Sussex) activity.

Alison M. Heru is a Professor of Psychiatry. She has written over 50 academic articles, book chapters and four textbooks, and published a column in *Clinical Psychiatric News* for many years. Her last position was Vice Chair of Clinical Services at the University of Colorado and prior to that she was the Interim Chair of the Department of Psychiatry.

Alessia McGowan is a University of Miami Fellow and second-year trainee in the Clinical Psychology PhD programme at the University of Miami. Her primary research interests include studying the cognitive, behavioural and sociocultural risk factors for psychosis and suicidality using large language models and other computational tools. She is also interested in promoting the adaptation of empirically supported treatment for mental illness to improve applicability and accessibility for individuals with marked cognitive impairment.

Kanchana Mohannathan has specialised in counselling, educational psychology and in constructing psychometric instruments. She has served in the faculty of Psychology (retired) in Women's Christian College, Chennai for over three decades and was Head of Psychology from 2020 to 2023. She was an Associate Professor in Psychology and during this period published several research papers, her major interest areas being youth, psycho-social factors in youth mental health and the efficacy of counselling related approaches. She has trained postgraduate students in counselling skills and guided postgraduate students and research scholars. In addition, she has coordinated the services offered to intellectually challenged children, a centre in the college campus. She also acquired some experience in working with children and adolescents during the early years of her career. This includes neurotypical children, children in conflict with the law and children with learning disability. She has enjoyed working and interacting with youth during the major part of her career. She believes in the importance of nurturing children and youth to give their 'best'.

Jennifer Nicholls is a graduate psychologist and credentialled coach working at the intersection of coaching psychology and applied qualitative research. She has worked as a Research Assistant on NHS-affiliated research projects, including Depict VR, where she led qualitative data collection and conducted reflexive thematic analysis. At Sussex Partnership NHS Foundation Trust, she contributed to the ECHOES project, leading data collection with young people, parents and teachers, facilitating focus groups and training sessions, and preparing qualitative datasets for inductive and deductive analysis. Alongside her research activity, she works as a coaching psychologist in applied settings, informing a practitioner-researcher approach that centres lived experience, reflexivity and the development of identity and agency within applied psychological and developmental contexts.

Preethi Premkumar is an experimental psychologist. She has published 54 journal articles in leading scientific journals. She has co-authored book chapters in three editions of the Essential Psychology book series. She studies family relationships and how they are linked to schizotypal personality and other mental health states. She has discovered how sensitivity to criticism and praise in families can link to schizotypy, depression, aggression and substance misuse. Designing novel experiments on family communication has helped her to decipher the brain signature for processing reward from praise and attending to rejection. She has published extensively on brain alterations in schizophrenia and on pharmacological interventions for obsessive-compulsive disorder. More recently, she has pioneered virtual-reality interventions for addressing social anxiety and perceived criticism.

Padmavati Ramachandran is a consultant psychiatrist in Chennai, India, and the Director of Schizophrenia Research Foundation (SCARF), a not-for-profit community-based mental health rehabilitation centre in Chennai. She has published over 100 journal articles on the nature and treatment of schizophrenia, including community-based interventions in South India. Her areas of interest are stigma in mental illness and in physical comorbidities in schizophrenia and community mental health. She won Young Women Scientist Award in 2000, awarded by the Tamil Nadu Science City (TANSA), Government of Tamil Nadu, India.

Dominic Rees-Roberts obtained his PhD in molecular parasitology and a Master's in Science Media Production at Imperial College London. He is the co-founder of BorderPoint Films, a creative company specialising in science-factual content. He is an experienced producer-director working on major factual series for leading national and international broadcasters. BorderPoint Films formed the collaboration with Dr Premkumar to develop Depict VR, a virtual-reality psychological application for addressing perceived criticism.

Genesis Saenz Escalante is a fifth-year clinical psychology PhD candidate at the University of Miami, supervised by Professor Amy Weisman de Mamani. Her interests lie at the intersection of psychology and culture, with a focus on how these factors relate to suicidal ideation and psychosis in marginalised populations, including queer communities and racial/ethnic marginalised groups. Genesis clinical interests centre on spiritually integrated, culturally informed therapy and the treatment of serious mental illness, guided by an integrative theoretical framework.

Sandhya Shivakumar is a passionate licensed clinical psychologist with a double master's degree from King's College London and Women's Christian College, Chennai, where she specialised in Counselling Psychology. She completed her MPhil in Clinical Psychology at Sri Ramachandra Medical College, Chennai, which involved two intensive years of supervised clinical training. She is currently pursuing her PhD at Women's Christian College. Her research interests span areas such as LGBTQ+ mental health, positive psychology and screen time in young children. Through her clinical work and research, she is committed to promoting evidence-based, culturally sensitive psychological care, with a special focus on child and family well-being.

Joanna Smogorzewska is a pedagogue and psychologist, PhD and Associate Professor at University of Warsaw, Faculty of Education, Warsaw. Her research interests concern mostly theory of mind and its development in the educational context, but also social and cognitive development of children in inclusive environment. She has conducted several big research projects in this area that have been financed by national grants institutions in Poland. She also regularly publishes results of her research internationally.

Amy Weisman de Mamani is a Professor at the University of Miami and a licensed clinical psychologist. Her research focuses on family and cultural factors that influence the course of serious mental illness. She has published two books and over 100 research articles related to mental illness. Her research has been funded by NIMH, The John Templeton foundation, the American Psychological Association and other agencies. In 2018, she received the Stanley Sue Award for Distinguished Contributions to Diversity in Clinical Psychology by APA's Division 12. In 2021, she received the Trailblazer Award from the Psychosis and Schizophrenia Spectrum Special Interest Group of the Association for Behavioral and Cognitive Therapies.

Ahmad Zandbagleh received a PhD degree in Electrical Engineering from the Iran University of Science and Technology (IUST), where he studied EEG-based analysis of schizotypy using advanced signal processing and machine learning methods. He is currently a Postdoctoral Researcher at the Institute of Psychology, Jagiellonian University, Poland, and is working on EEG-based studies of disorders of consciousness and associated neurophysiological biomarkers. His research interests include biomedical signal processing, cognitive neuroscience, and neuroimaging, with a focus on AI-based diagnostic tools and neurophysiological data analysis. He has contributed to several international EEG-based clinical studies, developed applications for monitoring heartrate variability for HBImed AG, and conducted extensive peer reviews for leading journals in neuroscience, psychiatry and biomedical engineering. His PhD viva was televised nationally as a selected thesis for its academic and public interest.

Abbreviations

3D	three-dimensional
4D	four-dimensional
ACC	anterior cingulate cortex
ADHD	Attention Deficit Hyperactivity Disorder
aPFC	anterior prefrontal cortex
app	application
ASC	academic self-concept
BFNE-R	Brief Fear of Negative Evaluation – Revised
BFT	behavioural family therapy
BOLD	blood-oxygen-level dependent
CA1/CA2/CA3	Cornu Ammonis regions 1, 2, and 3 of the hippocampus
CAMHS	Children and Adolescent Mental Health Services
CBT	cognitive behavioural therapy
CEN	central executive network
CFI	Camberwell Family Interview
CHI	clinical high-risk
CIT-S	culturally informed therapy for schizophrenia
COVID-19	Coronavirus disease 19
CR	conditioned response
CS	conditioned stimulus
dACC	dorsal anterior cingulate cortex
DG	dentate gyrus
DHH children	deaf or hard-of-hearing children
DLPFC	dorso-lateral prefrontal cortex
DMHIs	digital mental health interventions
EE	expressed emotion
EEG	electroencephalography
EMA	ecological momentary assessment
EOI	emotional over-involvement
ERP	event-related potential
FAS	family attitude scale
FFT	family focused therapy

FI	family intervention
fMRI	functional magnetic resonance imaging
FMSS	Five-Minute Speech Sample
FNE	fear of negative evaluation
fNIRS	functional near-infrared spectroscopy
FPE	fear of positive evaluation
FPES	fear of positive evaluation scale
GAD	generalized anxiety disorder
HR	heart rate
IFG	inferior frontal gyrus
Lab-TAB	laboratory temperament assessment battery
LEE	Level of Expressed Emotion
LPP	late positive potential
MDD	Major Depressive Disorder
MFGT	multi-family group therapy
MHRA	Medical Health Regulation Authority
mPFC	medial prefrontal cortex
NHS	National Health Service
NOS	not otherwise specified
O-LIFE	Oxford–Liverpool Inventory of Feelings and Experiences
PC	perceived criticism
PCC	posterior cingulate cortex
PCM	perceived criticism measure
PFC	prefrontal cortex
pgACC	pregenual anterior cingulate cortex
PPI	patient and public involvement
preCUN	precuneus
pSTS	posterior superior temporal sulcus
rACC	rostral anterior cingulate cortex
RewP	reward positivity
ROI	region of interest
SAD	social anxiety disorder
SB	subiculum
SD	standard deviation
SES	socio-economic status
SFG	superior frontal gyrus
sgACC	subgenual anterior cingulate cortex
SMA	supplementary motor area
SMI	serious mental illness
SNS	sympathetic nervous system
SPQ	Schizotypal Personality Questionnaire
SUD	Substance Use Disorder
T1, T2, T3	time 1, time 2, time 3
TAU	treatment as usual

tDCS	transcranial direct current stimulation
ToM	theory of mind
TPJ	temporoparietal junction
UR	unconditioned response
US	unconditioned stimulus
VLPFC	ventrolateral prefrontal cortex
vmPFC	ventromedial prefrontal
VR	virtual reality
VRET	virtual-reality-based exposure therapy

Introduction

Criticism is defined as a personal remark of dislike or disapproval about what the person does according to the theory of expressed emotion by Leff and Vaugh (1985). The *Oxford Dictionary* defines criticism as 'the act of expressing disapproval of someone or something and opinions about their faults or bad qualities; a statement showing disapproval'. In a literary context, the *Oxford Dictionary* defines criticism as 'the work or activity of making fair, careful judgments about the good and bad qualities of someone or something'. A criticism is defined both by its content and the tone of the speaker. Criticism is a natural part of our daily communication and our development. Criticism can be seen as a means to correct a person for their mistake. For instance, parents criticising their child during early development is important for disciplining and correcting the behaviour of the child. It serves to change the way we think and change the power dynamics in conversation. Criticism can also be used to blame a person for their actions, direct a person to take responsibility for actions in a social situation and confer responsibility on that person to change their behaviour. This book primarily focuses on the deleterious effects of criticism on mental health, but it also considers how school pupils flourish from an appropriate understanding of criticism from a teacher when it is taken as an opportunity to learn and grow.

In addition, criticism can be experienced in a range of social settings, such as the family, education and the workplace, and can be interpersonal or aimed at oneself. The aim of this book is to explore the psychology and purpose of criticism in different social settings. The book provides a comprehensive account of why people are critical of others, how criticism conditions our behaviours and how we respond to criticism. The book also aims to explain the relationship between perceiving criticism and mental health. The brain responds to criticism via the centres for salience, reward and emotion regulation, and these responses vary according to the type of mental distress and age of the person. There are several cognitive, behavioural and social interventions to mitigate the expression and perception of criticism.

DOI: 10.4324/9781003388159-1

Thus, Chapter 1 explains the evidence for criticism towards patients with serious mental illness within the framework of expressed emotion from a close relative. Chapter 2 presents the seminal studies on criticism from families towards patients with schizophrenia and the development of the concept of expressed emotion and the expressed emotion scale. It also reviews the key experimental studies on perceived criticism and its relationship to a range of mental health states, such as schizotypy, depression, aggression and substance use. Chapter 3 explains how criticism applies to educational settings, especially when teachers apply criticism to school pupils and how criticism motivates school pupils to improve in their academic performance. Chapter 3 also considers how theory of mind relates to sensitivity to criticism from a teacher and their peers, and how this relationship differs between cultures. It also considers how children who are deaf and hard of hearing respond to a teacher's critique. Chapter 4 looks at how culture impacts the perception of criticism and its relationship with mental health states. Chapter 5 examines the neurobiology of perceived criticism, such as the brain reward system and problem-solving system. Chapter 6 addresses the therapeutic approaches to processing and responding to criticism constructively and changing the way we communicate with family. Lastly, Chapter 7 presents Depict VR, a virtual-reality mental health application for helping young people to discuss their experiences of criticism with a trusted confidante. Chapter 7 gives an insider's view into designing a digital mental health intervention and the challenges with adopting it in services at scale. Chapter 8 suggests further topics for understanding criticism, such as early development and the workplace.

Each chapter also contains suggestions on 'How to…' minimise the psychological impact of criticism. The 'How to…' guides provide tips for minimising the psychological impact of criticism based on five key issues raised in the chapter. For instance, in Chapter 1 on the history of criticism within the context of expressed emotion, the techniques used in family intervention to reduce the impact of criticism include psychoeducation about the symptoms of mental distress. Chapter 2 and Chapter 6 consider the role of flexibility and cohesion in family interactions and conversation-oriented and conformity-oriented communication styles. Thus, the 'How to…' guides suggest communication techniques that achieve more balanced family interactions that are consensual and permit openness to new ideas.

0.1 A rationale for the book

This book is the first book to our knowledge to comprehensively explore the meaning of criticism in communication. No book synthesises the vast body of literature that exists on criticism. Criticism is often made without our awareness of it. Criticism is widespread across all spheres of life, such as journalism, political debates and academic argument. Yet, we need to know how profound and often insidious the effects of criticism are on our thinking and behaviour. In this growing age of social media and social networking where expression of negative feedback is rife, people need to develop skills to overcome criticism. The book sheds light on the curious phenomenon of criticism and its constructive and harmful consequences, and increases our awareness of criticism in our thoughts and speech. The book also examines the relationship of perceived criticism to our cognitive abilities and brain responses.

This book can be used by family counsellors, clinical psychologists, academic psychologists, education developers, public-speaking experts, politicians and journalists to gain insight into the significance of this style of communication. Furthermore, the book examines the neural underpinnings of criticism. Thus, the book would also appeal to neuroscientists interested in studying the biological basis of emotion. The book will also appeal to the layperson seeking to understand the nature of criticism in communication. In turn, the book can be used as a practical guide for improving communication styles.

0.2 Audience for the book

The book intends to be a practical guide for families, people in close relationships and other peer, teachers and professional relationships. Additionally, the book would be relevant in the following academic and applied contexts:

1) Higher education institutions including universities and colleges
   a Clinical/Counselling training courses, particularly those with a focus on systemic formulations
   b Well-being services within the institution, aimed at providing support for students
2) Counselling accreditation or governance bodies such as British Association for Counselling and Psychotherapy, Association for Behavioral and Cognitive Psychotherapies or National Counselling Society
3) Hospitals, especially mental health or psychiatry units
4) Organisations related to non-mental health-care professionals such as social workers, occupational therapists.

By presenting empirical scientific evidence about transactional criticism, the book would appeal to students on undergraduate and postgraduate mental health courses, such as counselling, clinical psychology, diplomas for improving access to psychological therapies and undergraduate and postgraduate psychology. The book may be included in student support services at different points in their journey through university. For instance, (1) it may be introduced at the induction to the university for students to better prepare for academic feedback; (2) it may be adopted by the student wellbeing services and advocated to students, as some distressed students may be distressed because of criticism received; and (3) in a staff lounge for staff to read in their spare time to deal with the feedback that they also receive from students.

Chapter 1

Expressed emotion in family members of individuals with severe mental illnesses

Amy Weisman de Mamani, Denise S. Chung-Zou, Genesis Saenz Escalante and Alessia McGowan

Abstract

This chapter provides an overview of research on the topic of expressed emotion (EE) within families of individuals with serious mental illness (SMI), such as schizophrenia and bipolar disorder. EE is a measure of the critical, hostile or emotionally overinvolved attitudes expressed by a family member, and it is a crucial construct in research on SMI as it strongly predicts the long-term outcomes of mental illness. This chapter begins with an overview of the EE construct and its association with the illness course for people with SMI, paying careful attention to how EE and illness prognosis vary across cultures. The chapter then examines how communication patterns within families, such as gossip, may be how EE attitudes are transmitted. Next, we examine how EE and critical comments could be perceived as social rejection and, in turn, impact clients' connections with others, potentially increasing loneliness. Finally, this chapter will examine research on biomarkers related to SMI that provide insight into how criticism and other markers of EE may be expressed physiologically. The chapter concludes with a summary of the materials reviewed and a discussion of their implications and directions for future research.

1.1 Introduction

This chapter provides an overview of research on the topic of expressed emotion (EE), especially the criticism component, in the family members of people with serious mental illness (SMI). We use the term SMI to refer to illnesses that include psychosis, with schizophrenia and bipolar disorder being the two most common forms. Schizophrenia is a chronic psychiatric disorder characterised by persistent psychotic symptoms and impaired functioning, while bipolar disorder involves recurrent episodes of mania and depression, and may also include psychotic features during mood episodes (American Psychiatric Association, 2002).

DOI: 10.4324/9781003388159-2

Psychosis is characterised by a significant impairment in reality testing, often manifesting through delusions, hallucinations, disorganised thinking and grossly disorganised or abnormal motor behaviour (American Psychiatric Association, 2002). For instance, an individual experiencing psychosis may believe they are being followed by government agents despite no evidence of such activity. Alternatively, they may hear voices commenting on their actions when no one is present. Such delusions suggest a disconnection from reality. People with psychosis usually experience delusions (false beliefs) and hallucinations (false sensory perceptions in absence of actual external stimuli). The presence of psychosis is frequently disruptive, impairing both social cognition and functional independence (Julayanont & Suryadevara, 2021). An example of impaired social cognition is where a person experiencing psychosis struggles to interpret social cues accurately, and this leads to inappropriate responses in conversation. An example of poor functional independence is where the person is unable to manage daily tasks, such as maintaining hygiene, preparing meals or handling finances independently. These difficulties can result in many individuals with SMI relying extensively on family members (van Husen et al., 2025). Supporting a family member with a SMI can be challenging. The unpredictable and bewildering nature of mental illness often makes it difficult for carers to understand these experiences, which, combined with the extensive demands of caregiving, often strains family dynamics (Fekadu et al., 2019; Kuipers et al., 2007). This may contribute to heightened tensions and negative interactions within the household (Marsh & Lefky, 2009; van Husen et al., 2025) and give rise to high EE.

EE refers to caregivers' attitudes towards a family member with a mental disorder and focuses on key dimensions, including criticism, hostility and emotional overinvolvement (EOI). A large body of research in the field of EE highlights how these heightened emotions in caregivers can have significant adverse effects on individuals with SMI. Traditionally, the construct was assessed through interviews, such as the Camberwell Family Interview (CFI; Leff Vaughn, 1984) or the Five-Minute Speech Sample (FMSS; Magaña et al., 1986). However, EE has also been assessed via self-report measures such as the Family Attitude Scale (FAS; Kavanagh et al., 1997) and the Level of Expressed Emotion scale (LEE; Cole Kazarian, 1988; Gerlsma & Hale, 1997). The LEE, FMSS and FAS have also been tailored to assess patients' perceptions of EE. The CFI, however, remains the gold standard for assessing EE, offering a comprehensive and nuanced evaluation of familial attitudes and interactions. According to Hooley and Parker (2006), alternative measures, such as self-report questionnaires and brief interviews, show moderate correspondence with CFI-based EE ratings, because they often lack the depth and contextual sensitivity of the full CFI.

1.2 Expressed emotion towards patients with severe mental illness

1.2.1 EE and relapse

There is substantial evidence that high EE (e.g. high degrees of criticism, hostility and EOI) is associated with poorer illness course and greater risk of relapse in individuals with schizophrenia and other psychosis spectrum disorders (Hooley & Parker, 2006), such as bipolar disorder (Kim & Miklowitz, 2004). In fact, a literature review by Kavanagh (1992) found that over twice as many (48%) people with schizophrenia living in high EE homes relapsed compared to those living in low EE homes (21%). Similarly, a meta-analysis of 26 studies affirmed that living in a high EE home environment is associated with more than twice the baseline recurrence rate of symptoms for schizophrenia patients (Butzlaff & Hooley, 1998). Although positive comments and warmth are components of EE, historically, they have received less attention in research, as they were not found to be as predictive of relapse as criticism, hostility and EOI (Butler et al., 2019; Hooley & Parker, 2006). Consequently, many studies have focused primarily on the negative dimensions of EE, contributing to its conceptualisation as a largely adverse family dynamic.

The predictive nature of EE seems to hold across diverse groups including gender, age, race and ethnicity. For example, Bebbington and Kuipers (1994b) found that the odds ratio for relapse in high EE homes was over four time greater than that of low EE homes and this pattern held for both men and woman. Furthermore, the contact time with a high EE relative contributes to the risk of relapse for psychosis, such that those in close contact with a high EE relative have a higher risk of relapse compared to those in close contact with a low EE relative (Bebbington & Kuipers, 1994a). Although most of the studies demonstrating a link between EE and illness prognosis were conducted on adults with SMI, research suggests that the predictive validity of EE is also true of younger people. For instance, adolescents with bipolar disorder living in high EE homes were found to endorse greater suicidal ideation than adolescents with bipolar disorder living in low EE homes (Ellis et al., 2014). Furthermore, Wedig and Nock (2007) found that when parents were highly critical, which is a key component of EE, adolescents with a range of mental health disorders were more likely to report self-injurious thoughts and suicidal behaviours. Interesting cultural patterns have also been observed in EE (reviewed further below and in Chapter 4), with relatively few exceptions such as Black Americans (Tompson et al., 1995). Yet, high EE based on criticism, hostility, EOI and positive comments, appears to be a robust predictor of poor course of illness in people with psychosis across diverse cultures. An international meta-analysis of 96 studies found that exposure to high EE was indicative of a 95% increased likelihood of relapse compared to low EE, and there was no effect of geographical region (O'Driscoll et al., 2019). The cultural differences may be more nuanced around the criteria and threshold for high EE, such as whether six criticisms or fewer count as high EE (Bebbington & Kuipers, 1994a, 1994b), and other factors as explained below.

1.2.2 EE, attributions and affect

An important question remains as to why some families express more criticism towards loved ones with SMI. Recent research by Audiffred-Jaramillo and García De Alba-García (2024) indicates that family members who possess greater knowledge about schizophrenia exhibit lower levels of EE, compared to those who are less informed. Earlier studies further emphasise the role of family attributions in understanding EE. For instance, Weisman and colleagues (1993) found, in a Mexican American sample, that families with high levels of EE often attributed the symptoms of schizophrenia to factors within the patient's personal control. This belief was associated with stronger negative emotions, such as anger and frustration. In contrast, when families with low EE were more likely to view the symptoms as outside the patient's control, they demonstrated more positive and supportive interactions. Weisman and colleagues (1998) replicated these findings in a sample of non-Hispanic White families, reinforcing the connection between attributions and EE across cultural contexts. Hinojosa-Marqués and colleagues (2020) similarly found that relatives who attributed blame to the patient and held emotionally negative representations of the illness were significantly more likely to express critical attitudes.

The findings from the studies discussed in the previous paragraph align with a social psychology framework known as Attribution-Affect theory (Schmidt & Weiner, 1988). Schmidt and Weiner (1988) posited that people's emotional responses are shaped by how they interpret the causes of events. For instance, if a teacher attributes a student's failure on a test to a controllable factor, such as not studying, the teacher is likely to feel anger and frustration. These feelings may lead to criticism of the student and reduced motivation to provide further assistance or support. Chapter 3 explains the impact of criticism on the academic performance of school pupils in an educational context further. In contrast, if the failure is attributed to an uncontrollable factor, such as a lack of ability, the teacher's emotional response is likely to be warmer and more empathetic. This shift in perception often results in greater expressions of support and a stronger willingness to offer help. See Figure 1.1 for a visual representation of this model.

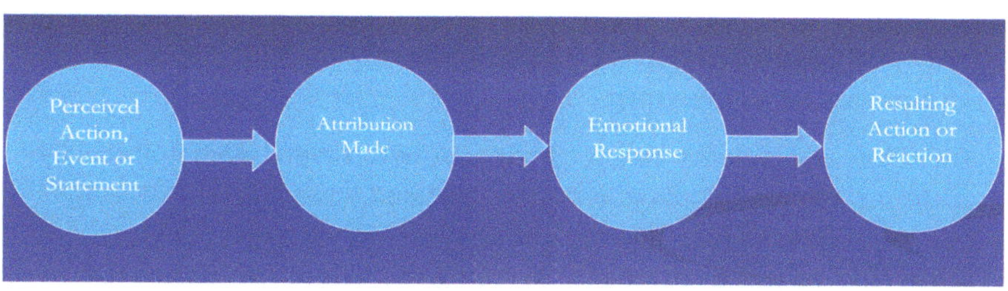

Figure 1.1 Attribution-affect theory.

The attribution-affect theory by Schmidt and Weiner (1988) could be used to understand EE and its connection to relapse. For instance, family members could attribute the symptoms or illness to factors they believe the person can and should control; e.g. if Mary would attend therapy and do her meditation exercises, she would stop hearing so many voices – a controllable attribution. It then seems plausible that such family members are more likely to react with negative emotional responses such as anger and frustration. These emotions often result in behaviours that are characteristic of high EE, including criticism and hostility directed towards the individual with SMI. Such perceptions and reactions may reduce the relative's motivation to offer support, such as driving the person to appointments, reminding them to take their medication, or providing helpful advice. This diminished support, combined with the psychological strain caused by exposure to criticism and hostility, may further exacerbate the person's symptoms, contributing to the established link between high EE and a poorer course of illness. Supporting this, Docherty and colleagues (2011) found that anxiety in individuals with schizophrenia coexisted with EE-related criticism, and together these two factors predict symptom exacerbation. Specifically, those with higher anxiety levels were more vulnerable to the negative effects of criticism, suggesting that emotional sensitivity may amplify the impact of high EE environments on clinical outcomes.

To reduce negative attributions and mitigate high EE responses, clinicians can support carers by fostering a more compassionate and informed understanding of SMI. Psychoeducation is key – helping relatives recognise that many symptoms which are not under the patient's voluntary control can shift attributions away from blame and towards empathy. Cognitive restructuring techniques can be used to challenge rigid beliefs, such as 'they're just being lazy', and replace them with more accurate interpretations like 'they're struggling with motivation due to their illness'. Encouraging carers to reflect on the emotional impact of their responses and promoting validation of the patient's experience can also reduce criticism and hostility. When carers feel heard and equipped with practical strategies, they are more likely to engage in supportive behaviours that enhance recovery and reduce relapse risk. Several existing therapies (Miklowitz & Goldstein, 1997; Weisman de Mamani, et al., 2021) offer techniques to achieve these goals.

How to resolve negative attributions from the carer about the patient's symptoms:

Clinicians can support carers of patients with severe mental illness by fostering a more compassionate and informed understanding of serious mental illness and help them to consider factors external to the patient that could be changed rather than trying to control the patient.

1.2.3 Culture and EE

EE is a reliable global predictor of schizophrenia outcomes (O'Driscoll et al., 2019). However, cultural differences in the prevalence of high EE and the behaviours that trigger criticism have been widely reported (Bebbington & Kuipers, 1994b). For instance, a series of studies conducted by the World Health Organization (Jablensky et al., 1992; Sartorius et al., 1974) highlight that traditional societies, which tend to place group goals over individualistic goals, often exhibit lower rates of high EE. In line with this, even within the U.S., Weisman de Mamani and colleagues (2007) found that White individuals were significantly more likely to be classified as high EE compared to Latine[1]/Hispanic individuals, based on both the CFI and the FMSS. In Asian countries, such as China and India, high EE rates are also lower, with approximately 25% of family members classified as high EE, compared to 67% of non-Hispanic White individuals in the U.S. (Leff et al., 1987; Ran et al., 2003; Vaughn et al., 1984). This disparity may be attributed to the centrality of collectivism and familism in traditional cultures, which fosters modesty, conformity and the suppression of negative emotions (Ran et al., 2003; Weisman de Mamani, et al., 2008). These cultural traits may contribute to reduced levels of EE, potentially explaining why individuals with schizophrenia in traditional societies often experience more favourable prognoses compared to those in less traditional settings.

Interestingly, African Americans are one of the few racial/cultural groups where high EE does not predict worse outcomes for SMI. In fact, some studies suggest the opposite. For example, Rosenfarb, Bellack and Aziz (2006) found that intrusive behaviour and higher levels of criticism were associated with better outcomes for African Americans with SMI. Similarly, Gurak and Weisman de Mamani (2017) reported that low-EE caregivers were linked to greater symptom severity in African Americans with schizophrenia. This may be due to cultural communication styles; African American speech patterns are often more animated and expressive than those of Anglo-Americans (Majors, 1991). Rogan and Hammer (1998) suggest that confrontational styles may be perceived as sincere and caring within African American communities, leading to a paradoxical effect where high EE mitigates rather than exacerbates symptoms.

Perceptions of EE also vary across cultures. Weisman and colleagues (2006) found that White and Hispanic/Latine family members who expressed criticism during the CFI were perceived as critical by their ill relatives, whereas no such association was observed for African Americans. For African American patients, perceived criticism was the sole predictor of symptom exacerbation (Tompson et al., 1995). This suggests that traditional EE assessment methods may have less predictive validity for Black ethnic minority populations, as the meaning of 'criticism' may differ across cultures. Addressing patients' perceptions of criticism could be particularly important in psychotherapy with African American families.

Finally, what is considered critical, hostile or emotionally overinvolved varies by culture. For instance, Kymalainen and colleagues (2006) found that White family members in the United States of America often criticised individual personality traits that disrupt autonomy, whereas Hispanic and Black families were more likely to criticise behaviours that violated collectivist norms. Kymalainen and colleagues (2006) interpreted their findings as evidence that cultural values significantly shape the nature of familial criticism. They suggested that in collectivist cultures, criticism is often rooted in preserving group harmony and interdependence, whereas in individualistic cultures, it tends to focus on traits that challenge personal autonomy. This cultural lens underscores the importance of tailoring mental health interventions to align with the values and communication styles of diverse populations.

How to address cultural variations in perception of criticism in therapy:

Clinicians working with families from diverse cultural backgrounds must recognise that expressions of criticism, hostility or emotional overinvolvement may carry different meanings depending on cultural norms and communication styles. Rather than assuming uniform impact, therapists should explore how both the patient and their relatives interpret these interactions. For example, what may be perceived as harsh criticism in one culture could be understood as concern or care in another, as seen in African American families where directness may signal emotional investment. Incorporating culturally sensitive assessments and engaging families in open dialogue about their values, expectations and relational norms can help reframe potentially harmful dynamics. By validating cultural expressions while gently guiding families toward more supportive communication, clinicians can reduce misinterpretations and foster therapeutic alliances that respect cultural identity while promoting recovery. In their book *Culturally Informed Therapy for Schizophrenia*, Weisman de Mamani and colleagues (2021) offer detailed suggests for how clinicians can tailor treatment to better incorporate clients' perceptions, values and worldviews in therapy.

1.3 The transmission of expressed emotion through gossip

As established above, *perceived* EE is linked to poor prognosis for individuals with psychosis, and for some groups it is the only predictor of illness course (e.g. African Americans; Tompson et al., 1995). Thus, it is important to also examine mechanisms by which EE may be transmitted indirectly in family networks. Gossip, broadly defined as evaluative talk exchanged informally about an absent third party, emerges as a promising area for future research for several reasons (Bosson et al., 2006; Mesoudi et al., 2006). Although gossip is often assumed to be derogatory or malicious, it broadly refers to informal talk about an absent person and may be positive, neutral, or simply informational (e.g. discussing life events, informing family about other members' care; Bosson et al., 2006; Mesoudi et al., 2006).

While information exchange can be evaluatively positive or negative (Mesoudi et al., 2006), it is most often framed as the communication of negative attitudes to others, such as criticism and hostility. It is important to note that gossip does not constitute EE. Instead, EE arises when gossip carries hostility or rejection, reflecting dislike of the individual rather than criticism of specific behaviours (Premkumar, et al., 2013). Second, individuals with SMI may be particularly vulnerable to targeted inter-family gossip due to the disruptive or troubling nature of some symptoms. Third, individuals with SMI may be more likely to perceive cues among family members as evidence of critical and persecutory attitudes about them. These interpretations align with the threat anticipation cognitive model (Freeman, 2007; Freeman & Garety, 2000), which posits that delusions emerge from anxiety-driven anomalous experiences and are shaped by pre-existing negative beliefs. Stressful interpersonal events may trigger ambiguous external perceptions (e.g. whispers or glances interpreted as persecutory) that individuals seek to make sense of through threat-based explanations (Freeman, 2007). In families with high EE, such perceptions may or may not be accurate, but the history of negative interactions may heighten individuals' tendency to interpret ambiguity as threatening, further reinforcing their sense of vulnerability.

Cognitive and interpersonal vulnerabilities associated with schizophrenia may shape how individuals perceive and react to gossip within their family networks. For example, Berry and colleagues (2012) found that insecure attachment was positively associated with both the severity and distress of auditory hallucinations, a common positive symptom. Attachment styles, shaped by early caregiving experiences, influence interpersonal relationships across the lifespan. Insecure attachment, often stemming from inconsistent or intrusive care in childhood, has been found to be associated with negative self-beliefs, as well as a heightened sensitivity to criticism and rejection (Bowlby, 1980). In families with high EE, individuals with schizophrenia may be more likely to anticipate rejection or interpret gossip as personally threatening. Even when the gossip is not factual, its perceived presence may exacerbate paranoia, reinforce stigma-related beliefs and may even result in worse symptom outcomes.

Research also indicates associations between perceived gossip and symptom severity in SMI. For instance, in a study investigating the content of delusions of reference in individuals with schizophrenia, Startup and Startup (2005) found that gossip was the most common delusion endorsed and was significantly related to increased hallucinations and persecutory delusions. Even when not directly observed, gossip may serve as a potent and covert mechanism of EE, further reinforcing feelings of exclusion, amplifying internalised stigma and exacerbating both psychological distress and illness trajectory among individuals with SMI.

In treatment contexts where a patient relies on family care, information shared by family members with practitioners may be perceived as gossip, particularly when, due to the chronic nature of schizophrenia, the patient is unable to advocate for themselves and may be left out of the conversation. In family therapy research, where some forms of talk may resemble gossip (e.g. parents talking with a therapist about their child without the child present), Parker and O'Reilly (2012) viewed gossip as social action instead of it being simply malicious. Drawing from naturally occurring family therapy sessions, authors identified how seemingly factual descriptions about another member (i.e. gossiping) may sometimes carry an underlying negative social action, particularly when family members describe children's behaviours in ways that distance themselves and preserve their own face. In relation to schizophrenia and EE, this suggests that gossip, even when framed as factual or informational, may be used to subtly convey criticism or hostility. Within families, such evaluative talk could reinforce high EE climates, where negative attributions and disapproval are indirectly communicated about the patient. As with therapy talk, what appears to be neutral information-sharing may in practice perform the social action of exclusion or rejection, thereby maintaining stigma and heightening the patient's sensitivity to gossip.

Critical, hostile and emotionally overinvolved attitudes conveyed through gossip may also be a way to informally police the behaviours of individuals with SMI. Gossip can reflect and reinforce carers' illness attributions, particularly when they interpret symptoms as the patient's personal failings rather than manifestations of the disorder. Gossip also often functions as a way to reinforce social norms and punish perceived transgressions, and its ability to reinforce stigma may have detrimental consequences in the care of individuals with SMI (Foster, 2004). For example, O'Reilly and colleagues (2019) found that family members frequently judged or excluded relatives with SMI due to behaviours associated with their illness, highlighting how such informal communication can reinforce carers' perceptions and justify their attitudes. By discussing the patient's behaviours with other family members, carers may maintain a sense of control and validate their own emotional responses, subtly empowering themselves within the family context. At the same time, gossip may also serve more prosocial or cathartic purposes; it can be a way for carers to seek advice, emotional support or practical guidance, particularly when they feel isolated or burdened by caregiving responsibilities. The content and context of gossip may be intimately tied to both the family's understanding of the illness and the patient's experience of stigma, rejection and emotional over-involvement, illustrating how informal communication channels can shape the dynamics of EE in schizophrenia.

How to address family gossip about a relative's SMI:

Family members need to be empathetic towards patients with SMI and understand the patient's psychotic experiences without judgement, as well as their experience of stigma, rejection and emotional over-involvement.

1.4 Perceived rejection and loneliness

Another potential consequence of EE behaviours, such as criticism and hostility, is the potential for perceived rejection of the individual with SMI and loneliness (Sündermann et al., 2013). A recent review paper suggests that, after simulated social exclusion, those across the psychosis spectrum experience levels of distress similar to healthy controls, but that this experience exacerbates psychotic symptoms (Lincoln et al., 2021), suggesting the importance of perceived rejection for this group. Moreover, hostility is a form of EE that occurs when a relative expresses a frank dislike of the individual with SMI (e.g. blaming who they are, rather than what they do). Such perceived rejection and social exclusion could stir up social anxiety and avoidance (Premkumar et al., 2015) as well as loneliness. A systematic review unveiled that higher rejection sensitivity, or disposition towards oversensitivity to social exclusion, is indeed associated with greater loneliness (Gao et al., 2017). This is also functionally important, as it has been found that for patients with schizophrenia who have cognitive impairment, sensitivity to rejection predicts communication disturbance and thought disorder (Grant & Beck, 2009) which could make social functioning even more difficult.

Resulting from rejection and exclusion, loneliness is defined as the subjective experience of social isolation and the mismatch between desired and achieved social connection (Russell et al., 2012). People with SMI tend to suffer from greater loneliness compared to the public, due to important reasons such as stigma, interpersonal competence, lower social support (Lim et al., 2018) and smaller social networks (Sündermann et al., 2013). This finding is salient because loneliness has been found to weaken immune functioning for those with SMI (Cole et al., 2015) and impacts cardiovascular health and is associated with early mortality to an extent similar to smoking 15 cigarettes a day (Holt-Lunstad et al., 2010). This finding is especially meaningful as persons with SMI already have significantly shorter average life expectancies than the general population by 15–20 years (Correll et al., 2022).

As loneliness is exacerbated by perceived rejection, and thought disorder and communication disturbances likely alter the perception of social experiences, it would be important to consider how those with SMI may interpret negative interactions. Framing this understanding, McCormickand colleagues (2023) argue that one's relational value to others, or the degree to which a relationship is regarded as important (Leary et al., 2001), may play a role in how people view themselves. Experiencing criticism and hostility (either directly or indirectly) may lower one's perceived relational value (Leary et al., 2001) and in turn exacerbate negative cognitive bias during social interactions (e.g. increasing social threat; Hawkley & Cacioppo, 2010; McCormick et al., 2023). For persons with SMI, who may already be sensitive to social rejection as well as fluctuations in their own relational value, criticism may add to existing fears of mental illness stigma and assumptions that they will be received poorly by others (Lysaker et al., 2010; McCormick et al., 2023). Moreover, metacognitive ability has been shown to be impaired in SMI (Lysaker et al., 2018). Considering the link between criticism and loneliness, without an integrated sense of oneself, individuals may inappropriately rely on critical, emotionally overinvolved comments from others to postulate an understanding of how they are viewed (like the fluctuations in relational value, described above).

In their review of the psychological mechanisms of isolation, Fulford and Holt (2023) explain that loneliness contributes to cognitive biases which reinforce social disconnection, which could be applied to our understanding of the consequences of EE. In a study sampling the public, conducted during the COVID-19 pandemic, chronic loneliness related to a preference for larger interpersonal distance, while acute loneliness linked with a preference for smaller interpersonal distance (Saporta et al., 2021). In other words, those with trait-level loneliness are prone to greater sensitivity to negative evaluation and social threats (e.g. hostility and criticism; EE) and tend to keep others away (Fulford & Holt, 2023), which should be kept in mind when considering individuals with SMI. A systematic review shows that for those with early psychosis, the number of friends (not family members) is significantly lower than that of healthy controls, and thus the social network is reduced and less satisfactory overall (Gayer-Anderson & Morgan, 2013), which is important context for recovery and rehabilitation from SMI. Indeed, the reinforcing nature of chronic loneliness is important to consider, as applied to persons with SMI, who are at risk of misunderstanding EE but still desire and benefit from meaningful relationships.

To address the issue of mental health outcomes, such as loneliness, that result from hostility, people with SMI and their loved ones should receive education regarding the potential for relationships to be restored, and psychiatric outcomes to be improved, though positive relational styles such as warmth. For example, positive affect from relatives, or EE warmth, has been found to prevent relapse at 6- and 12-month follow-up, in persons who have experienced first-episode psychosis (Lee et al., 2014). Moreover, having a positive family environment, in which relatives display warmth and give positive remarks, predicted fewer symptoms and better social functioning at 3-month follow up for adolescents at risk for developing psychosis (O'Brien et al., 2006). As social functioning and loneliness are negatively related with one another (e.g. Culbreth et al., 2021), encouraging a warm family environment may have more positive health sequelae that should be explored in future investigations. In sum, drawing from existing research, families of individuals with SMI should feel confident that their social behaviours have a tangible impact on their loved ones, and can be altered if necessary. Indeed, greater agreeableness in social interactions explains the relationship between greater psychosis-like experiences and lesser perceived rejection (Premkumar et al., 2018).

How to handle rejection and loneliness:

Creating a positive and encouraging family atmosphere without being overbearing toward patients with SMI, and fostering agreeableness in social interactions can reduce perceived rejection.

1.5 Biological markers of EE in individuals with SMI

1.5.1 Brain-based responses to high EE

While psychosocial approaches highlight the interpersonal consequences of EE, examining neural responses offers critical insight into the underlying mechanisms by which emotionally charged environments contribute to symptom exacerbation and relapse in serious mental illness. Thus, the physiological ramifications of EE in individuals with SMI are reviewed here.

Exposure to high EE environments triggers distinctive patterns of brain activation and connectivity in individuals with SMI. For instance, neuroimaging studies reveal that criticism or hostile emotional input over-activates limbic emotion-processing regions while disrupting activation in prefrontal regulatory circuits (Hooley, 2007; Hooley et al., 2012; Rylands et al., 2011). In other words, these studies have found that when individuals with SMI are exposed to criticism, their brains respond as if under threat, activating regions involved in detecting danger and emotional distress (the amygdala), whereas areas responsible for emotion regulation and reflective thinking become less active (see Figure 5.3, Chapter 5). In one such study, individuals with major depressive disorder (MDD) in remission were asked to listen to critical comments from their mothers while in the functional magnetic resonance imaging (fMRI) machine (Hooley, 2007; Hooley et al., 2005). Despite being symptom-free at the time of assessment, those in the group with MDD showed increased amygdala activation, a region in the emotion-processing system, and blunted dorsolateral prefrontal cortex (DLPFC) activation, a region involved in modulating emotion regulation, compared to healthy controls (Hooley et al., 2005, 2009). As the DLPFC is implicated in emotion regulation and cognitive control, this finding suggests that individuals with SMI may have difficulty coordinating activation in regulatory brain regions under social-evaluative stress (Hooley et al., 2005).

In individuals with schizophrenia, emerging evidence similarly points to altered fronto-limbic function in high-EE contexts. A recent functional near-infrared spectroscopy (fNIRS) study used audio recordings to simulate high-EE family interactions, finding that patients with schizophrenia exhibited disrupted cortical connectivity when hearing critical/hostile comments (Wang et al., 2024). Compared to healthy participants, those with schizophrenia showed reduced functional connectivity among the medial prefrontal cortex, left ventrolateral prefrontal cortex (PFC), and left superior temporal gyrus during high-EE exposure (Wang et al., 2024). These regions are involved in social-emotional processing and language, suggesting that high EE may also transiently impair the coordination of brain networks responsible for interpreting and regulating emotional speech for individuals with SMI. Furthermore, the degree of decoupling (i.e. reduced coordination or communication between brain regions) between left ventrolateral PFC and superior temporal gyrus correlated with patients' negative symptom severity (Wang et al., 2024), suggesting that individuals with more profound social withdrawal or blunted affect may experience even greater neural disruption from a critical environment. These patterns observed in schizophrenia and depression align with the stress-vulnerability model of SMI, such that aversive emotional signals (such as harsh criticism) hyper-activate threat-responsive circuitry (amygdala and related networks) while attenuating top-down emotion regulation regions, leaving the individual neurologically primed for affective dysregulation and symptom exacerbation (Walker & Diforio, 1997).

1.5.2 Psychophysiological markers of EE-related stress

The stressful nature of high EE is also evident in psychophysiological reactions. Individuals with SMI, as well as those at risk for SMI display heightened vegetative nervous system arousal (i.e. activation of the system responsible for involuntary physiological functions) when exposed to critical or hostile comments (Hooley & Gotlib, 2000). Heart rate (HR), skin conductance and cortisol levels tend to spike in response to EE-related stressors, reflecting activation of the sympathetic nervous system (SNS). In a controlled experiment, Weintraub et al. (2019) examined youth at clinical high risk (CHR) for psychosis as they listened to audio-recorded comments that were critical, praising, or neutral. Both the high-risk and healthy control groups showed immediate increases in HR and skin conductance during a critical comment; however, CHR individuals experienced prolonged physiological arousal during the recovery period after the criticism ended (Weintraub et al., 2019). Interestingly, the same high-risk individuals also showed greater reactivity to positive emotional input: hearing praise from a speaker produced a strong reduction in

HR and negative affect. Authors interpreted this finding to indicate that CHR individuals may experience praise as especially rewarding due to increased loneliness and reduced access to affirming social interactions (Weintraub et al., 2019). This high responsivity to positive emotional input may be a promising avenue for intervention in high EE environments.

Similarly, among patients with schizophrenia, early studies found that high EE family interactions provoke greater autonomic arousal. In a classic case assessment, a young man with schizophrenia underwent continuous skin conductance monitoring while interacting one-on-one with his high-EE parent and his low-EE parent separately (Tarrier & Barrowclough, 1984). The man's skin conductance was significantly higher in the presence of the high-EE parent compared to his low-EE parent (Tarrier & Barrowclough, 1984). More recent research has extended these early observations using refined physiological measures and larger samples. For example, Weintraub and colleagues (2019) found that youth at CHR exhibit similarly heightened autonomic arousal in response to critical comments, along with delayed physiological recovery, suggesting that this stress sensitivity may emerge even before illness onset (Weintraub et al., 2019). Such heightened arousal in high-EE environments has been observed in other schizophrenia patient populations and is thought to mediate the link between EE and relapse (Hooley, 2007). Prolonged or repeated surges in HR, blood pressure and stress hormones (like cortisol) in reaction to familial criticism could cumulatively strain an already vulnerable system, potentially precipitating symptom surges. In fact, individuals with schizophrenia often have baseline autonomic irregularities (e.g. reduced HR variability) consistent with chronic stress exposure (Haigh et al., 2021). High-EE environments likely exacerbate these psychophysiological burdens.

1.5.3 *Effects on cognitive and affective functioning*

The neurobiological and physiological responses to high EE can have downstream effects on patients' cognitive and emotional functioning for individuals with SMI. Cognitively, the stress of intense criticism or hostility may momentarily degrade processes like attention, working memory and self-regulation (Nuechterlein & Dawson, 1984). This theory was substantiated by a more recent study, which found that the combination of criticism and deficits in attention and immediate memory was the strongest predictor of unusual thought content (Kéri & Kelemen, 2009). This picture is consistent with neuroimaging findings that PFC activity (a brain region ascribed to attention and immediate memory) is suppressed during high-EE exposure in vulnerable individuals (Hooley et al., 2005). Affectively, high EE interactions can trigger intense negative emotions (anger, anxiety, sadness) and dysregulated mood in SMI individuals (Cuellar et al., 2009). For example, Cutting and colleagues (2006) found that schizophrenia patients who perceived their relatives as highly critical showed elevated subjective stress and were more likely to experience positive symptom exacerbation following stressful family encounters (Cutting & Docherty, 2000). Overall, the hostile emotional climate of high EE is detrimental to cognitive clarity and emotional well-being in SMI, often creating a vicious cycle wherein stress impairs functioning, which then may lead relatives to become even more critical, further worsening the patient's condition.

1.6 Integration and clinical implications

The research converges to portray a coherent biopsychosocial narrative: Individuals with SMI are particularly vulnerable to the effects of EE as evidenced by measurable stress reactions in the brain and body that, in turn, can destabilise their mental state. These acute responses may cumulatively tax the individual's stress response systems (e.g. hypothalamic–pituitary–adrenal axis). As a result, the person's cognitive and emotional resources are progressively eroded – they may become more preoccupied with avoiding criticism, less able to concentrate or reason through problems, and more prone to mood swings or psychotic thinking under stress.

How to address altered physiological stress and cognitive disorganisation:

Recognising these mechanisms has important clinical implications. First, it reinforces the rationale for family interventions in serious mental illness. Psychoeducation and family therapy aimed at reducing EE by teaching relatives to express emotions in more constructive, non-critical ways are empirically supported to reduce relapse rates (Pharoah et al., 2010). The biological evidence adds weight to these outcomes: by keeping the family atmosphere calmer and more supportive, deleterious brain-body stress responses may be mitigated. Second, cognitive-behavioural strategies can be useful for individuals with SMI to reframe critical remarks in less personal, threatening ways, potentially engaging frontal regulatory circuits rather than purely emotional reactivity. Finally, clinicians should be aware that even in the absence of reported distress, the patient's heart rate, cortisol or limbic activity may be spiking. Thus, assessments of the family environment and patient's stress reactivity should be included in treatment planning. By integrating neurobiological insights with psychosocial interventions, mental health professionals can better buffer patients from the toxic effects of high EE and improve long-term outcomes.

1.7 Conclusions and guidelines for clinicians working with families with SMI

In this chapter, we reviewed research on EE in families of individuals with SMI. The evidence suggests that living with, or being surrounded by family members who display critical, hostile or other high-EE attitudes can lower mental health and heighten the progression of the illness for people with SMI. As reviewed above, critical and hostile comments can lead to low self-esteem, loneliness, and greater symptom severity in people with SMI, and can have negative impacts on their brains and bodies. Helping families recognise that even when criticism is conveyed to people with SMI through the grapevine (family gossip) it can be damaging to mental health. Thus, educating family members about EE and negative gossip and their impacts on loved ones with SMI mental and physical health, coupled with clear guidelines for improving communication, may help to improve the illness course for people with SMI. One technique for reducing criticism in the family members of people with SMI is to teach them to focus more on what they would like to see rather than criticising what they don't like. For example, coaching family members to say things like, 'I would appreciate it if you would remember to take your medication every morning without me needing to remind you', would likely trigger less stress and encourage greater compliance from them than would more hostile or critically phrased comments such as, 'You are so irresponsible. I'm tired of nagging you to comply with even the most basic responsibilities, like taking your medications.' Communication training programs and family-focused interventions, such as culturally informed therapy for schizophrenia (Weisman de Mamani, 2021), offer promising approaches to achieving these goals and will be discussed further in Chapter 6.

Note

1 **Latine** is a gender-inclusive alternative to *Latino/a* that aligns with traditional Spanish phonetics (Cano & Gelpí-Acosta, 2022), whereas **Latinx** incorporates the letter 'x', which is not commonly used in Spanish pronunciation.

References

American Psychiatric Association. (2002). *Diagnostic and Statistical Manual of Mental Disorders* (Fifth Edition, Text Revision (DSM-5-TR) ed.). American Psychiatric Association.

Audiffred-Jaramillo, R., & Alba-García, J. E. G. D. (2024). Cultural beliefs about the etiology of schizophrenia and expressed emotion in Mexican families. *Revista Colombiana De Psiquiatría*, *53*(4), 435–442. 10.1016/j.rcp.2022.07.003

Bebbington, P., & Kuipers, L. (1994a). The clinical utility of expressed emotion in schizophrenia. *Acta Psychatr Scand*, *89*(382), 46–53. 10.1111/j.1600-0447.1994.tb05865.x

Bebbington, P., & Kuipers, L. (1994b). The predictive utility of expressed emotion in schizophrenia: an aggregate analysis. *Psychological Medicine*, *24*(3), 707–718. 10.1017/S0033291700027860

Berry, K., Wearden, A., Barrowclough, C., Oakland, L., & Bradley, J. (2012). An investigation of adult attachment and the nature of relationships with voices. *British Journal of Clinical Psychology*, *51*(3), 280–291. 10.1111/j.2044-8260.2011.02027.x
Bosson, J. K., Johnson, A. B., Niederhoffer, K., & Swann, William B. Jr., (2006). Interpersonal chemistry through negativity: Bonding by sharing negative attitudes about others. 10.1111/j.1475-6811.2006.00109.x
Bowlby, J. (1980). *Loss: sadness and depression*. Penguin Books.
Butler, R., Berry, K., Ellett, L., & Bucci, S. (2019). An experimental investigation of the impact of critical and warm comments on state paranoia in a non-clinical sample. *Journal of Behavior Therapy and Experimental Psychiatry*, *62*, 30–37. 10.1016/j.jbtep.2018.08.008
Butzlaff, R. L., & Hooley, J. M. (1998). Expressed emotion and psychiatric relapse: A Meta-analysis. *Archives of General Psychiatry*, *55*(6), 547–552. 10.1001/archpsyc.55.6.547
Cano, M., & Gelpí-Acosta, C. (2022). Variation in US drug overdose mortality within and between Hispanic/Latine subgroups: a disaggregation of national data. *SSM-Mental Health*, *2*, 100095. 10.1016/j.ssmmh.2022.100095
Cole, J. D., & Kazarian, S. S. (1988). The level of expressed emotion scale: A new measure of expressed emotion. *Journal of Clinical Psychology*, *44*(3), 392–397.
Cole, S. W., Levine, M. E., Arevalo, J. M. G., Ma, J., Weir, D. R., & Crimmins, E. M. (2015). Loneliness, eudaimonia, and the human conserved transcriptional response to adversity. *Psychoneuroendocrinology*, *62*, 11–17. 10.1016/j.psyneuen.2015.07.001
Correll, C. U., Solmi, M., Croatto, G., Schneider, L. K., Rohani-Montez, S. C., Fairley, L., Smith, N., Bitter, I., Gorwood, P., Taipale, H., & Tiihonen, J. (2022). Mortality in people with schizophrenia: a systematic review and meta-analysis of relative risk and aggravating or attenuating factors. *World Psychiatry*, *21*(2), 248–271. 10.1002/wps.20994
Cuellar, A. K., Johnson, S. L., & Ruggero, C. J. (2009). Affective reactivity in response to criticism in remitted bipolar disorder: A laboratory analog of expressed emotion. *Journal of Clinical Psychology*, *65*(9), 925–941. 10.1002/jclp.20596
Culbreth, A. J., Barch, D. M., & Moran, E. K. (2021). An ecological examination of loneliness and social functioning in people with schizophrenia. *Journal of Abnormal Psychology*, *130*(8), 899–908. 10.1037/abn0000706
Cutting, L. P., Aakre, J. M., & Docherty, N. M. (2006). Schizophrenic patients' perceptions of stress, expressed emotion, and sensitivity to criticism. *Schizophrenia Bulletin*, *32*(4), 743–750. 10.1093/schbul/sbl001
Cutting, L. P., & Docherty, N. M. (2000). Schizophrenia outpatients' perceptions of their parents: Is expressed emotion a factor? *Journal of Abnormal Psychology*, *109*(2), 266–272. 10.1037/0021-843X.109.2.266
Docherty, N. M., St-Hilaire, A., Aakre, J. M., Seghers, J. P., McCleery, A., & Divilbiss, M. (2011). Anxiety interacts with expressed emotion criticism in the prediction of psychotic symptom exacerbation. *Schizophrenia Bulletin*, *37*(3), 611–618. https://doi.org/10.1093/schbul/sbp123
Ellis, A. J., Portnoff, L. C., Axelson, D. A., Kowatch, R. A., Walshaw, P., & Miklowitz, D. J. (2014). Parental expressed emotion and suicidal ideation in adolescents with bipolar disorder. *Psychiatry Research*, *216*(2), 213–216. 10.1016/j.psychres.2014.02.013
Fekadu, W., Mihiretu, A., Craig, T. K. J., & Fekadu, A. (2019). Multidimensional impact of severe mental illness on family members: systematic review. *BMJ Open*, *9*(12), e032391. 10.1136/bmjopen-2019-032391
Foster, E. K. (2004). Research on gossip: Taxonomy, methods, and future directions. *Review of General Psychology*, *8*(2), 78–99. 10.1037/1089-2680.8.2.78

Freeman, D. (2007). Suspicious minds: The psychology of persecutory delusions. *Clinical Psychology Review*, *27*(4), 425–457. 10.1016/j.cpr.2006.10.004
Freeman, D., & Garety, P. A. (2000). Comments on the content of persecutory delusions: Does the definition need clarification? *British Journal of Clinical Psychology*, *39*(4), 407–414. 10.1348/014466500163400
Fulford, D., & Holt, D. J. (2023). Social withdrawal, loneliness, and health in schizophrenia: psychological and neural mechanisms. *Schizophrenia Bulletin*, *49*(5), 1138–1149. 10.1093/schbul/sbad099
Gao, S., Assink, M., Cipriani, A., & Lin, K. (2017). Associations between rejection sensitivity and mental health outcomes: A meta-analytic review. *Clinical Psychology Review*, *57*, 59–74. 10.1016/j.cpr.2017.08.007
Gayer-Anderson, C., & Morgan, C. (2013). Social networks, support and early psychosis: a systematic review. *Epidemiology and Psychiatric Sciences*, *22*(2), 131–146. 10.1017/S2045796012000406
Gerlsma, C., & Hale, W., 3. (1997). Predictive power and construct validity of the Level of Expressed Emotion (LEE) scale: Depressed out-patients and couples from the general community. *British Journal of Psychiatry*, *170*(6), 520–525. 10.1192/bjp.170.6.520
Grant, P. M., & Beck, A. T. (2009). Evaluation sensitivity as a moderator of communication disorder in schizophrenia. *Psychological Medicine*, *39*(7), 1211–1219. 10.1017/S0033291709005479
Gurak, K., & Weisman de Mamani, A. (2017). Caregiver expressed emotion and psychiatric symptoms in African-Americans with schizophrenia: An attempt to understand the paradoxical relationship. *Family Process*, *56*(2), 476–486. 10.1111/famp.12188
Haigh, S. M., Walford, T. P., & Brosseau, P. (2021). Heart rate variability in schizophrenia and autism. *Frontiers in Psychiatry*, *12*, 760396. 10.3389/fpsyt.2021.760396
Hawkley, L. C., & Cacioppo, J. T. (2010). Loneliness matters: A theoretical and empirical review of consequences and mechanisms. *Annals of Behavioral Medicine*, *40*(2), 218–227. 10.1007/s12160-010-9210-8
Hinojosa-Marqués, L., Domínguez-Martínez, T., Kwapil, T. R., & Barrantes-Vidal, N. (2020). Predictors of criticism and emotional over-involvement in relatives of early psychosis patients. *PloS One*, *15*(6), e0234325. 10.1371/journal.pone.0234325
Holt-Lunstad, J., Smith, T. B., & Layton, J. B. (2010). Social relationships and mortality risk: A meta-analytic review. *PLoS Medicine*, *7*(7), e1. 10.1371/journal.pmed.1000316
Hooley, J. M. (2007). Expressed emotion and relapse of psychopathology. *Annual Review of Clinical Psychology*, *3*(1), 329–352. 10.1146/annurev.clinpsy.2.022305.095236
Hooley, J. M., & Gotlib, I. H. (2000). A diathesis-stress conceptualization of expressed emotion and clinical outcome. *Applied & Preventive Psychology*, *9*(3), 135–151. 10.1016/S0962-1849(05)80001-0
Hooley, J. M., Gruber, S. A., Parker, H. A., Guillaumot, J., Rogowska, J., & Yurgelun-Todd, D. (2009). Cortico-limbic response to personally challenging emotional stimuli after complete recovery from depression. *Psychiatry Research: Neuroimaging*, *171*(2), 106–119. 10.1016/j.pscychresns.2008.04.001
Hooley, J. M., Gruber, S. A., Scott, L. A., Hiller, J. B., & Yurgelun-Todd, D. (2005). Activation in dorsolateral prefrontal cortex in response to maternal criticism and praise in recovered depressed and healthy control participants. *Biological Psychiatry*, *57*(7), 809–812. 10.1016/j.biopsych.2005.01.012
Hooley, J. M., & Parker, H. A. (2006). Measuring expressed emotion: An evaluation of the shortcuts. *Journal of Family Psychology*, *20*(3), 386–396. 10.1037/0893-3200.20.3.386
Hooley, J. M., Siegle, G., & Gruber, S. A. (2012). Affective and neural reactivity to criticism in individuals high and low on perceived criticism. *PloS One*, *7*(9), e44412. 10.1371/journal.pone.0044412

Jablensky, A., Sartorius, N., Ernberg, G., Anker, M., Korten, A., Cooper, J. E., Day, R., & Bertelsen, A. (1992). Schizophrenia: manifestations, incidence and course in different cultures A World Health Organization Ten-Country Study. *Psychological Medicine Monograph Supplement*, *20*, 1–97. 10.1017/S0264180100000904

Julayanont, P., & Suryadevara, U. (2021). Psychosis. *Continuum* (Minneapolis, Minn.), *27*(6), 1682–1711. 10.1212/CON.0000000000001013

Kavanagh, D. J. (1992). Recent developments in expressed emotion and schizophrenia. *British Journal of Psychiatry*, *160*(5), 601–620. 10.1192/bjp.160.5.601

Kavanagh, D. J., O'Halloran, P., Manicavasagar, V., Clark, D., Piatkowska, O., Tennant, C., & Rosen, A. (1997). The family attitude scale: Reliability and validity of a new scale for measuring the emotional climate of families. *Psychiatry Research*, *70*(3), 185–195. 10.1016/S0165-1781(97)00033-4

Kéri, S., & Kelemen, O. (2009). The role of attention and immediate memory in vulnerability to interpersonal criticism during family transactions in schizophrenia. *British Journal of Clinical Psychology*, *48*(1), 21–29. 10.1348/014466508X342926

Kim, E. Y., & Miklowitz, D. J. (2004). Expressed emotion as a predictor of outcome among bipolar patients undergoing family therapy. *Journal of Affective Disorders*, *82*(3), 343–352. 10.1016/j.jad.2004.02.004

Kuipers, E., Watson, P., Onwumere, J., Bebbington, P., Dunn, G., Weinman, J., Fowler, D., Freeman, D., Hardy, A., & Garety, P. (2007). Discrepant illness perceptions, affect and expressed emotion in people with psychosis and their carers. *Social Psychiatry and Psychiatric Epidemiology*, *42*(4), 277–283. 10.1007/s00127-007-0165-4

Kymalainen, J. A., Weisman, A. G., Rosales, G. A., & Armesto, J. C. (2006). Ethnicity, expressed emotion, and communication deviance in family members of patients with schizophrenia. *The Journal of Nervous and Mental Disease*, *194*(6), 391–396. 10.1097/01.nmd.0000221171.42027.5a

Leary, M. R., Cottrell, C. A., & Phillips, M. (2001). Deconfounding the effects of dominance and social acceptance on self-esteem. *Journal of Personality and Social Psychology*, *81*(5), 898–909. 10.1037//0022-3514.81.5.898

Lee, G., Barrowclough, C., & Lobban, F. (2014). Positive affect in the family environment protects against relapse in first-episode psychosis. *Social Psychiatry and Psychiatric Epidemiology*, *49*(3), 367–376. 10.1007/s00127-013-0768-x

Leff, J., Wig, N. N., Ghosh, A., Bedi, H., Menon, D. K., Kuipers, L., Korten, A., Ernberg, G., Day, R., & Sartorius, N. (1987). Expressed emotion and schizophrenia in north India. III. Influence of relatives' expressed emotion on the course of schizophrenia in Chandigarh. *British Journal of Psychiatry*, *151*(2), 166–173. 10.1192/bjp.151.2.166

Leff, J. P., & Vaughn, C. (1984). The expressed emotion scales. In *Expressed emotion in families: Its significance for mental illness* (pp. 37–63). Guilford Press.

Lim, M. H., Gleeson, J. F. M., Alvarez-Jimenez, M., & Penn, D. L. (2018). Loneliness in psychosis: a systematic review. *Social Psychiatry and Psychiatric Epidemiology*, *53*(3), 221–238. 10.1007/s00127-018-1482-5

Lincoln, S. H., Johnson, T., Winters, A., & Laquidara, J. (2021). Social exclusion and rejection across the psychosis spectrum: A systematic review of empirical research. *Schizophrenia Research*, *228*, 43–50. 10.1016/j.schres.2020.11.056

Lysaker, P. H., Gagen, E., Moritz, S., & Schweitzer, R. D. (2018). Metacognitive approaches to the treatment of psychosis: a comparison of four approaches. *Psychology Research and Behavior Management*, *11*, 341–351. 10.2147/PRBM.S146446

Lysaker, P., Yanos, P., Outcalt, J., & Roe, D. (2010). Association of stigma, self-esteem, and symptoms with concurrent and prospective assessment of social anxiety in schizophrenia. *Clinical Schizophrenia & Related Psychoses*, *4*(1), 41–48. 10.3371/CSRP.4.1.3

Magaña, A. B., Goldstein, M. J., Karno, M., Miklowitz, D. J., Jenkins, J., & Falloon, I. R. H. (1986). A brief method for assessing expressed emotion in relatives of psychiatric patients. *Psychiatry Research*, *17*(3), 203–212. 10.1016/0165-1781(86)90049-1

Majors, R. (1991). *Nonverbal behaviors and communication styles among African Americans* (3rd ed.). Cobb & Henry Publishers.

Marsh, D. T., & Lefky, H. P. (2009). Serious mental illness: Family experiences, needs, and interventions. In J. H. Bray & M. Stanton (Eds.), *The Wiley-Blackwell handbook of family psychology* (pp. 742–754). Blackwell. https://doi.org/10.1002/9781444310238.ch53

McCormick, B. P., Brusilovskiy, E., Nagata, S., Townley, G., Snethen, G., & Salzer, M. S. (2023). The role of acceptance in everyday loneliness among adults with serious mental illness. *Community Mental Health Journal*, *60*, 308–316. 10.1007/s10597-023-01172-4

Mesoudi, A., Whiten, A., & Dunbar, R. (2006). A bias for social information in human cultural transmission. *British Journal of Psychology*, *97*(3), 405–423. 10.1348/000712605X85871

Miklowitz, D. J., & Goldstein, M. J. (1997). *Bipolar disorder: A family-focused treatment approach*. Guilford Press.

Nuechterlein, K. H., & Dawson, M. E. (1984). A heuristic vulnerability/stress model of schizophrenic episodes. *Schizophrenia Bulletin*, *10*(2), 300–312. 10.1093/schbul/10.2.300

O'Brien, M. P., Gordon, J. L., Bearden, C. E., Lopez, S. R., Kopelowicz, A., & Cannon, T. D. (2006). Positive family environment predicts improvement in symptoms and social functioning among adolescents at imminent risk for onset of psychosis. *Schizophrenia Research*, *81*(2), 269–275. 10.1016/j.schres.2005.10.005

O'Driscoll, C., Sener, S. B., Angmark, A., & Shaikh, M. (2019). Caregiving processes and expressed emotion in psychosis, a cross-cultural, meta-analytic review. *Schizophrenia Research*, *208*, 8–15. 10.1016/j.schres.2019.03.020

O'Reilly, C. L., Paul, D., McCahon, R., Shankar, S., Rosen, A., & Ramzy, T. (2019). Stigma and discrimination in individuals with severe and persistent mental illness in an assertive community treatment team: Perceptions of families and healthcare professionals. *International Journal of Social Psychiatry*, *65*(7–8), 570–579. 10.1177/0020764019867358

Parker, N., & O'Reilly, M. (2012). 'Gossiping' as a social action in family therapy: The pseudo-absence and pseudo-presence of children. *Discourse Studies*, *14*(4), 457–475. 10.1177/1461445612452976

Pharoah, F., Jair, J. M., Rathbone, J., & Wong, W. (2010). Family intervention for schizophrenia. *Cochrane Database of Systematic Reviews*, *2012*(11), CD. 10.1002/14651858.cd000088.pub3

Premkumar, P., Onwumere, J., Albert, J., Kessel, D., Kumari, V., Kuipers, E., & Carretié, L. (2015). The relation between schizotypy and early attention to rejecting interactions: The influence of neuroticism. *The World Journal of Biological Psychiatry*, *16*(8), 587–601. 10.3109/15622975.2015.1073855

Premkumar, P., Onwumere, J., Betts, L., Kibowski, F., & Kuipers, E. (2018). Schizotypal traits and their relation to rejection sensitivity in the general population: Their mediation by quality of life, agreeableness and neuroticism. *Psychiatry Research*, *267*, 201–209. S0165-1781(17)31903-0 [pii]

Premkumar, P., Williams, S. C., Lythgoe, D., Andrew, C., Kuipers, E., & Kumari, V. (2013). Neural processing of criticism and positive comments from relatives in individuals with schizotypal personality traits. *The World Journal of Biological Psychiatry: The Official Journal of the World Federation of Societies of Biological Psychiatry*, *14*(1), 57–70. 10.3109/15622975.2011.604101 [doi]

Ran, M., Leff, J., Hou, Z., Xiang, M., & Chan, C. L. (2003). The characteristics of expressed emotion among relatives of patients with schizophrenia in Chengdu, China. *Culture, Medicine and Psychiatry*, *27*(1), 95–106. 10.1023/A:1023636021995

Rogan, R. G., & Hammer, M. R. (1998). An exploratory study of message affect behavior: A comparison between African Americans and Euro-Americans. *Journal of Language and Social Psychology*, *17*(4), 449–464. 10.1177/0261927X980174002

Rosenfarb, I. S., Bellack, A. S., & Aziz, N. (2006). Family interactions and the course of schizophrenia in African American and White patients. *Journal of Abnormal Child Psychology*, *115*(1), 112–120. 10.1037/0021-843X.115.1.112

Russell, D. W., Cutrona, C. E., McRae, C., & Gomez, M. (2012). Is loneliness the same as being alone? *The Journal of Psychology*, *146*(1-2), 7–22. 10.1080/00223980.2011.589414

Rylands, A. J., McKie, S., Elliott, R., Deakin, J. F. W., & Tarrier, N. (2011). A functional magnetic resonance imaging paradigm of expressed emotion in schizophrenia. *The Journal of Nervous and Mental Disease*, *199*(1), 25–29. 10.1097/NMD.0b013e3182043b87

Saporta, N., Scheele, D., Lieberz, J., Stuhr-Wulff, F., Hurlemann, R., & Shamay-Tsoory, S. (2021). Opposing association of situational and chronic loneliness with interpersonal distance. *Brain Sciences*, *11*(9), 1135. 10.3390/brainsci11091135

Sartorius, N., Shapiro, R., & Jablensky, A. (1974). The international pilot study of schizophrenia. *Schizophrenia Bulletin*, *1*(11), 21–34. 10.1093/schbul/1.11.21

Schmidt, G., & Weiner, B. (1988). An attribution-affect-action theory of behavior: Replications of judgments of help-giving. *Personality & Social Psychology Bulletin*, *14*(3), 610–621. 10.1177/0146167288143021

Startup, M., & Startup, S. (2005). On two kinds of delusion of reference. *Psychiatry Research*, *137*(1), 87–92. 10.1016/j.psychres.2005.07.007

Sündermann, O., Onwumere, J., Bebbington, P., & Kuipers, E. (2013). Social networks and support in early psychosis: potential mechanisms. *Epidemiology and Psychiatric Sciences*, *22*(2), 147–150. 10.1017/S2045796012000601

Tarrier, N., & Barrowclough, C. (1984). Psychophysiological assessment of expressed emotion in schizophrenia: A case example. *British Journal of Psychiatry*, *145*(2), 197–200. 10.1192/bjp.145.2.197

Tompson, M. C., Goldstein, M. J., Lebell, M. B., Mintz, L. I., Marder, S. R., & Mintz, J. (1995). Schizophrenic patients' perceptions of their relatives' attitudes. *Psychiatry Research*, *57*(2), 155–167. 10.1016/0165-1781(95)02598-Q

van Husen, G., Burger, T. J., de Koning, M. B., de Wit, M. A. S., Segeren, M. W., & Beekman, A. T. F. (2025). Needs of the network: A qualitative study of the needs of family members, partners and close friends of people with a severe mental illness (SMI). *BMC Psychiatry*, *25*(1), 220–314. 10.1186/s12888-025-06607-8

Vaughn, C. E., Snyder, K. S., Jones, S., Freeman, W. B., & Falloon, I. R. H. (1984). Family factors in schizophrenic relapse: Replication in California of British research on expressed emotion. *Archives of General Psychiatry*, *41*(12), 1169–1177. 10.1001/archpsyc.1984.01790230055009

Walker, E. F., & Diforio, D. (1997). Schizophrenia: A neural diathesis-stress model. *Psychological Review*, *104*(4), 667–685. 10.1037/0033-295X.104.4.667

Wang, C., Zhang, Y., Chong, J. S., Zhang, W., Zhang, X., McIntyre, R. S., Li, Z., Ho, R. C. M., Tang, T. B., & Lim, L. G. (2024). Altered functional connectivity subserving expressed emotion environments in schizophrenia: An fNIRS study. *Schizophrenia Research*, *270*, 178–187. 10.1016/j.schres.2024.06.019

Wedig, M. M., & Nock, M. K. (2007). Parental expressed emotion and adolescent self-injury. *Journal of the American Academy of Child & Adolescent Psychiatry*, *46*(9), 1171–1178. 10.1097/chi.0b013e3180ca9aaf

Weintraub, M. J., Weisman de Mamani, A., Villano, W. J., Evans, T. C., Millman, Z. B., Hooley, J. M., & Timpano, K. R. (2019). Affective and physiological reactivity to emotional comments in individuals at elevated risk for psychosis. *Schizophrenia Research, 206*, 428–435. 10.1016/j.schres.2018.10.006

Weisman, A., López, S. R., Karno, M., & Jenkins, J. (1993). An attributional analysis of expressed emotion in Mexican-American families with schizophrenia. *Journal of Abnormal Psychology, 102*(4), 601–606. 10.1037/0021-843X.102.4.601

Weisman, A. G., Nuechterlein, K. H., Goldstein, M. J., & Snyder, K. S. (1998). Expressed emotion, attributions, and schizophrenia symptom dimensions. *Journal of Abnormal Psychology, 107*(2), 355–359. 10.1037/0021-843X.107.2.355

Weisman, A. G., Rosales, G. A., Kymalainen, J. A., & Armesto, J. C. (2006). Ethnicity, expressed emotion, and schizophrenia patients' perceptions of their family members' criticism. *The Journal of Nervous and Mental Disease, 194*(9), 644–649. 10.1097/01.nmd.0000235504.39284.f1

Weisman de Mamani, A., Dunham, R., Aldebot, S., Tuchman, N., Wasserman, S., Loue, S., & Sajatovic, M. (2008). Family-focused psychoeducational programs for minorities with serious mental illness. In S. Loue & M. Sajatovic (Eds.), *Determinants of minority mental health and wellness* (pp. 1–18). Springer New York. 10.1007/978-0-387-75659-2_12

Weisman de Mamani, A., McLaughlin, M., Altamirano, O., Lopez, D., & Ahmad, S. S. (2021). *Culturally informed therapy for schizophrenia: A family-focused cognitive behavioral approach*. Oxford University Press.

Weisman de Mamani, A. G., Kymalainen, J. A., Rosales, G. A., & Armesto, J. C. (2007). Expressed emotion and interdependence in White and Latino/Hispanic family members of patients with schizophrenia. *Psychiatry Research, 151*(1), 107–113. 10.1016/j.psychres.2006.11.007

Chapter 2

Measuring sensitivity to criticism and its relationship to mental health

Alice Betteridge and Preethi Premkumar

Abstract

This chapter discusses the measurement of criticism following the concept of expressed emotion and the relapse of mental disorder. This concept explains how the emotion expressed by a close relative of a patient diagnosed with a mental disorder includes criticism, hostility, emotional over-involvement and positive comments. Besides the measurement of expressed emotion (EE) from the close relative, the criticism perceived by the patient can be measured in several ways, including standard audio-comments of criticism that mimics EE-criticism, and these measurements are related to mental health outcomes in both clinical and non-clinical populations. Furthermore, criticism perceived by a person, either with or without a mental disorder, such as intimate couples, can be reciprocated and in turn increase one's own level of depression and anxiety. The level of perceived criticism by patients with psychosis also relates to carer attributes, such as the burden of care and having optimistic or pessimistic expectations for the patient. When presented as standard auditory vignettes, the arousal of standard criticism and standard praise, and their relevance to close relationships, relate to a range of mental health problems, such as schizotypal personality, substance abuse, childhood trauma and paranoia. These mental health outcomes of perceived criticism have given rise to interventions to challenge beliefs and attributions of family members and to work with them to improve resilience to stressful situations.

2.1 Introduction

Criticism is intended to correct a person for their mistake with the intention of changing the way the person thinks and acts. Yet, criticism can have different consequences based on how it is levelled at the person, i.e. constructive or unconstructive. Constructive criticism is meant to be helpful and acknowledge poor performance, and it is considerate and encouraging (Tortoriello & Hart,

DOI: 10.4324/9781003388159-3

2019). Unconstructive criticism can be used to threaten a person, blame them for their actions and direct a person to take responsibility for their actions (Tortoriello & Hart, 2019). As explained in Chapter 1, excessive criticism from a carer towards a patient with serious mental illness increases the risk of relapse.

2.1.1 The construct of expressed emotion

The construct of expressed emotion (EE) defines criticism as a personal remark of dislike or disapproval about what the person does (Brown et al., 1972; Leff & Vaughn, 1984a). Families who express a high number of these comments would be classified as being high EE families; however, it is important to note the tone of these comments. Families can express dissatisfaction towards their family member but still be classed as low EE families, as the key difference is this critical tone and sense of blaming for their behaviours (Domínguez-Martínez et al., 2014; Leff, Julian & Vaughn, 1985). This chapter follows this definition of criticism, that is expressing disapproval using a high tone (Magaña et al., 1986), and understanding sensitivity to such criticism using vignettes in an experimental setting has produced new insights into mental distress (Premkumar et al., 2019, 2020).

The construct of EE focuses on the mental health of patients with a psychiatric disorder and considers the role that the carer plays in the prognosis of patients with a psychiatric disorder. The theory of EE states that EE increases the likelihood of a patient with mental health problems relapsing (Bebbington & Kuipers, 1994; Butzlaff & Hooley, 1998), with a more recent review of literature suggesting that critical comments from carers is the main contributing factor for predicting relapse following treatment of first-episode psychosis (Alvarez-Jimenez et al., 2012). EE is a rating of criticism, hostility, emotional over-involvement and warmth expressed by a caregiver towards a patient with a diagnosis of mental disorder (see section 2.3.1). Thus, the construct of EE places criticism more broadly alongside other attitudes of the carer towards the patient in understanding the relationship between the patient and the carer. However, some sources consider criticism to be the most important component of high EE (Onwumere et al., 2009). Critical EE has has been found to relate to other aspects of psychotic disorders including predicting the onset of first-episode psychosis and increasing the severity of their symptoms (Izon et al., 2018). This is thought to be due to critical families causing the development of a negative self-concept which exacerbates positive symptoms (Barrowclough et al., 2003).

The construct of EE has clear criteria about the content of a comment and the tone of the speaker for the comment to be regarded as criticism (Leff & Vaughn, 1984b). These criteria provided clear guidelines for preparing experimental stimuli in a laboratory setting (see section 2.4.1). And these criteria were developed following the seminal studies of families of patients with schizophrenia (Brown et al., 1962, 1966, 1972). Brown et al. (1962) found that patients with schizophrenia were more likely to deteriorate on returning from hospital after remission if they had prolonged contact with their close relative who had certain relational characteristics. Brown et al. (1962) speculated that patients would be more likely to relapse if they returned to live with a close relative who showed hostility or dominating behaviour and had prolonged contact with them (Brown and colleagues 1962). The concept of EE as criticism had not emerged then. Instead, hostility was the closest observed phenomenon, and it was assessed by an overall attitude of the relative rejecting the patient over the course of the interview. There, Brown and colleagues (1962) examined the clinical progress of 128 male patients with schizophrenia who were discharged from hospitals in London. In that study, researchers interviewed the close relative of the patient at three time points:

1) before the patient returned home;
2) two weeks after the patient returned home from hospital;
3) when the patient was readmitted to hospital following a relapse or after one year, which ever was earlier.

Interestingly, Brown and colleagues (1962) did not find that hostility influenced the likelihood of relapse. The likelihood of relapse was no greater among relatives who were hostile (80%) than not hostile (74%). Instead, emotional over-involvement (EOI) was the key determinant of relapse. The likelihood of relapse was 76% if the relative was overinvolved and 28% if the relative was not overinvolved. Crucially, the time spent with the overinvolved relative determined clinical outcome. More patients deteriorated when they spent more than 35 hours per week (96%) with a close relative who was emotionally overinvolved than when they spent less than 35 hours per week with a close relative who was emotionally overinvolved (50%) (Brown et al., 1962). EOI denotes excessive anxiety, over-protection and concern for the welfare of the patient. Thus, EOI is detrimental to the prognosis of schizophrenia. Positive comments, which include praises, are closely related to EOI because in excess, positive comments denote warmth which can be seen as being overbearing. Given that EOI predicted relapse, positive comments are also of interest (Brown et al., 1972). Positive comments denote 'Sympathy and concern, interest in the other as a person, and expressed enjoyment in mutual activities', and positive comments (or praises) co-exist with high EOI, as does criticism with hostility. Overall, these seminal studies emphasise the importance of looking at both criticism and praise together when assessing the clinical outcome of EE.

2.1.2 *How expressed emotion is measured*

The Camberwell Family Interview: The Camberwell Family Interview (CFI) was the first measure of EE to be developed and it is the gold standard measurement of expressed emotion. It uses observational techniques in semi-structured interviews for rating EE based on family members' speech, expressions and tone. The CFI originated from the family interviews conducted in these seminal studies (Brown et al., 1962, 1966, 1972). An early family adjustment measure (Brown et al., 1972) was refined into the CFI (Leff & Vaughn, 1984a; Vaughn & Leff, 1976a; Vaughn, & Leff, 1976b). The earlier family adjustment measure defined the rating of criticism as follows (Brown et al., 1972):

> For a remark to be judged critical in content there had to be a clear and unambiguous statement of resentment, disapproval or dislike. Any remark could be rated critical on tone alone, and in making the ratings most emphasis was laid on the interviewer's judgement of tone of voice.

In contrast, a positive comment (hereafter termed as praise) constitutes warmth (Brown et al., 1972). It is defined as:

> a statement which expresses praise, approval or appreciation of the behaviour or personality of the person to whom it refers … A positive remark, unlike warmth, is defined primarily by its content. The meaning of the remark should express praise, appreciation or approval without ambiguity.

The CFI addresses aspects of the individual's mental illness, and levels of stress within the household associated the individual's abilities to contribute to overall family functioning. Verbal behavioural communications give ratings for all the five components of expressed emotion (Amaresha & Venkatasubramanian 2012; Wearden et al., 2000).

1) **Criticism** – assessing the quantity of critical comments
2) **Hostility** – attitudes rated as being present or absent from communication
3) **Emotional Over-Involvement** – verbalisations of extreme over-protective behaviours
4) **Warmth** – verbalisations of kindness and concern shown through vocal qualities, i.e. tone of voice, and behavioural indicators, i.e. smiling
5) **Positive comment** – quantity of statements expressing support or appreciation

From this, the family member is then classified as displaying either high or low EE, with high EE being high in critical comments, hostility and/or emotional overinvolvement (Avraam et al., 2022; Brown et al., 1972; Leff & Vaughn, 1984a). Thus, criticism and praise constitute two ends of the emotional spectrum in relationships, and both are unhelpful in excess. As will become apparent below, the appraisals of criticism and praise relate to vulnerability for schizophrenia differently. Furthermore, different thresholds were set for the frequency of criticism to count as high EE during the seminal studies, beginning with seven or more but the threshold was adjusted to six or more because the lower threshold gave a better separation of relapse rates of schizophrenia between those families classed as high EE and those classed as low EE (Magaña et al., 1986; Vaughn, & Leff, 1976a).

How to show appreciation:

Regularly express praise and gratitude for each other's actions and efforts. Simple acknowledgements create a positive environment and make it easier to handle criticism because family members feel valued.

Five-Minute Speech Sample (FMSS): The FMSS (Magaña et al., 1986) can also be used to measure family members' EE and works in a similar way to the CFI (Sher-Censor, 2015). The family member must speak about the individual for five minutes uninterrupted, with the idea that speaking uninterrupted for this length of time would maximise their projections of internal feelings (Gottschalk & Gleser, 2023). This speech is then assessed for EE components. Although this method has been criticised for being less nuanced that the CFI, it is appraised as a valid measure for EE with the benefit of being drastically shorter and less time consuming (Amaresha & Venkatasubramanian, 2012; Gottschalk, 1969). Here, a relative is classed as high EE for expressing (a) any criticism based on either content or tone at any point during the five-minute speech, (b) a negative opening statement, or (c) an overall negative relationship rating based on a tally of a weak positive relationship statement, a strong positive relationship statement, a weak negative relationship statement and a strong negative relationship statement.

2.1.3 Psychometric measures

From these observational techniques, various self-report psychometric measures have been developed.

Level of Expressed Emotion scale: The Level of Expressed Emotion (LEE) scale measures the emotional environment of an individual's most important relationship (Cole & Kazarian, 1988). The LEE scale is a simplified measure of EE and the scale asks how the individual perceives EE in their close relative. It measures the content of EE from this close relative from the perspective of the individual. The 38-item scale measure irritability, intrusiveness, lack of emotional support and criticism from the relative. This self-reported scale is quicker to administer than the 45-minute CFI, although it is an indirect measure of EE since the person perceives EE in their relative instead of directly enquiring about EE with the relative in an interview. Irritability on the LEE scale resembles hostility in the CFI measure of EE. Intrusiveness on the LEE scale resembles EOI in the CFI measure of EE. There is also a version that family members can complete to provide their perspective which measures for intrusiveness, emotional response, attitude towards illness, and tolerance and expectations.

Family Emotional Involvement and Criticism scale: Family Emotional Involvement and Criticism Scale (FEICS) assesses emotional over-involvement and perceived criticism (Shields et al., 1992). The decision to focus solely on these two components of EE was informed by previous research, which showed the strongest associations with relapse rates in mental healthcare at the time. The scale asks about the quantity of behaviours displayed by individuals' family members.

Family Attitude Scale: The Family Attitude Scale (FAS) places its emphasis on criticism and hostility (Kavanagh et al., 1997). The FAS can be completed by either the individual or the family member perspective, asking the reader to rate how often statements are true. The scale gives an overall score, with higher scores indicating higher levels of criticism expressed from the family members and higher levels of burden felt by the family members.

Perceived Criticism Measure: Perceived Criticism (PC) measure is the most efficient of all available psychometric measures, taking approximately one minute to complete (Hooley & Teasdale, 1989). It is founded on the claim that criticism is the most important of all EE components and therefore asks one question, 'How critical is your partner/relative of you?', which the person rates on a scale of 1 to 10 from 'Not at all critical' to 'Very critical indeed'. However, a two-item version of this measure also asked the person to rate 'how critical the patients considered themselves to be of their spouses' and this version has been seldom used as are other variations of the original single-item measure (Parra Castaneda et al., 2022).

2.2 The impact of EE-criticism and perceived criticism on patient mental health outcomes

The attributes of both the carers and the patients determine carer EE. A greater number of criticisms from the carer uttered during the CFI corresponded with heightened anxiety of patients with psychosis (n=86), and lower self-esteem and an avoidant coping style of their carer (Kuipers et al., 2006). Here, a third of patients living with a high EE carer encountered high criticism. The findings reinforced the role of carer criticism in anxiety of patients with psychosis. Nonetheless, the patient's anxiety did not explain the relationship between the patient's PC of the carer and the carer's level of criticism as measured by the CFI (Onwumere et al., 2009), which suggests that factors other than the patient's affect could influence their perception of their carer's criticism, such as the patients' arousal level and knowledge of criticism.

Furthermore, patient perceived criticism was associated with the carer's burden in terms of the carer lacking support from a confidante (Onwumere et al., 2009), and this suggests that support for patients must draw on support from wider social networks. When carers were optimistic about the consequences of the illness and about the illness of the patient as a whole, such discrepancies between the carer and the patients were associated with more anxiety in the patient (Kuipers et al., 2007). In addition, when carers were pessimistic about the future of the illness, such as the view that there was little that the patient could do to control their symptoms, the patients reported higher self-esteem while carers themselves reported more stress and lower self-esteem (Kuipers et al., 2007). Finally, more divergence between carers and patients about the consequence of the illness corresponded with carers expressing more EOI towards the patient rated during the CFI. In summary, patients are adept at perceiving their carer's criticism. Such PC co-exists with the burden sustained by carers, and expectations of the carer about the illness corresponds with anxiety of patients with psychosis.

Patients' PC of their carer was systematically reviewed across the literature among patients with a severe mental illness, such as depression, bipolar disorder and anxiety (Parra Castaneda et al., 2022). The studies included ratings from patients of their partner, parent or their family as a whole, and the review examined the relationship between PC and patient characteristics, illness factors and treatment outcomes (Parra Castaneda et al., 2022). With regards to the quality of the relationship between the patient and their carer, greater PC was associated with lower relationship satisfaction in patients with anxiety and depression. PC was associated with poorer social functioning in patients with anxiety disorder and patients with depression. Additionally, PC predicted relapse of depression in some studies, but not others, and it predicted relapse in patients with first-episode psychosis. PC also predicted the severity of social anxiety disorder in patients with this diagnosis, and poorer treatment outcomes, such as poorer improvement in symptoms, in patients with anxiety disorders. The review highlights the broad implications of PC for the severity of mental illness, recovery and social functioning.

Notwithstanding the noted dearth of literature on the impact of PC on carer wellbeing and their roles as a carer (Parra Castaneda et al., 2022), three studies reported its relationship between PC and caregiver burden. Carers of patients with psychosis carry undue burden and burnout as they grapple with the nature of symptoms (Onwumere et al., 2016, 2018). They can experience poor psychological functioning, stress disorders and social isolation (Onwumere et al., 2016). Carer burnout, in terms of a sense of lack of achievement and emotional exhaustion, was related to carer depression and anxiety in patients with early psychosis (Onwumere et al., 2018). Parents formed the majority of carers (85%) in this representative sample of carers of patients with early psychosis (n=169), and 60% reported above-threshold levels of burnout. Alleviating carer burnout is a key pathway to care of patients with severe mental illness, and primary care practitioners must recognise this burnout and facilitate communication between patients and carers (Onwumere et al., 2016).

2.3 Impact of EE on mental health in the non-clinical population

There is consistent evidence that EE is related to more depression in patients with schizophrenia (Bentsen et al., 1998; Docherty et al., 2011; Kuipers et al., 2006). More criticism from the relative when interacting with the patient alongside poorer patient attention predicted unusual thinking in patients with schizophrenia (Kéri & Kelemen, 2009; Rosenfarb et al., 2000). However, EE may not necessarily be an epiphenomenon of mental disorder, and it could exist on a continuum from normal to subclinical and clinical populations (Goldstein, 1985; McFarlane & Cook, 2007). Greater PC by adolescents of their parents coincides with a higher level of depression, aggression and delinquency (Hale et al., 2011). EE also increases antisocial behaviour in young children (Caspi et al., 2004) and behavioural inhibition of children of mothers with anxiety disorder (Hirshfeld et al. 1997). These findings emphasise the need to monitor non-clinical populations that are exposed to criticism for vulnerability for mental disorders.

How to deal with criticism towards adolescents:

Given that criticism is linked to greater level of depression, aggression and delinquency in adolescents, parents could express the criticism constructively without a raised tone. Parents could also offer alternative ways of dealing the situation.

2.3.1 EE reciprocity

Early attempts at understanding the psychological effect of criticism focused on the transaction between patients and their close relative during a problem-solving exercise. This is because EE may reflect the direct dyadic interaction between the patient and their relative (Gerlsma et al., 2009; Goldstein et al., 1989; Kuipers et al., 1983; Miklowitz et al., 1989; Strachan et al., 1989). EE reciprocity is defined as the concordance of EE level (high/low) between the patient and their close relative. Thus, it is important to study the live interaction between the patient and their close relative.

In married couples, affective linkage is where the negative emotions of one partner are more likely to affect the emotions of the other partner (Gottman & Levenson, 1985). Here, affective linkage was more common in distressed couples than non-distressed couples. More depression and dejection in the wife were associated with both the husband and wife expressing more sadness during interpersonal interaction (Geist & Gilbert, 1996). Anger and hostility in wives were associated with more anger and contempt expressed by both the wife and husband during interaction (Geist & Gilbert, 1996). Studies of close relationships in healthy populations suggest several reasons for relational discord. Conflict may occur due to relational competence, such as use of idiosyncratic strategies to resolve conflict (Klein & Milardo, 1993), a sense of obligation (Stein, 1993) and external manifestation of internal dialectics of each individual (Baxter & Montgomery, 1993). This understanding of how criticism manifests as relational discord offers ways into minimise the discord.

A study of EE reciprocity based on 40 healthy couples (Gerlsma et al., 2009) found that the more a partner PC, the more likely EE was to concur between partners, and the greater the partner's own depressive and marital complaints. This finding suggests that partners agree considerably in the amount of criticism they perceive from each other (Gerlsma et al., 2009). However, another study examined EE in both partners and found that only one out of 40 married couples (2%) was dual high EE (Brückner et al., 2008).

EE reciprocity may be higher in other close relationships where there is vulnerability for mental disorder. In a study of adolescents with mild behavioural disturbance (Goldstein, 1985), 11 out of 45 parent–adolescent dyads (24%) were dual high EE. And such parental EE coincided with a negative affect style during a problem-solving interaction between the parent and their adolescent and greater communication deviance between parents of the adolescent (Goldstein, 1985). Furthermore, parental EE increased the likelihood of the adolescent with mild behavioural disturbance subsequently having a diagnosis on the schizophrenia spectrum (Goldstein, 1985). Considering these two studies together, it seems that the likelihood of EE reciprocity is higher in clinical, than non-clinical, populations.

How to deal with criticism between couples:

Couples who experience affective linkage could use non-verbal means of appreciation in the face of criticism, such as by writing statements that reaffirm their confidence in their partner. These constructive written statements could remind couples of what works well in their relationships.

How to reinforce each other's strengths:

Instead of focusing on each other's weaknesses, regularly acknowledge each other's positive traits. For example, compliment your family member's kindness or resilience, especially in difficult situations. This approach makes critical conversations feel more balanced and supportive.

Listening to criticism can be challenging at times, especially when it is not accompanied by guidance on how to grow from the criticism. Share your learning from the feedback with that person. Ask the person who criticised you to suggest how they might respond in that situation and what might be a good way to address the criticism.

2.3.2 *Impact of EE on mental health in at-risk populations*

EE has been found to impact the mental health of individuals who are deemed to be at risk of the development of a psychiatric disorder, most frequently psychosis. Approximately one-third of individuals deemed to have an At-Risk Mental State (ARMS) had relatives who displayed high levels of EE, much higher than the general population (Izon et al., 2018). These families display higher levels of criticisms, increased hostility and lower levels of nurturing behaviours (Welsh & Tiffin, 2015). Within this population, the individual suffers negative consequences, displaying a range of poor skills and functioning including poorer perceived problem-solving skills and increased negative symptoms, which is a reduction of usual behaviours and abilities for things such as communication, motivation and displays of emotion (O'Brien et al., 2006; Schlosser et al., 2010). For those who go on to develop psychotic symptoms, similar relationships are found, where increased criticisms and conflictual communications from family members were associated with worsening symptoms and decreased functioning.

Contrastingly, families who structured their critical comments in a more constructive way by focusing on problem-solving showed enhanced social functioning in their relationship with an ARMS (O'Brien et al., 2009). Additionally, families who displayed more of the positive components of EE, that is warmth and positive regard, showed a decrease in negative and disorganised symptoms, which is unusual or bizarre behaviour, and improvements in social functioning over time (Izon et al., 2018; O'Brien et al., 2006, 2008; Tsai et al., 2015).

2.4 Experimental investigation of criticism and praise

Inviting the close relative and the index participant to take part in a dyadic interaction is an elaborate process and raises hurdles with participant recruitment and engagement (Magaña et al., 1986). Practically, asking the relative to pre-record a bank of criticisms about the index participant and for these criticisms to then be delivered to the index participant in the laboratory is time consuming and raises ethical issues about asking the relative to generate such material. Instead, a bank of standard auditory criticism and praise could imitate the remarks of a close relative and obviate the need for the relative to be present to deliver these comments to research participants (Servaas et al., 2013). Such a bank of standard EE-like criticism and praise could reduce the difficulties that researchers encounter when recruiting service users and their carers for research (e.g. Garety et al., 2008) and benefit the wider scientific community (Premkumar et al., 2019, 2020). Hearing standard criticism and standard praise from a confederate could even lower variation in affective reactivity to different family members arising from different family histories of interaction with each family member (Cuellar et al., 2009). Such experimental investigation of criticism and praise could help to understand how participants experience support, intrusion, rejection or neglect in relationships (Newsom et al., 2005). Sexagenarians (participants in their 60s) recollected the number of positive and negative social exchanges in the previous month. Viewing positive social exchanges as a means of informational and emotional support was associated with more distress (Newsom et al., 2005). This suggests that partners were more likely to offer affirming social exchanges when their partner was distressed. Appraising negative social exchanges as denoting unsympathetic behaviour was also associated with more distress in this sample of sexagenarians. In a similar manner, a bank of standard criticism and praise could prompt recollection of recent social exchanges and reliably relate to distress.

How to acknowledge others' emotions:

Start interactions by validating the other person's feelings and emotions; for example, 'I can see this is difficult for you.' This approach helps family members feel understood, making them more open to any feedback that follows.

Another advantage of having a bank of standard criticism and praise is that the gender of the actor could be varied and allow the participant to imagine different types of EE relatives speaking to them, and so the comments could reflect a range of family relationships. More salience is attached to the female voice, than the male voice (Paulmann & Kotz, 2008). This is because mothers play a greater role in child development. Maternal warmth, rather than paternal warmth, relates to attachment quality in adolescents (Jacobsen et al., 2000). Accordingly, female carers perceive their caring role as more burdensome than male carers do (Fernando et al., 2017). However, Hooley (1986) found that carer gender did not affect the likelihood of patients with depression having a high EE carer. Nonetheless, gender differences in EE remain with mothers expressing more EOI than fathers (Cutting & Docherty, 2000).

How to deal with incidental criticism:

Prepare a bank of criticisms that reflect your personal relationships. Exposure to them could help to lower arousal to criticism, regulate emotion and alter appraisal

Practise how to provide constructive criticism, rather than hostile criticism. Write down a typical criticism and make it constructive. Here's an example of a criticism: 'You spend too much time watching television. We don't get enough time to talk to each other.' Change it to a constructive criticism: 'We could watch the television. Let's also try to spend more time doing other things like reading together and chatting to each other.'

2.4.1 Appraisal of standard auditory criticism and praise

Arousal could be higher from criticism than praise if people are more vigilant for threat in social situations (Green & Phillips, 2004; Lang, 1995). Criticism may be perceived as more relevant among those living in high EE households than those in low EE households and when families express criticism and conflict (Narayan et al., 2015; Onwumere et al., 2009). The relevance of criticism may also be higher when families use rigid rather than flexible styles of communicating (Olson et al., 2019). In such situations, standard criticism could seem more relevant than praise because people need to appraise conflict flexibly (Gruber et al., 2013). Likewise, praise may be appraised as less arousing or relevant if the close relative is emotionally over-involved (Barber, 1996). Equally, the arousal and relevance of praise could be higher than that of criticism if families are supportive (Swenson et al., 2016).

Gender differences: The gender of the participant may also affect the appraisal of EE. Cuellar et al. (2009) found that women with bipolar disorder perceive more negativity in standard criticism than men, perhaps because women are more reactive to hostile marital interactions than men (Kiecolt-Glaser et al., 1994). Gender differences in social conformity may also explain gender differences in appraisal of criticism. For instance, adolescent girls with bipolar disorder may be more used to hearing parental criticism than boys, because girls are expected to conform to social norms (Coville et al., 2008).

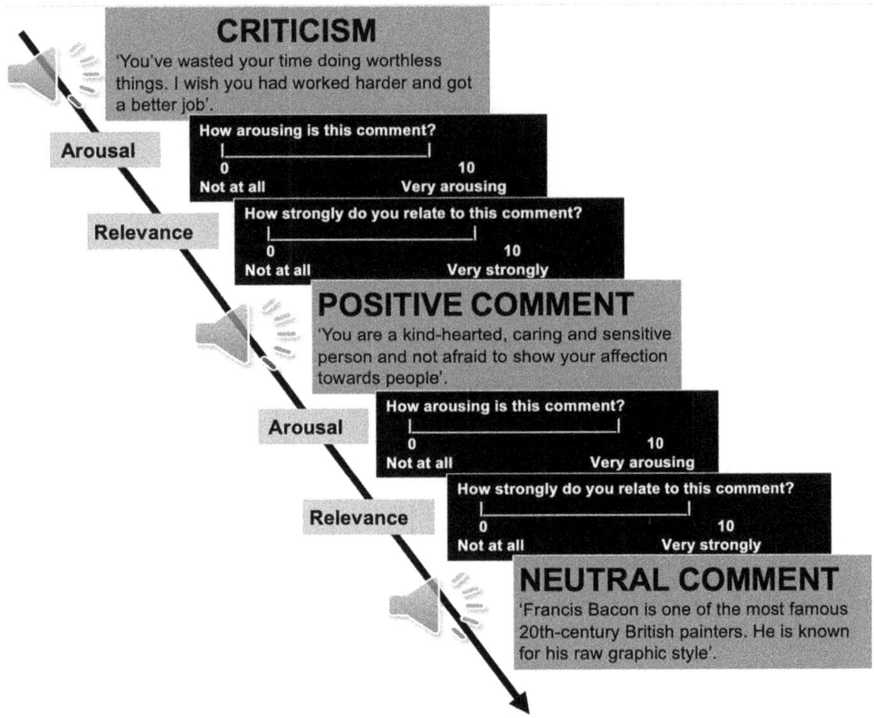

Figure 2.1 Affective evaluation task of standard criticism and standard praise.

A bank of standard auditory criticism and praise was developed by Premkumar and colleagues (2019, 2020). It is ecologically valid because appraisal of the comments related to valid measures of mental wellbeing and EE. Forty standard criticisms, 40 standard praises and 40 standard neutral comments were administered to 98 participants from the non-clinical population (Premkumar et al., 2019, 2020) (Figure 2.1). Criticism included phrases such as, 'You spend too much time running around and not accomplishing anything; you should use your time more wisely.' A positive comment could be, 'You have a lot of energy. You wake up early and keep busy till late. Your energy and enthusiasm are amazing.' A neutral comment could be, 'Most places will have a dry evening with some late sunshine, although one or two showers will continue in coastal areas.' Neutral comments covered scientific facts on astronomy and nature or art. The comments were played in a male and female voice using the conventions of rating criticism and praise for EE in the CFI. Participants were asked to rate each comment on how relevant the comment was to them and how arousing the comment was. Arousal refers to the level of energy and interest in the situation and can range from calm to excited (Bradley & Lang, 1999). These scales were rated on 11-point Likert scales.

2.4.2 *Relationships among sensitivity to criticism, schizotypy and aggression*

Schizotypy is a personality trait denoting a sub-clinical level of characteristics of schizophrenia (Lenzenweger, 2018), and schizotypy has three main dimensions. Positive schizotypy includes perceptual aberrations and magical thinking, such as hearing voices and delusional beliefs. Another dimension is negative schizotypy, and negative schizotypy refers to a state of withdrawal in mood, poor speech and having a low appetite for pleasure. A third dimension is disorganisation, and disorganisation resembles thought disorder in schizophrenia (Tompson et al., 1997) because it is characterised by incoherent speech, thinking illogically, poor concentration and social anxiety (Mason & Claridge, 2006). When the abovementioned bank of criticisms and praises was administered to 98 young volunteers, the relevance of criticism was found to co-exist with a greater level of all three schizotypal dimensions (Premkumar et al., 2019). Here, schizotypy was measured with the Oxford-Liverpool Inventory of Feelings and Experiences (O-LIFE), a self-report measure consisting of 104 questions about schizotypy (Mason et al., 1995). Meanwhile, arousal from criticism coincided with a greater level of cognitive disorganisation which was again measured through the O-LIFE. It was argued that disorganisation among all the schizotypal dimensions is most salient in the context of social judgements, such as sensitivity to criticism and rejection (Premkumar et al., 2018). This is because criticism and rejection can be seen to weaken social connection and destabilise the person. It appears that social integrity is fundamental for logical thinking because in essence we are socially constructed beings (Burr, 2004). These findings also support the affective explanation of the link between carer criticism and patient relapse in patients with psychosis, where carer criticism is associated with anxiety in patients (Kuipers et al., 2006), since heightened patient arousal is related to relapse of patients living with high EE relatives (Tarrier, 1989). Anxiety in schizotypy goes to form disorganisation (Premkumar et al., 2021). Therefore, it is meaningful that the relationship between arousal from criticism and disorganisation found in the non-clinical population (Premkumar et al., 2019) parallels the relationship between carer criticism and anxiety in patients with psychosis (Kuipers et al., 2006). Furthermore, when patients with schizophrenia perceive criticism from their carer, this perception coexists with the carers being rated as "high EE" on the CFI (Cutting et al., 2006; Onwumere et al., 2009). These findings also suggest that patients with schizophrenia and individuals with high schizotypal traits make reliable judgements of criticism from their close relative (Onwumere et al., 2009; Premkumar et al., 2019; Scazufca et al., 2001). The finding of an association between arousal from criticism and the disorganisation in schizotypy (Premkumar et al., 2019) corresponds with the finding in patients between PC and psychopathology (Onwumere et al., 2009), and it suggests that PC relates to the distress and anxiety arise from the primary positive and negative psychosis-like experiences.

The relevance of criticism also related to perception of the level of EE as measured by the Level of Expressed Emotion scale (Cole & Kazarian, 1988; Gerlsma & Hale, 1997). In the sample of 98 young healthy volunteers (Premkumar et al., 2019), rating criticism as relevant coincided with participants rating their close relative as being irritable and critical towards them on the LEE scale. Furthermore, in the same sample of 98 young healthy volunteers (Premkumar et al., 2019), rating praise as less relevant coincided with participants rating their close relative as being intrusive on the LEE scale and being disorganised on the questionnaire about schizotypal traits. What these findings indicate is that how people respond to criticisms and praises in the laboratory resonates with their daily experiences of close relationships and they carry that emotional burden with them to other social contexts. The experiments also show that people in the general population make sound judgements of EE in their close relative. Thus, the standard measure of criticism and praise reflect family EE and ratings on this instrument can indicate vulnerability for schizophrenia.

Premkumar and colleagues (2020) also sought to understand how rating of the standard criticism and praise could explain how schizotypal personality co-exists with depression and aggression in the non-clinical population. EE is related to depression in patients with schizophrenia (Bentsen et al., 1998; Docherty et al., 2011; Kuipers et al., 2006). EE is related to aggression since, patients with schizophrenia can display reactive aggression on provocation and EE as hostility from a carer might coincide with such aggressive behaviour (Onwumere et al., 2014; Wildman et al., 2023). For instance, schizophrenia patients can make three times as many criticisms and a third as few autonomous responses when interacting with a high EE parent than a low EE parent (Goldstein et al., 1989; Strachan et al., 1989; Woo et al., 2004). Likewise, schizophrenia patients can display more anxious/agitated and hostile/unusual behaviour when interacting with a high EE parent. Patients with severe mental illness can also be violent. The rate of violence from patients with serious mental illness towards carers is varied, ranging from 21% to 77% across studies (Wildman et al., 2023). However, suggestions of carer burden being a factor in patient violence is unsubstantiated through correlational analyses (Onwumere et al., 2016). Instead, carers who have sustained violence verbally report low self-esteem and burden from years of violence, experiencing immense isolation and exhaution (Wildman et al., 2023).

In the study by Premkumar and colleagues (2020), the same 98 participants as in the above study (Premkumar et al., 2019) also rated their level of depression and aggression. Cognitive disorganisation was found to be a key schizotypal dimension in the path to aggression as anger, with depression and the relevance of standard criticism playing a role in this pathway. The relevance of praise also played a role alongside depression in the path from cognitive disorganisation to aggression as anger. These findings suggest that PC and perceived praise are closely associated with schizotypy as disorganisation. This finding is meaningful because disorganisation consists of communication disorder, incoherent speech, illogical thinking and social anxiety, all of which are linked to social interaction.

The path from disorganisation to aggression was explained by depression, heightened sensitivity to criticism, diminished sensitivity to praise and perceiving irritability from a close relative. It was suggested that social anxiety could arise from sensitivity to criticism, reduced sensitivity to praise and noticing irritability from a close relative, and such social anxiety could turn into anger. Thinking catastrophically about situations is a key feature of depression, and such thoughts could increase sensitivity to criticism and praise and increase anger in social situations. In both models (Figure 2.2a and b), anger rather than verbal aggression corresponded with schizotypy, depression and perceived EE. This suggests that aggression is internalised as anger rather than being communicated verbally. In a non-clinical population and the absence of caregiver burden, the link between schizotypal traits and reactive aggression in the context of perceived EE may be more subtle than in a clinical population.

How to use forgiveness:

Make forgiveness a habit by letting go of minor grievances and misunderstandings. Actively forgiving each other nurtures a supportive environment, reducing the weight of critical feedback.

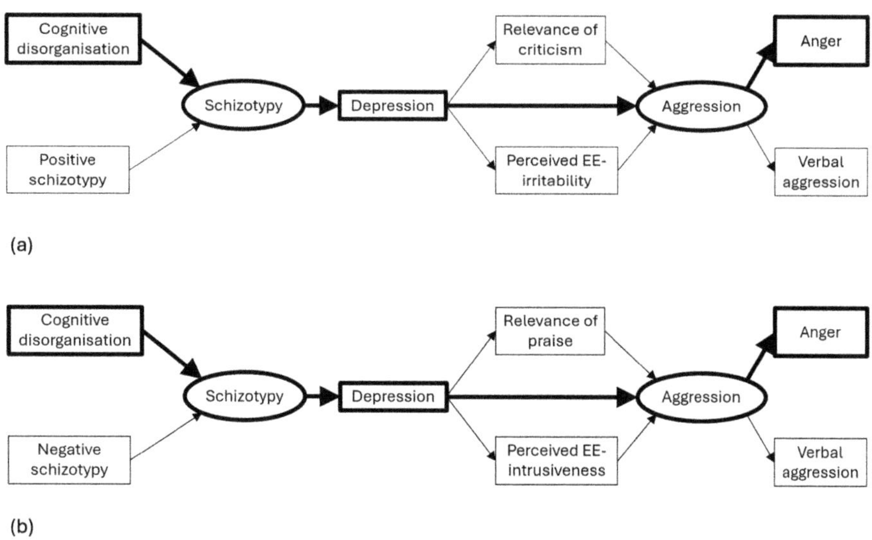

Figure 2.2 Path from disorganisation in schizotypy to aggression via (a) depression, relevance of criticism and perceived irritability from a close relative where aggression branches into anger and verbal aggression and (b) depression, relevance of praise and perceived intrusiveness from a close relative where aggression branches into anger and verbal aggression. The highlighted path indicates the strongest path from schizotypy to anger.

Relationship between sensitivity to criticism, substance use and schizotypy: The validity of the instrument of standard criticism and praise extends beyond non-clinical schizotypal traits to individuals with a history of substance abuse disorder (SUD) (Wang et al., 2021) and individuals with anxiety and depression. Individuals with SUD have challenging family relationships and encounter EE, and PC can trigger relapse of substance use (Fals-Stewart et al., 2001). Thus, Wang and colleagues studied sensitivity to criticism in individuals who had a past history of substance use and were currently abstinent (n=23). Some participants had comorbid mental disorder besides a history of substance use (n=16). The relevance of criticism and arousal of criticism were compared between these groups of individuals with a history of substance use and a group of healthy individuals who were matched for age and gender (n=30). The SUD group without comorbid mental disorder found the criticism more arousing than the healthy controls, while the SUD group with comorbid mental disorder found the criticism more relevant to their personal relationships than the healthy controls. Furthermore, greater arousal from criticism coincided with cognitive disorganisation in the SUD individuals in line with the findings by Premkumar and colleagues (2019). These findings highlight the strained nature of the relationships of individuals with a history of SUD. Individuals with SUD may struggle to regulate their emotions in the face of criticism, and the increased attention to criticism may destabilise the individuals with SUD (Wang et al., 2021). Besides, the sensitivity to criticism coexists with disorganisation and thought disturbance that characterise schizotypy in individuals with a history of SUD which suggests that SUD are susceptible to comorbid vulnerability for schizophrenia due to interpersonal stress.

How to address sensitivity to criticism:

Divert attention from the event and focus on a something you enjoy doing outside the interaction, such as music or art. Also, find an opportunity to speak calmly and kindly to your close relative.

2.4.3 Understanding sensitivity to criticism in the context of paranoia and early childhood experiences

Such social trauma and sensitivity to criticism can perpetuate paranoia since paranoia is vulnerable to interpersonal sensitivity (Meisel et al., 2018). Paranoia is the unfounded belief that others have hostile intentions and want to cause personal harm (Freeman & Loe, 2023; Garety & Freeman, 2013; Meisel et al., 2018). Paranoia increases when being discriminated, experiencing childhood mistreatment and having negative self-belief and social anxiety among other factors (Freeman & Loe, 2023). Thus, Butler and colleagues (2019) tested the impact of listening to standard criticism and warmth on paranoia in healthy individuals. They also examined how self-esteem explained this effect. Criticism increased paranoia and self-esteem explained this increase in paranoia after listening to criticism. Criticism is a form of social threat and the study (Butler et al., 2019) shows that perceiving such social threat can heighten paranoia by increasing the false beliefs of about the self and others paranoia. Being criticised is a form of verbal pain that increases anger (Premkumar et al., 2020). Sustaining such social pain can be internalised as anger, in turn damaging self-esteem and increasing paranoia, which at a mild level constitutes thoughts that people are trying to harm you, but at a severe level constitutes delusional beliefs of people or even organisations conspiring against you and belief in conspiracy theories (Meisel et al., 2018).

Adverse relationships during early development may also impact sensitivity to criticism and praise (Zhang et al., 2022). When healthy university students listened to standard criticism and praise, greater pleasantness of criticism corresponded with higher levels of childhood physical abuse and physical neglect. This finding suggests that childhood abuse diminishes sensitivity to criticism in a way that distorts the perception of criticism as not threatening, possibly through internalising the criticism through self-criticism and submissiveness (Zhang et al., 2022).

How to reconcile the criticism:

Unfair criticism can increase paranoia and stir misconceptions that others are trying to harm you. Criticism can also lower self-esteem. Seeking reassurance from friends and others with who you have good relationships can dispel these misconceptions.

2.5 Expressed emotion interventions

From the EE research, interventions have been proposed and trialled (see Chapter 6). Early family interventions focus on family members' expressions of emotion and aim to reduce these to a healthier level (Barrowclough & Tarrier, 1998). These include criticism, expressions of dissatisfaction towards the individual's actions and hostility towards personal traits. They also target family members' level of emotional over-involvement including addressing relatives' feelings of distress, self-sacrificing coping strategies and overprotective behaviours. These interventions have been trialled from the 1980s and have been consistently found to improve relapse rates of patients with schizophrenia through to more modern day (Bird et al., 2010).

How to keep criticism constructive:

When expressing critical feedback, focus on behaviours or tasks rather than the person's personal attributes. Also consider sharing these in private to make feedback feel less like judgement and more like constructive support.

Additionally, interventions have been proposed that allow the individual to become more imperturbable towards the negative aspects of EE. Encouraging the individual to challenge the beliefs and attributions of family members who display high EE would encourage the relative to move away from blaming behaviours, becoming more sensitive to the individuals challenging attributes (Domínguez-Martínez et al., 2014).

How to use calm communication:

Set aside time for relaxed discussions to calmly express how certain comments affect you. Waiting for emotions to settle allows for open, honest conversations and reduces defensiveness, making it easier to set boundaries and understand unfair criticism.

Finally, interventions have been proposed which enable family members to work together to gain both perspectives of the situation. This encourages families to communicate to improve their resilience to stressful environments as a way of reducing negative EE (Meneghelli et al., 2011).

How to reduce stress in family situations:

Stress can lead to criticism, so families can work together to ease tense moments by using humour or sharing a reassuring word. For example, recalling a funny memory to lighten the atmosphere. This approach can lower overall stress levels, helping everyone to feel calmer and less likely to be critical of one another or make it easier to accept and give feedback constructively.

Change amount of flexibility:

- Make a list of family norms, e.g. household chores, shopping, paying bills
- Rate on a scale of 1 to 10 how strictly family members adhere to them
- Write down how you can increase or decrease these scores

Define boundaries and sharing time and space together. Are all family members involved in making decisions about family activities?

The perspective of the intervention and evaluation of this differs depending upon which perspective is being reflected in the chosen EE measure. Some families have high amounts of critical EE, in which case observational methods such as the CFI would be appropriate and interventions that target the family members or unit as a whole. Meanwhile, individuals may have differing perceptions of EE in their family members, in which case self-report methods such as the LEE would be appropriate, alongside interventions that aim to increase the resilience of the individual against critical comments.

2.6 Conclusion

To conclude, sensitivity to criticism can be measured psychometrically, experimentally and through dyadic interaction to understand the impact of criticism from a close relative, friend or a stranger on the mental health of individuals in clinical and non-clinical populations. These proxy modes of assessing sensitivity to criticism can circumvent the gold-standard method of assessing the EE using the CFI, which can be tedious. In close relationships, such as couples and parent–child dyads, the criticism is reciprocated and perpetuates depression and marital distress in healthy couples and thought disorder in adolescents. The impact of criticism on the mental health of patients extends to the mental health of healthy individuals. PC in patients corresponds with carer EE and co-exists with the carer's attitudes towards mental illness and expectations for the patient. Burden and burnout from caregiving can heighten EE.

Creating standard vignettes of criticism and praise simulates the transactions between people and rating these experimental vignettes as relevant and arousing is consistent with the irritability and criticism that people perceive in their close relative. Rating standard criticism as relevant and arousing co-occurs with schizotypal traits, predominantly cognitive disorganisation, but also positive schizotypy and negative schizotypy. Such a finding of PC and its relationship with disorganisation in individuals with schizotypal traits parallels the affective route to PC in patients with schizophrenia, and it suggests the key role of anxiety in the path from PC to vulnerability for schizophrenia. Individuals with a history of SUD have a heightened sensitivity to criticism. Meanwhile, sensitivity to criticism is reminiscent of childhood abuse and instils paranoia and social threat in the general population.

There are self-guided way to remediate sensitivity to criticism, such as self-exposure to such standard remarks to desensitise oneself and writing strengthening statements about the person's virtues that can remind the person of their good qualities. Diverting attention away from the criticism through engaging in one's interests could reduce ruminating over the criticism. Improving communication styles will also diffuse the impact of criticism, such as being constructive, reassuring the person of the relative's/friend's confidence in the person's thoughts and actions, validating the person for their strengths. Reaching out for social support from those you trust could also reinstate self-esteem and self-confidence.

References

Alvarez-Jimenez, M., Priede, A., Hetrick, S. E., Bendall, S., Killackey, E., Parker, A. G., McGorry, P. D., & Gleeson, J. F. (2012). Risk factors for relapse following treatment for first episode psychosis: a systematic review and meta-analysis of longitudinal studies. *Schizophrenia Research*, *139*(1–3), 116–128.

Amaresha, A. C., & Venkatasubramanian, G. (2012). Expressed emotion in schizophrenia: an overview. *Indian Journal of Psychological Medicine*, *34*(1), 12–20. 10.4103/0253-7176.96149

Avraam, G., Samakouri, M., Tzikos, A., & Arvaniti, A. (2022). High expressed emotion and warmth among families of patients with schizophrenia in Greece. *Healthcare (Basel)*, *10*(10), 1957. 10.3390/healthcare10101957

Barber, B. K. (1996). Parental psychological control: Revisiting a neglected construct. *Child Development*, *67*(6), 3296–3319. 10.1111/j.1467-8624.1996.tb01915.x

Barrowclough, C., & Tarrier, N. (1998). The application of expressed emotion to clinical work in schizophrenia. *In Session: Psychotherapy in Practice*, *4*(3), 7–23.

Barrowclough, C., Tarrier, N., Humphreys, L., Ward, J., Gregg, L., & Andrews, B. (2003). Self-esteem in schizophrenia: Relationships between self-evaluation, family attitudes, and symptomatology. *Journal of Abnormal Psychology*, *112*(1), 92.

Baxter, L. A., & Montgomery, B. M. (1993). The social side of personal relationships: A dialectical perspective. In S. Duck (Ed.), *Social contexts and relationships* (pp. 305–350). Sage Publications.

Bentsen, H., Notland, T. H., Boye, B., Munkvold, O., Bjøge, H., Lersbryggen, A. B., Uren, G., Oskarsson, K. H., Berg-Larsen, R., Lingjærde, O., & Malt, U. F. (1998). Criticism and hostility in relatives of patients with schizophrenia or related psychoses: Demographic and clinical predictors. *Acta Psychiatrica Scandinavica*, *97*(1), 76–85. 10.1111/j.1600-0447.1998.tb09967.x

Bird, V., Premkumar, P., Kendall, T., Whittington, C., Mitchell, J., & Kuipers, E. (2010). Early intervention services, cognitive–behavioural therapy and family intervention in early psychosis: Systematic review. *The British Journal of Psychiatry*, *197*(5), 350–356.

Bradley, M. M., & Lang, P. J. (1999). *Affective Norms for English Words (ANEW): Instruction manual and affective ratings* (Technical Report C-1 ed.). The Center for Research in Psychophysiology.

Brown, G. W., Birley, J. L. T., & Wing, J. K. (1972). Influence of family life on the course of schizophrenic disorders: A replication. *British Journal of Psychiatry, 121*(562), 241–258. 10.1192/bjp.121.3.241
Brown, G. W., Bone, M., Dalison, B., & Wing, J. K. (1966). *Schizophrenia and social care: A comparative follow-up study of 339 schizophrenic patients*. London: Oxford University Press. 10.1016/S0033-3506(66)80062-8
Brown, G. W., Monck, E. M., Carstairs, G. M., & Wing, J. K. (1962). Influence of family life on the course of schizophrenic illness. *British Journal of Preventive & Social Medicine, 16*(2), 55–68. 10.1136/jech.16.2.55
Brückner, E., Peter, H., Rufer, M., Bandelow, B., Dahme, B., Hand, I., & Mueller-Pfeiffer, C. (2008). Expressed emotion in the partners of a non-clinical adult sample: A comparison with relatives of patients with schizophrenia and depression.
Burr, V. (2004). *Social constructionism* (2nd ed.). Taylor & Francis. 10.4324/9780203694992
Butler, R., Berry, K., Ellett, L., & Bucci, S. (2019). An experimental investigation of the impact of critical and warm comments on state paranoia in a non-clinical sample. *Journal of Behavior Therapy and Experimental Psychiatry, 62*, 30–37. 10.1016/j.jbtep.2018.08.008
Caspi, A., Moffitt, T. E., Morgan, J., Rutter, M., Taylor, A., Arseneault, L., Tully, L., Jacobs, C., Kim-Cohen, J., & Polo-Tomas, M. (2004). Maternal expressed emotion predicts children's antisocial behavior problems: Using monozygotic-twin differences to identify environmental effects on behavioral development. *Developmental Psychology, 40*(2), 149–161. 10.1037/0012-1649.40.2.149
Cole, J. D., & Kazarian, S. S. (1988). The level of expressed emotion scale: A new measure of expressed emotion. *Journal of Clinical Psychology, 44*(3), 392–397.
Coville, A. L., Miklowitz, D. J., Taylor, D. O., & Low, K. G. (2008). Correlates of high expressed emotion attitudes among parents of bipolar adolescents. *Journal of Clinical Psychology, 64*(4), 438–449. 10.1002/jclp.20463
Cuellar, A. K., Johnson, S. L., & Ruggero, C. J. (2009). Affective reactivity in response to criticism in remitted bipolar disorder: A laboratory analog of expressed emotion. *Journal of Clinical Psychology, 65*(9), 925–941. 10.1002/jclp.20596
Cutting, L. P., Aakre, J. M., & Docherty, N. M. (2006). Schizophrenic patients' perceptions of stress, expressed emotion, and sensitivity to criticism. *Schizophrenia Bulletin, 32*(4), 743–750. 10.1093/schbul/sbl001
Cutting, L. P., & Docherty, N. M. (2000). Schizophrenia outpatients' perceptions of their parents: is expressed emotion a factor? *Journal of Abnormal Psychology, 109*(2), 266–272. 10.1037/0021-843X.109.2.266
Docherty, N. M., St-Hilaire, A., Aakre, J. M., Seghers, J. P., McCleery, A., & Divilbiss, M. (2011). Anxiety interacts with expressed emotion criticism in the prediction of psychotic symptom exacerbation. *Schizophrenia Bulletin, 37*(3), 611–618. https://doi.org/10.1093/schbul/sbp123
Domínguez-Martínez, T., Medina-Pradas, C., Kwapil, T. R., & Barrantes-Vidal, N. (2014). Relatives′ illness attributions mediate the association of expressed emotion with early psychosis symptoms and functioning. *Psychiatry Research, 218*(1–2), 48–53.
Fals-Stewart, W., O'Farrell, T. J., & Hooley, J. M. (2001). Relapse among married or cohabiting substance-abusing patients: The role of perceived criticism. *Behavior Therapy, 32*(4), 787–801. 10.1016/S0005-7894(01)80021-6
Fernando, S. M., Deane, F. P., McLeod, H. J., & Davis, E. L. (2017). A carer burden and stigma in schizophrenia and affective disorders: Experiences from Sri Lanka. *Asian Journal of Psychiatry, 26*, 77–81. 10.1016/j.ajp.2017.01.023
Freeman, D., & Loe, B. S. (2023). Explaining paranoia: cognitive and social processes in the occurrence of extreme mistrust. *BMJ Mental Health, 26*(1), e300880. 10.1136/bmjment-2023-300880
Garety, P. A., Fowler, D. G., Freeman, D., Bebbington, P., Dunn, G., & Kuipers, E. (2008). Cognitive-behavioural therapy and family intervention for relapse prevention

and symptom reduction in psychosis: Randomised controlled trial. *British Journal of Psychiatry*, *192*(6), 412–423. 10.1192/bjp.bp.107.043570
Garety, P. A., & Freeman, D. (2013). The past and future of delusions research: From the inexplicable to the treatable. *British Journal of Psychiatry*, *203*(5), 327–333. 10.1192/bjp.bp.113.126953
Geist, R. L., & Gilbert, D. G. (1996). Correlates of expressed and felt emotion during marital conflict: Satisfaction, personality, process, and outcome. *Personality and Individual Differences*, *21*(1), 49–60. 10.1016/0191-8869(96)00049-9
Gerlsma, C., & Hale, W., 3. (1997). Predictive power and construct validity of the Level of Expressed Emotion (LEE) scale. Depressed out-patients and couples from the general community. *British Journal of Psychiatry*, *170*(6), 520–525. 10.1192/bjp.170.6.520
Gerlsma, C., van Duijn, M. A. J., Hale, W. W., & van Hout, W. J. P. J. (2009). Perceived criticism: Associations with perceiver characteristics and interpersonal behaviour. *Psychiatry Research*, *170*(2), 234–240. 10.1016/j.psychres.2008.09.007
Goldstein, M. J. (1985). Family factors that antedate the onset of schizophrenia and related disorders: The results of a fifteen year prospective longitudinal study. *Acta Psychiatrica Scandinavica*, *71*, 7–18. 10.1111/j.1600-0447.1985.tb08520.x
Goldstein, M. J., Miklowitz, D. J., Strachan, A. M., Doane, J. A., Nuechterlein, K. H., & Feingold, D. (1989). Patterns of expressed emotion and patient coping styles that characterise the families of recent onset schizophrenics. *British Journal of Psychiatry*, *155*, 107–111. 10.1192/S0007125000296074
Gottman, J. M., & Levenson, R. W. (1985). A valid procedure for obtaining self-report of affect in marital interaction. *Journal of Consulting and Clinical Psychology*, *53*(2), 151–160. 10.1037/0022-006X.53.2.151
Gottschalk, L. A. (1969). The measurement of hostile aggression through the content analysis of speech—Some biological and interpersonal aspects. In S. Garattini, & E. B. Sigg (Eds.), *Aggressive behaviour* (pp. 299–316). Excerpta Medica Foundation.
Gottschalk, L. A., & Gleser, G. C. (2023). *The measurement of psychological states through the content analysis of verbal behavior* (1st ed.). University of California Press.
Green, M. J., & Phillips, M. L. (2004). Social threat perception and the evolution of paranoia. *Neuroscience & Biobehavioral Reviews*, *28*(3), 333–342. 10.1016/j.neubiorev.2004.03.006
Gruber, J., Kogan, A., Quoidbach, J., & Mauss, I. B. (2013). Happiness is best kept stable: Positive emotion variability is associated with poorer psychological health. *Emotion (Washington, D.C.)*, *13*(1), 1–6. 10.1037/a0030262
Hale, W. W., Raaijmakers, Q. A. W., van Hoof, A., & Meeus, W. H. J. (2011). The predictive capacity of perceived expressed emotion as a dynamic entity of adolescents from the general community. *Social Psychiatry and Psychiatric Epidemiology*, *46*(6), 507–515. 10.1007/s00127-010-0218-y
Hooley, J. M. (1986). Expressed emotion and depression: Interactions between patients and high- versus low- expressed-emotion spouses. *Journal of Abnormal Psychology*, *95*(3), 237–246. 10.1037/0021-843X.95.3.237
Hooley, J. M., & Teasdale, J. D. (1989). Predictors of relapse in unipolar depressives: Expressed emotion, marital distress, and perceived criticism. *Journal of Abnormal Psychology*, *98*(3), 229–235. 10.1037//0021-843x.98.3.229
Izon, E., Berry, K., Law, H., & French, P. (2018). Expressed emotion (EE) in families of individuals at-risk of developing psychosis: A systematic review. *Psychiatry Research*, *270*, 661–672.
Jacobsen, T., Hibbs, E., & Ziegenhain, U. (2000). Maternal expressed emotion related to attachment disorganization in early childhood: A preliminary report. *Journal of Child Psychology and Psychiatry*, *41*(7), 899–906. 10.1111/1469-7610.00677
Kavanagh, D. J., O'Halloran, P., Manicavasagar, V., Clark, D., Piatkowska, O., Tennant, C., & Rosen, A. (1997). The family attitude scale: Reliability and validity of a new

scale for measuring the emotional climate of families. *Psychiatry Research*, *70*(3), 185–195. 10.1016/S0165-1781(97)00033-4
Kéri, S., & Kelemen, O. (2009). The role of attention and immediate memory in vulnerability to interpersonal criticism during family transactions in schizophrenia. *British Journal of Clinical Psychology*, *48*(1), 21–29. 10.1348/014466508X342926
Kiecolt-Glaser, J. K., Malarkey, W. B., Cacioppo, J. T., & Glaser, R. (1994). *Stressful personal relationships: Immune and endocrine function*. Elsevier Science & Technology.
Klein, R., & Milardo, R. M. (1993). Third party influence on the management of personal relationships. In S. Duck (Ed.), *Social contexts and relationships* (pp. 55–77). Sage Publications.
Kuipers, E., Bebbington, P., Dunn, G., Fowler, D., Freeman, D., Watson, P., Hardy, A., & Garety, P. (2006). Influence of carer expressed emotion and affect on relapse in non-affective psychosis. *British Journal of Psychiatry*, *188*(2), 173–179. 10.1192/bjp.bp.104.007294
Kuipers, E., Watson, P., Onwumere, J., Bebbington, P., Dunn, G., Weinman, J., Fowler, D., Freeman, D., Hardy, A., & Garety, P. (2007). Discrepant illness perceptions, affect and expressed emotion in people with psychosis and their carers. *Social Psychiatry and Psychiatric Epidemiology*, *42*(4), 277–283. 10.1007/s00127-007-0165-4
Kuipers, L., Sturgeon, D., Berkowitz, R., & Leff, J. (1983). Characteristics of expressed emotion: Its relationship to speech and looking in schizophrenic patients and their relatives. *British Journal of Clinical Psychology*, *22*(4), 257–264. 10.1111/j.2044-8260.1983.tb00612.x
Lang, P. J. (1995). The emotion probe: Studies of motivation and attention. *American Psychologist*, *50*(5), 372–385. 10.1037/0003-066X.50.5.372
Leff, J. P., & Vaughn, C. (1984a). *Expressed emotion in families: Its significance for mental illness*. Guilford Press.
Leff, J. P., & Vaughn, C. (1984b). The expressed emotion scales. *Expressed emotion in families: Its significance for mental illness* (pp. 37–63). Guilford Press.
Lenzenweger, M. F. (2018). Schizotypy, schizotypic psychopathology, and schizophrenia: Hearing echoes, leveraging prior advances, and probing new Angles. *Schizophrenia Bulletin*, *44*, S564–S569. 10.1093/schbul/sby083
Magaña, A. B., Goldstein, M. J., Karno, M., Miklowitz, D. J., Jenkins, J., & Falloon, I. R. H. (1986). A brief method for assessing expressed emotion in relatives of psychiatric patients. *Psychiatry Research*, *17*(3), 203–212. 10.1016/0165-1781(86)90049-1
Mason, O., & Claridge, G. (2006). The Oxford-Liverpool Inventory of Feelings and Experiences (O-LIFE): Further description and extended norms. *Schizophrenia Research*, *82*(2), 203–211. 10.1016/j.schres.2005.12.845
Mason, O., Claridge, G., & Jackson, M. (1995). New scales for the assessment of schizotypy. *Personality and Individual Differences*, *18*(1), 7–13. 10.1016/0191-8869(94)00132-C
McFarlane, W. R., & Cook, W. L. (2007). Family expressed emotion prior to onset of psychosis. *Family Process*, *46*(2), 185–197. 10.1111/j.1545-5300.2007.00203.x
Meisel, S. F., Garety, P. A., Stahl, D., & Valmaggia, L. R. (2018). Interpersonal processes in paranoia: a systematic review. *Psychological Medicine*, *48*(14), 2299–2312. 10.1017/S0033291718000491
Meneghelli, A., Alpi, A., Pafumi, N., Patelli, G., Preti, A., & Cocchi, A. (2011). Expressed emotion in first-episode schizophrenia and in ultra high-risk patients: Results from the Programma2000 (Milan, Italy). *Psychiatry Research*, *189*(3), 331–338.
Miklowitz, D. J., Goldstein, M. J., Doane, J. A., Nuechterlein, K. H., Strachan, A. M., Snyder, K. S., & Magana-Amato, A. (1989). Is expressed emotion an index of a transactional process? I. Parents' affective style. *Family Process*, *28*(2), 153–167. 10.1111/j.1545-5300.1989.00153.x

Narayan, A., Cicchetti, D., Rogosch, F. A., & Toth, S. L. (2015). Interrelations of maternal expressed emotion, maltreatment, and separation/divorce and links to family conflict and children's externalizing behavior. *Journal of Abnormal Child Psychology*, *43*(2), 217–228. 10.1007/s10802-014-9911-8

Newsom, J. T., Rook, K. S., Nishishiba, M., Sorkin, D. H., & Mahan, T. L. (2005). Understanding the relative importance of positive and negative social exchanges: Examining specific domains and appraisals. *The Journals of Gerontology: Series B*, *60*(6), P304–P312. 10.1093/geronb/60.6.P304

O'Brien, M. P., Gordon, J. L., Bearden, C. E., Lopez, S. R., Kopelowicz, A., & Cannon, T. D. (2006). Positive family environment predicts improvement in symptoms and social functioning among adolescents at imminent risk for onset of psychosis. *Schizophrenia Research*, *81*(2-3), 269–275.

O'Brien, M. P., Zinberg, J. L., Bearden, C. E., Lopez, S. R., Kopelowicz, A., Daley, M., & Cannon, T. D. (2008). Parent attitudes and parent adolescent interaction in families of youth at risk for psychosis and with recent-onset psychotic symptoms. *Early Intervention in Psychiatry*, *2*(4), 268–276.

O'Brien, M. P., Zinberg, J. L., Ho, L., Rudd, A., Kopelowicz, A., Daley, M., Bearden, C. E., & Cannon, T. D. (2009). Family problem solving interactions and 6-month symptomatic and functional outcomes in youth at ultra-high risk for psychosis and with recent onset psychotic symptoms: A longitudinal study. *Schizophrenia Research*, *107*(2-3), 198–205.

Olson, D. H., Waldvogel, L., & Schlieff, M. (2019). Circumplex model of marital and family systems: An update. *Journal of Family Theory & Review*, *11*(2), 199–211. 10.1111/jftr.12331

Onwumere, J., Grice, S., Garety, P., Bebbington, P., Dunn, G., Freeman, D., Fowler, D., & Kuipers, E. (2014). Caregiver reports of patient-initiated violence in psychosis. *Canadian Journal of Psychiatry*, *59*(7), 376–384. 10.1177/070674371405900705

Onwumere, J., Kuipers, E., Bebbington, P., Dunn, G., Freeman, D., Fowler, D., & Garety, P. (2009). Patient perceptions of caregiver criticism in psychosis: Links with patient and caregiver functioning. *The Journal of Nervous and Mental Disease*, *197*(2), 85–91. 10.1097/NMD.0b013e3181960e57

Onwumere, J., Shiers, D., & Chew-Graham, C. (2016). Understanding the needs of carers of people with psychosis in primary care. *British Journal of General Practice*, *66*(649), 400–401. 10.3399/bjgp16X686209

Onwumere, J., Sirykaite, S., Schulz, J., Man, E., James, G., Afsharzadegan, R., Khan, S., Harvey, R., Souray, J., & Raune, D. (2018). Understanding the experience of 'burnout' in first-episode psychosis carers. *Comprehensive Psychiatry*, *83*, 19–24. 10.1016/j.comppsych.2018.02.003

Parra Castaneda, K., Reynolds, N., & Onwumere, J. (2022). The role of perceived criticism in patient and caregiver outcomes in severe mental health disorders: A systematic review. *Health Sciences Review (Oxford, England)*, *3*, 100023. 10.1016/j.hsr.2022.100023

Premkumar, P., Alahakoon, P., Smith, M., Kumari, V., Babu, D., & Baker, J. (2021). Mild-to-moderate schizotypal traits relate to physiological arousal from social stress. *Stress (Amsterdam, Netherlands)*, *24*(3), 303–317. 10.1080/10253890.2020.1797674

Premkumar, P., Dunn, A. K., Onwumere, J., & Kuipers, E. (2019). Sensitivity to criticism and praise predicts schizotypy in the non-clinical population: The role of affect and perceived expressed emotion. *European Psychiatry*, *55*, 109–115. [pii]

Premkumar, P., Kuipers, E., & Kumari, V. (2020). The path from schizotypy to depression and aggression and the role of family stress. *European Psychiatry*, *63*(1), e79. 10.1192/j.eurpsy.2020.76 [doi]

Premkumar, P., Onwumere, J., Betts, L., Kibowski, F., & Kuipers, E. (2018). Schizotypal traits and their relation to rejection sensitivity in the general population: Their mediation by quality of life, agreeableness and neuroticism. *Psychiatry Research*, *267*, 201–209. [pii]

Rosenfarb, I. S., Nuechterlein, K. H., Goldstein, M. J., & Subotnik, K. L. (2000). Neurocognitive vulnerability, interpersonal criticism, and the emergence of unusual thinking by schizophrenic patients during family transactions. *Archives of General Psychiatry*, *57*(12), 1174–1179. 10.1001/archpsyc.57.12.1174

Scazufca, M., Kuipers, E., & Menezes, P. R. (2001). Perception of negative emotions in close relatives by patients with schizophrenia. *British Journal of Clinical Psychology*, *40*(2), 167–175. 10.1348/014466501163616

Schlosser, D. A., Zinberg, J. L., Loewy, R. L., Casey-Cannon, S., O'Brien, M. P., Bearden, C. E., Vinogradov, S., & Cannon, T. D. (2010). Predicting the longitudinal effects of the family environment on prodromal symptoms and functioning in patients at-risk for psychosis. *Schizophrenia Research*, *118*(1-3), 69–75.

Servaas, M. N., Riese, H., Renken, R. J., Marsman, J. C., Lambregs, J., Ormel, J., & Aleman, A. (2013). The effect of criticism on functional brain connectivity and associations with neuroticism. *PloS One*, *8*(7), e69606. 10.1371/journal.pone.0069606

Sher-Censor, E. (2015). Five Minute Speech Sample in developmental research: A review. *Developmental Review*, *36*, 127–155. 10.1016/j.dr.2015.01.005

Shields, C. G., Franks, P., & Harp, J. J. (1992). Development of the Family Emotional Involvement and Criticism Scale (FEICS): A self-report scale to measure expressed emotion. *Journal of Marital and Family Therapy*, *18*(4), 395. 10.1111/j.1752-0606.1992.tb00953.x

Stein, C. H. (1993). Felt obligation in adult family relationships. In S. Duck (Ed.), *Social contexts and relationships* (pp. 78–99). Sage Publications.

Strachan, A. M., Feingold, D., Goldstein, M. J., Miklowitz, D. J., & Nuechterlein, K. H. (1989). Is expressed emotion an index of a transactional process? II. Patient's coping style. *Family Process*, *28*(2), 169–181. 10.1111/j.1545-5300.1989.00169.x

Swenson, S., Ho, G. W. K., Budhathoki, C., Belcher, H., Tucker, S., Miller, K., & Gross, D. (2016). Parents' use of praise and criticism in a sample of young children seeking mental health services. *Journal of Pediatric Health Care*, *30*(1), 49–56. https://doi.org/10.1016/j.pedhc.2015.09.010

Tarrier, N. (1989). Arousal levels and relatives' Expressed emotion in remitted schizophrenic patients. *British Journal of Clinical Psychology*, *28*(2), 177–180. 10.1111/j.2044-8260.1989.tb00828.x

Tompson, M. C., Asarnow, J. R., Hamilton, E. B., Newell, L. E., & Goldstein, M. J. (1997). Children with schizophrenia-spectrum disorders: Thought disorder and communication problems in a family interactional context. *Journal of Child Psychology and Psychiatry*, *38*(4), 421–429. 10.1111/j.1469-7610.1997.tb01527.x

Tortoriello, G. K., & Hart, W. (2019). Trait interpersonal vulnerability attenuates beneficial effects of constructive criticism on failure responses. *The British Journal of Psychology*, *110*(3), 594–613. 10.1111/bjop.12356

Tsai, K. H., López, S., Marvin, S., Zinberg, J., Cannon, T. D., O'Brien, M., & Bearden, C. E. (2015). Perceptions of family criticism and warmth and their link to symptom expression in racially/ethnically diverse adolescents and young adults at clinical high risk for psychosis. *Early Intervention in Psychiatry*, *9*(6), 476–486.

Vaughn, C., & Leff, J. (1976b). The measurement of expressed emotion in the families of psychiatric patients. *British Journal of Social and Clinical Psychology*, *15*(2), 157–165. 10.1111/j.2044-8260.1976.tb00021.x

Vaughn, C. E., & Leff, J. P. (1976a). The influence of family and social factors on the course of psychiatric illness. A comparison of schizophrenic and depressed neurotic patients. *British Journal of Psychiatry*, *129*(2), 125–137. 10.1192/bjp.129.2.125

Wang, G. Y., Premkumar, P., Lee, C. Q., & Griffiths, M. (2021). The role of criticism in expressed emotion among psychoactive substance users: An experimental vignette study. *International Journal of Mental Health and Addiction*, *21*(1), 258–272. https://doi.org/10.1007/s11469-021-00591-2

Welsh, P., & Tiffin, P. A. (2015). Adolescent family perceptions in the At-Risk Mental State for psychosis. *Early Intervention in Psychiatry*, *9*(4), 316–323.

Wildman, E. K., MacManus, D., Harvey, J., Kuipers, E., & Onwumere, J. (2023). Prevalence of violence by people living with severe mental illness against their relatives and its associated impacts: A systematic review. *Acta Psychiatrica Scandinavica*, *147*(2), 155–174. 10.1111/acps.13516

Woo, S. M., Goldstein, M. J., & Nuechterlein, K. H. (2004). Relatives' affective style and the expression of subclinical psychopathology in patients with schizophrenia. *Family Process*, *43*(2), 233–247. 10.1111/j.1545-5300.2004.04302008.x

Zhang, X., Luo, L., Hu, J., Gao, Z., & Gao, S. (2022). More exposure to childhood trauma associates with reduced displeasure at self-referential criticism. *Journal of Child & Adolescent Trauma*, *15*(3), 893–898. 10.1007/s40653-021-00429-y

Chapter 3

Sensitivity to criticism in relation to children's theory of mind and functioning at school

Joanna Smogorzewska

Abstract

This chapter focuses on the relationship between sensitivity to criticism and theory of mind among preschool and school-age children and its role in children's functioning in educational context, mostly for their academic achievement. The chapter begins by defining the concepts of feedback, criticism and sensitivity to criticism. Next, the chapter describes the concept of theory of mind and its relation to academic achievement are. Building on previously published research, the relation between theory of mind and sensitivity to criticism is presented, and the importance of this relation for children's functioning at school, mostly for their academic achievement, is highlighted.

3.1 Introduction

Sensitivity to criticism in the context of education has specific implications. On the one hand, it concerns the emotions that children feel after receiving certain feedback from the teacher. These emotions can be linked with children's perception of their ability as pupils after receiving the information they perceive as critical. On the other hand, sensitivity to criticism is about the extent to which children are motivated to change or improve the work that was commented on by the teacher. What is especially important in this situation is the ability to understand and reflect on the true message that lies behind the teacher's feedback. Although the criticism can take diverse forms, it is important to notice that the aim of the teacher's critique is not to cause harm to someone but to improve his/her knowledge and correct mistakes. Importantly and ideally, the critique from the teacher should be constructive, contain strong and weaker points of the assessed work, and concern the work itself so as not to harm the children's feelings. Studies conducted in this area show that theory of mind (ToM) is an important ability in helping children to understand the intentions of the teacher and, as a result, to improve their academic achievement.

DOI: 10.4324/9781003388159-4

In this chapter, I will first discuss the issues connected with feedback and criticism in the context of education, mostly academic achievement. Furthermore, I will focus on ToM as the ability of children to understand the intentions of teachers behind the criticism, and how this is related to children's academic achievement. Finally, I will analyse the role of ToM and sensitivity to criticism in improving academic achievement of school-aged children.

3.2 Feedback and criticism in the educational context

Analysing a teacher's feedback is an important element of research about the effectiveness of education in general, and specifically about academic achievement. It is well recognised that a teacher's feedback is a significant and important predictor of students' academic improvement and achievement (Hattie & Timperley, 2007). However, the impact of feedback can vary based on different factors, such as the type of feedback, i.e. positive or negative, or the way the feedback is provided, i.e. whether it is supportive or it gives a direct advice. The feedback that the teacher delivers can take the form of criticism especially when noting mistakes that the student made, the progress they showed or the level of effort they presented while learning (Hyland & Hyland, 2001; Ruiz-Primo & Li, 2013). One of the risks while providing feedback is that at least some children may perceive the criticism that they receive not as a way of support, but as a personal attack on themselves. Therefore, the criticism, which is mostly about mistakes, may turn out to be less effective than constructive feedback, in relation to tasks, processes and the engagement (Hattie & Timperley, 2007).

When the criticism takes a personal form and concerns the child directly, in most cases it contains less detailed information regarding the quality of the tasks performed as well as fewer hints showing how the tasks should be corrected or how to further develop the skills based on what has already been done, in comparison to the feedback directed to the work done (Cutting & Dunn, 2002). This type of teacher feedback may also have other negative consequences that can decrease the self-confidence of children and lead to a self-fulfilling prophecy in which students follow their teachers' opinions and expectations and do not believe in themselves and in their own abilities (Cutting & Dunn, 2002; Hyland & Hyland, 2001; Ruiz-Primo & Li, 2013).

Investigating different types of feedback, its form and the way it is given is obviously not enough to understand the mechanisms that lie behind its effectiveness and impact on academic achievement (Hattie & Timperley, 2007; Jónsson et al., 2018). Therefore, research needs to be complemented with characteristics of students and their learning contexts because these two elements can influence the teachers' critique, its content and the way it is delivered (Hattie & Timperley, 2007; Jónsson et al., 2018). As studies show, ToM is one of the student's characteristics that is perceived as important for how the critique is received, understood and used by the students. Therefore, ToM can influence children's academic achievement.

3.3 Theory of mind

ToM has been studied thoroughly since the 1970s (Premack & Woodruff, 1978). It is the ability to understand that people possess and understand mental states, such as desires, beliefs, emotions or intensions, which are crucial for their behaviours and for making predictions about behaviours of others (Wellman et al., 2001). One of the key elements of ToM is understanding of other people's false beliefs, which is an ability to understand that other people can have beliefs about the world or the situation that do not have to be true and can be different from one's own beliefs (e.g. Wellman et al., 2001). The first-order false belief is the ability to understand that other people's beliefs can be false and different from the child's belief; so the child can say: 'He thinks that…, but I know it is not true.' The second-order false belief, concerns the ability to understand that one person can have a false belief about another person's belief; therefore, the child can say: 'He thinks that she thinks…, but I know that what he thinks is not true.'

Since the concept of ToM was conceived, research on ToM has gone through different stages. The first stage mostly concerned how ToM develops. The majority of early research on ToM was devoted to children of preschool age (Wellman et al., 2001). It was believed that children start to understand the mental states of others after a certain age (4–5-year-olds). However, it was later discovered that not only some elements of ToM understanding are observed among much younger children than preschoolers (e.g. Baillargeon, 2004; Meltzoff, 2007; Moore, 2006; Onishi & Baillargeon, 2005), but also that ToM can develop even after the preschool years, giving children, adolescents and adults a chance for advanced understanding of different complex concepts of social situations, such as misunderstanding, analysing ambiguous social information and interpreting white lies (e.g. Białecka-Pikul et al., 2017; Osterhaus & Koerber, 2021; Peterson et al., 2005; Smogorzewskaet al., 2018).

The second stage of research on ToM concerned factors that can influence its development. Thanks to robust analyses of diverse elements, currently we know quite a lot about positive and negative influences on ToM. The factors can be divided into three main groups. The first concerns individual characteristics of a child. Therefore, it is now clear that cognitive and social abilities support the development of ToM. For instance, the better language abilities and language understanding that children have, the better for their ToM development (Milligan et al., 2007). In addition, the better development of executive function in children, the better they understand others (Devine & Hughes, 2014). Social openness and ease also support the development of ToM (e.g., Fink et al., 2015; Imuta et al., 2016; Slaughter et al., 2015). At the same time, having disability suppresses, but does not stop, the development of understanding of mental states (Peterson et al., 2005, 2012; Thirion-Marissiaux & Nader-Grosbois, 2008a, 2008b; Yirmiya et al., 1998). The second group of factors consists of characteristics of a family in which children develop: the socio-economic status (SES), parenting styles, as well as everyday interactions between parents and their child (Devine & Hughes, 2018). It has been shown that higher family SES, authoritative, democratic style of up-bringing, as well as 'parental talk', based on mental-state verbs (such as to like, to know, to think, to feel), and 'parental mind-mindedness', i.e. understanding the child as a separate human being, who has its own mental states, foster the development of ToM in children (see Devine & Hughes, 2018; Miller, 2016 for review of studies). The third group of factors important for ToM development are social factors that go beyond the family. The research shows that what is especially important for ToM development is a diverse environment in which the children are raised and educated. Studies that bring these kind of results are most often conducted within the school classrooms and show that a more diverse environment favours the development of ToM for children individually. For instance, the diversity may concern the level of ToM among peers, ethnic diversity of the classroom or having peers with disability in the classroom (Devine et al., 2024; Lecce et al., 2024; Smogorzewska et al., n.d.).

The third and most current stage of research on ToM focuses on the importance of ToM for children's social and cognitive functioning, in both the shorter and longer term. The research shows that children with better developed ToM have more friends, are accepted more by peers and show more prosocial behaviours towards others in comparison with peers with lower level of understanding of others (e.g., Fink et al., 2015; Imuta et al., 2016; Slaughter et al., 2015). Other research also shows that ToM protects children from feeling lonely since children with higher ToM abilities report feeling less lonely (e.g., Caputi et al., 2017; Devine & Hughes, 2014; Yu et al., 2024). However, what is more important in the context of the topic of this chapter is that ToM turns out to be significantly linked with cognitive functioning of children, particularly their academic achievement. This finding raises the possibility that ToM can be linked to how children attend to criticism.

3.4 Theory of mind and academic achievement

The relationship between ToM and academic achievement is tested within different aspects of ToM and within diverse areas of academic functioning. ToM is tested as understanding of false beliefs, understanding of emotions and advanced ToM; and it covers abilities beyond the preschool age. Academic achievement in the context of ToM has mainly been explained through language abilities (e.g., verbal abilities, reading, narrative comprehension, knowledge of letters of the alphabet and phonemic awareness) and mathematical competence.

The most reliable conclusions about the relationship between ToM and academic achievement can be drawn from longitudinal research. These studies show meaningful links between children's ToM and academic achievement, although the links are not very strong. It is probably because many other factors exist that influence the academic achievement of students besides ToM. Proficiency in ToM is meaningful for academic success (Astington et al., 2005; Blair & Razza, 2007; Guajardo & Cartwright, 2016; Lecce et al., 2011, 2014, 2017, 2021; Lockl et al., 2017). The predictive role of ToM has been shown to be equally important for both language and mathematical abilities in most studies (Dore et al., 2018; Ebert, 2020; Florit et al., 2020; Smith et al., 2019; Trentacosta & Izard, 2007). An exception was seen in one study, in which it was shown that while the relation exists between ToM and reading comprehension, a relationship does not exist between ToM and mathematical competence (Lecce et al., 2021). Importantly, although most studies used false-belief understanding to represent ToM and examine its relationship with academic achievement, the understanding of emotions, which is another facet of ToM, is as predictive of academic achievement as is understanding of false beliefs (Astington et al., 2005; Ebert, 2020; Florit et al., 2020). Importantly, even though controlling for different variables, such as verbal and nonverbal abilities, SES and sex, and using them as mediators and moderators may weaken the relation between ToM and academic achievement, these variables do not fully explain the relation between the two or cause the relation between the two to disappear.

It is possible to distinguish between two related but distinct perspectives that aim to explain the relationship between ToM and academic achievement. The first one relies on metacognition as an important skill for both ToM and academic achievement (Roebers et al., 2014). High ToM abilities in children let them display more metacognitive knowledge and behaviours. What this means is that children are more conscious of their own cognitive abilities and how to use them. This, in turn, may lead to higher academic achievement (Dunlosky & Metcalfe, 2009; Schneider et al., 2008; Wellman, 2017). Importantly, it has already been mentioned that ToM is significantly linked to cognitive skills, such as language and executive functions (Devine & Hughes, 2014; Milligan et al., 2007); therefore, a common ground exists between ToM and cognitive function without a doubt. The second perspective which is more relevant to the topic of this chapter is the importance of the relationship between children and their teachers (Lockl et al., 2017; Magro et al., 2024; Smogorzewska et al., 2025). Based on the attachment theory (Bowlby, 1982), it has been stated that positive and close relationships between children and their teachers can support children in social functioning and in different areas of school life, i.e. in establishing bonds with peers (Buyse et al., 2011), developing their social identity (Alderman, 2004) and in general, shaping their emotional and behavioural skills (Ahnert et al., 2012). Moreover, higher ToM abilities make it possible for children to understand teachers' intentions and instructions better (Astington et al., 2005). Through better communication and understanding between children and their teachers, it is possible for children to create new knowledge and find new methods and strategies for learning (Davis, 2003; Garner & Waajid, 2008; Hamre & Pianta, 2001). Close relationships with teachers are possible thanks to a good level of understanding between the child and the teacher, and this makes it possible for a child to be more open for a critique from the teacher and improve their own academic achievement. Thus, a healthy relationship between the child and their teacher is conducive for the teacher to give appropriate constructive feedback to the child and for the child to receive the feedback constructively.

3.5 Theory of mind and sensitivity to criticism in relation to children's functioning at school

The amount of research on the relationship between ToM and sensitivity to criticism and in turn functioning at school is limited. Nonetheless, these studies explain some of the mechanisms behind the link between ToM and academic achievement. The first piece of research that analysed the relationship between ToM and sensitivity to a teacher's criticism was a study conducted by Dunn (1995). In this study, the procedure for assessing children's reactions to teachers' criticism was developed by Heyman and colleagues (1992). The study was longitudinal and 46 children participated in the study when they were 40, 68 and 75 months old. The children's ToM was tested by two tasks on understanding of emotion and five false-belief tasks and children were asked to give explanations of the situation for each task. ToM was examined at the first timepoint, while the sensitivity to criticism was assessed at the third timepoint when children were 75 months old. The procedure of assessing sensitivity to criticism was interactive. First, children listened to the stories and were asked to assume the role of the key character in the following stories: (1) s/he prepared a painting that represents family members; and (2) s/he did a maths task (wrote numbers in order from 1 to 10). In each of these stories, the key character in the story worked hard on the task, but made a small mistake. In the first story, the feet of a child were missing from the picture that the key character painted. In the second story, the number 8 was missing from the list of numbers that the key character wrote. While listening to the stories, the children were asked to act with a puppet and assume that the puppet was a teacher. In one story, but not the other (changed randomly between the two stories), the child was criticised by the teacher (the puppet). For example, in the case of the first story the criticism from the teacher was: 'There are no feet on that child. That's not what I call drawing people the right way. I'm disappointed in you' (Heyman et al., 1992, p. 404). There were two scenarios, one of which only featured a failure without any critique, and the other featured a failure that was followed by a critique of the mistake. After listening to each scenario, the children were asked to evaluate their work; i.e. they were asked to assess how good they were at completing the task and to assess the product of their work. Additionally, the authors used a separate task to assess children's understanding of situations in which one could feel two emotions of opposite valence at the same time (Gordis et al., 1989). The results showed that children who were successful in false-belief tasks earlier were more sensitive to the teacher's criticism by judging their work as poorer than those children whose earlier understanding of false beliefs was weaker. In contrast, there was no correlation between understanding of emotions as assessed by Gordis and colleagues (1989) task and sensitivity to criticism. The conclusion from this study was that children who have a better ToM in terms of understanding of false beliefs are more sensitive to judgements from others and are more aware of others' thinking. However, it does not mean that it is easier for these children to function at school. Instead, it can be even more difficult for them, as they are especially aware of what others are thinking about them and their work.

How to handle the teacher's feedback:

It is very important to teach children how to handle with the teacher's feedback, mostly to teach them to understand that the teacher, in most of the cases, has good intentions, i.e. s/he wants to help their students, and not to harm them.

Focusing on understanding of false beliefs, Cutting and Dunn (2002) extended the abovementioned piece of research (Dunn, 1995). Here, the authors wanted to find out if the link between *earlier* understanding about false beliefs and *current* sensitivity to criticism was determined by *current* understanding about false beliefs. Therefore, they replicated the study by Dunn (1995), but assessed understanding of false beliefs not only prior to assessing sensitivity to criticism, but also concurrently with the sensitivity to criticism. One hundred and forty-one participants took part in the study at two timepoints, first when children were aged around four years old (T1, average age = 4.16 years), and second when they were aged around five years old (T2, mean age = 5.13 years). At T1, children performed a range of tasks, namely false belief, understanding of emotion, verbal ability and family background. First, children were asked to solve seven false-belief tasks that involved predicting, explaining or recalling a false belief. Four of the seven false-belief tasks were tasks about an unexpected location and the other three false-belief tasks were tasks about unexpected content. Next, understanding of emotion was assessed at T1 with two procedures in two ways. The first involved understanding of typical (e.g. being happy during a happy event) and atypical emotions (e.g. being sad during a happy event) for a given situation concerning emotions of an imaginary character. Second, understanding of emotion was assessed by asking participants to give examples of situations in which children themselves, their mothers and their friends feel four emotions, namely happy, sad, angry and scared.

The procedure of assessing sensitivity to criticism at T2 in the study by Cutting and Dunn (2002) was identical to the one presented in the study by Dunn (1995), namely in the form of two stories. As before, both stories were associated with making an error that could be viewed as failures, but only one (randomly assigned from one participant to another) was followed by criticism from the teacher. However, the difference between this study (Cutting & Dunn, 2002) and the earlier study (Dunn, 1995) was that after listening to the stories, the children were asked a series of questions. The first question concerned the emotional response to the critique by the teacher, i.e. whether they felt happy, sad or angry. The second question was about the rating of their own ability concerning maths/painting skills; thus, they were asked to assess their imaginary product (i.e. having the numbers written or having the portrait of the family painted). The third question was what they would do and say to the child who made a mistake mentioned during the critique; here, children were asked to act as a teacher and were asked how they would respond to a child who made a mistake. ToM understanding at T2 was measured with first- and second-order false-belief tasks (two story-book false-belief tasks; each story first involved a first-order false belief and then a second-order false belief). Both tasks were based on the procedure developed by Sullivan and colleagues (1994) (see details in Cutting & Dunn, 2002, p. 853).

ToM understanding at T2 was also measured by an emotion understanding task involving understanding of mixed emotions – understanding of situations in which it is possible to feel two opposite emotions. During each wave, the tasks differed because during the second wave children were significantly older than during the first wave. The research yielded interesting results. Firstly, it was obvious that children's emotional response, ability rating and teacher's response were significantly more negative when the story included criticism by the teacher in comparison with the story of a failure without the teacher's criticism. Further, it turned out that children with higher understanding of false beliefs and understanding of emotions at both T1and at T2 were more sensitive to criticism, but only in terms of rating their own ability. Therefore, children with better understanding of ToM assessed their own abilities lower than children with weaker ToM abilities. Moreover, it was demonstrated that preschool children who had well-developed social cognition skills were more sensitive to both criticism and failure a year later, while those who had good concurrent ToM skills reacted only to the explicit criticism and not failure depicted in the story. These results suggest that having more advanced ToM skills at the age of 4 may lead children to experience a different, but not necessarily more advantageous, social world than children whose early social understanding is less advanced (Cutting & Dunn, 2002). The authors drew important implications from these findings. They remind, on one hand, that it is important to consider children's representations of themselves, because the beginning of school is a time when children develop their self-concept and self-esteem (Cutting & Dunn, 2002). On the other hand, the authors state that being sensitive to criticism may help children to learn better from constructive criticism. This issue was addressed in further studies.

How to scaffold theory of mind in children when exposed to criticism:

Developing theory of mind skills in children may help them to understand more nuanced feedback in the future. Moreover, it is important to care about children's self-concept and self-esteem, because at the beginning of school they initiate comparisons with others, which can influence their overall well-being.

Since those initial studies, research has explored the relationship between ToM, sensitivity to criticism and academic performance. The first study to show the associations between ToM, sensitivity to teacher's criticism and academic achievement of children was conducted by Lecce and colleagues (2011). Sixty Italian children took part in this longitudinal study with three time points. They were tested in their last year of preschool (average age = 5.6 years), first year of school (average age = 6.5 years) and in their second year of primary school (average age = 7.5). At T1 and T2, children's understanding of false beliefs was assessed with a battery of six tasks involving first- and second-order false beliefs (Hughes et al., 2000). At T3, children's abilities were assessed with the ToM Test (Pons, F. & Harris, 2002) that was more suitable for children aged 7 years. Emotion understanding at T1 and T2 concerned mixed emotion understanding (Gordis et al., 1989), while at T3 emotion understanding was tested with the Test of Emotion Comprehension (Pons, et al., 2004). Scores on emotion understanding tasks at T1 and T2 were combined with scores on false-belief understanding tasks at T1 and T2, because of high correlations between the constructs, but these concepts were kept separate at T3 as the correlations between them were insignificant. Sensitivity to criticism was assessed with the same procedure as in papers of Dunn (1995) and Cutting and Dunn (2002). The only difference at T3 was that after listening to the stories, children were asked two, not three, questions concerning emotional response and ability rating. Academic achievement of children was assessed by their teachers using the academic competence subscale from the Social Skills Rating System questionnaire (Gresham & Elliott, 1990). While using the questionnaire, the teachers needed to rate each child's performance in comparison with other children in the classroom using a five-point Likert scale. Additionally, children's verbal abilities and social skills were measured at each timepoint. The authors assumed that children's earlier ToM would predict their later academic achievement. It turned out that children who got higher ratings from teachers on academic performance showed higher levels of ToM, verbal ability and social skills both concurrently and longitudinally. Furthermore and similar to the findings of Cutting and Dunn (2002), they found that better ToM development in children was associated with higher sensitivity to criticism. Here, sensitivity to criticism was determined by a self-ability rating; i.e. children answered the question of how they rate their own ability as 'good' or 'not good'. Additionally, it was demonstrated that the relationship between ToM and sensitivity to criticism in children is independent of their concurrent social skills. Moreover, the results have shown that children's earlier sensitivity to teacher's criticism predicted teachers' later ratings of children's academic achievement.

The last, but not least, discovery was that children's sensitivity to criticism partly explained the relationship between ToM at T1 and teachers' ratings of children's academic achievement at T3. This means that not only were children who earlier revealed better understanding of false belief more sensitive to teachers' criticism, but they were also assessed higher on academic achievement by their teachers later on. The result concurs with the conclusions drawn by Cutting and Dunn (2002) that even though sensitivity to criticism may have emotional costs for the children, it also can help children to learn better. The authors highlighted that it is possible that better ToM means that children are able to engage more in understanding the meaning of teacher's criticism, which in turn help them in improving their academic performance. The results mean that children are reflective practitioners. They are able to properly interpret the criticism, reflect on it and use it constructively, as well as apply it to different academic situations.

The next study by Lecce and colleagues (2014) brought similar results, even though some changes were implemented. Again, the study was longitudinal, but the gap between the second and third measurement point was significantly longer than in previous studies. Forty-nine children participated in the study when they were in kindergarten (average age = 5.6 years), the first grade (average age = 6.5 years) and the fifth grade (average age = 10.2 years). ToM was measured in the same way at T1 and T2 as in the previous study (Lecce et al., 2011). At T3, ToM was assessed with four Strange Stories (White et al., 2009), a task that is suitable for older children. Sensitivity to criticism was also measured in the same way at T2 as in the previous study (Lecce et al., 2011). Academic achievement was assessed directly at T3 in terms of reading comprehension (Cornoldi & Colpo, 1995) and mathematical abilities (Cornoldi et al., 2002), as well as indirectly with teachers' ratings using the academic competence subscale of the Social Skills Rating System (Gresham & Elliott, 1990). At each time-point, verbal abilities of the children were also assessed by the Peabody Picture Vocabulary Test (Dunn & Dunn, 1981). The results of the study were consistent with those of the previous study (Lecce et al., 2011), showing that children with higher ToM were more sensitive to the teacher's criticism (they rated their own abilities as lower) than those with lower ToM and had higher overall academic achievement. However, the key difference from the previous study (Lecce et al., 2011) was that the gap between second and third measurement point was much longer (four years) compared to the previous study (one year). This difference in the T2/T3 lag between the two studies shows that the tested relationship exists not only in short term, but also in long-term development.

How to help children handle criticism from their teacher:

Developing theory of mind in children is not only important to understanding the intentions of the critique, it also has consequences for children's academic achievement. It helps children to learn more effectively.

The next study in chronological order did not analyse academic achievement, but greatly enhanced understanding of the relationship between ToM and sensitivity to criticism. Mizokawa (2015) proposed three new elements to the puzzle. The first was that she verified the relationship between each of the first- and second-order understandings of false belief and sensitivity to criticism. Secondly, she compared the reactions of children not only to the teacher's criticism, but also to peers' criticism. Thirdly, she added a novel component to the sensitivity to criticism measure. Here, apart from well-known questions, Mizokawa (2015) asked children about 1) their motivation to keep trying after listening to the critique, and 2) why the teacher said what s/he said (only in the cases where the teacher's feedback followed the failure). Eighty-nine Japanese children aged 6.4 years on average participated in the study. Children's ToM was assessed with four stories – two concerning first-order, and two concerning second-order false-belief tasks (Harris et al., 1989; Sullivan et al., 1994). In the case of the sensitivity to criticism tasks, children were split into two groups: 'teacher feedback' or 'peer feedback' conditions. Three stories were presented to the children. The first two stories were just the same as in previous studies, namely imagining they did a mathematical task involving writing numbers and imagining that they prepared a painting of their family members (Heyman et al., 1992). 'Just failure' and 'failure with criticism' conditions were counterbalanced between the stories, except that in the 'teacher feedback condition' children were criticised by a teacher, and in the 'peer feedback condition' children were criticised by a peer. The third story was used for debriefing and children received a compliment from the teacher for a great performance on doing a puzzle and helping a peer, and were given an apology for the earlier criticism.

After listening to the stories, children were asked questions concerning emotional response and ability rating as used in previous studies, as well as questions on different themes. The first theme concerned motivation, to determine whether children have motivation to continue the task regardless of the critique, 'If the teacher/friend asked you to do the task again, would you do it or would you do something else nice instead?' The second theme concerned memory, to check whether the children remembered the criticism they received (the results of children who did not answer the question properly were not analysed). The third theme concerned intentions (only in the teacher condition), to check whether the children understood the real intentions behind what the teacher had said, i.e. because s/he thinks the child is no good, or because s/he just think the child did a 'good job' but missed something that should be corrected. Additionally, linguistic abilities of the children were assessed and controlled for in the analyses with the Picture Vocabulary Test-Revised (Ueno et al. n.d.), but linguistic abilities turned out not to be associated with children's responses to failure and criticism in either condition. The results revealed that children's emotional response, ability rating and motivation to keep trying after listening to the critique were lower in the 'failure with criticism' condition in comparison to the 'just failure' condition. Moreover, children assessed their abilities significantly lower after receiving criticism from the teacher than from the peer.

Further, the author divided the children into three groups according to their ToM abilities. Group 1 included children who failed the second-order false-belief tasks and were also weak in solving the first-order false-belief tasks (low-ToM). Group 2 included children who failed second-order false-belief tasks, but passed the first-order false-belief tasks (moderate-ToM). Group 3 included children who passed both first- and second-order false-belief tasks (high-ToM). The study found that in the 'teacher feedback condition', ToM level differentiated between the children's rating of their ability to do the two pretend tasks (writing numbers and painting their family) and motivation to keep trying after listening to the critique. Here, the moderate-ToM group rated their abilities higher than the other groups. Moreover, the high-ToM group was more motivated to keep trying after criticism than the two other groups. However, the levels of ToM did not distinguish between emotional response or understanding of the teacher's intentions. In the 'peer feedback condition', the ToM level did not distinguish emotional response, ability rating ('how good I was in imaginary maths/painting task') or motivation to keep trying after listening to the critique between the three groups of children with different levels of ToM. To conclude, the study revealed new information that children rate their abilities lower only in the teacher-criticism but not peer-criticism condition. Moreover, it turned out that the level of ToM is important not only for ability rating, but also for motivation to persevere after teacher's critique. The result has shown that probably the ToM skills matter more in the case of the teacher's assessment than in the case of peers' assessment. It may suggest that the credibility and experience of the adult is more important in the child's evaluation of their ability and motivation to learn from mistakes than in the case of the peers. Children may impute the thoughts of teachers more than those of their peers out of a sense of duty and moral obligation.

How to motivate children to persevere following criticism:

It is important for the teachers to teach children to be persistent in trying, because children have the tendency to give up easily. Moreover, teachers must remember that they are important figures for their young students and children learn from them in not only direct, but also indirect way.

3.5.1 *Culture, criticism and theory of mind in young children*

The aim of the next study was to analyse whether there are differences in relationship between ToM and sensitivity to criticism between Eastern (Japan) and Western/Southern (Italy) cultures (Mizokawa & Lecce, 2017). Previous studies have demonstrated that children from Eastern countries, e.g. China and Japan, show a delay in ToM development in comparison with children from English-speaking Western countries (Hughes et al., 2014; Liu et al., 2008; Wellman et al., 2001), although no such differences were noticed between Eastern and Southern European countries, such as Italy. Furthermore, the authors stated that almost no studies exist on the social correlates of ToM, such as sensitivity to criticism, that compare different cultures (Mizokawa & Lecce, 2017). Thus, in this study (Mizokawa & Lecce, 2017), a group of Japanese (n = 76, mean age = 6.32) and Italian (n = 76, mean age = 6.5) children were randomly assigned to the teacher or peer conditions in terms of who provided the critique. Children participated in the same procedure of sensitivity to criticism assessment as in the previous study (Mizokawa, 2015) and answered three questions concerning emotional response (how they felt after listening to the story: whether or not they were happy, sad or angry), ability rating (whether their work was good or not) and motivation (whether they are ready to continue the activities described in the stories). Children's ToM was assessed with two second-order false-belief stories. Additionally, verbal abilities controlled for differences in performance in both Japanese and Italian children. Results revealed that children from both countries showed more negative emotions and rated their abilities lower in the 'failure with criticism' condition in comparison with the 'just failure' condition, regardless of whether the critique was from the teacher or peers. Furthermore, while Japanese children showed more positive emotions, they rated their abilities lower after the teacher's criticism than after the peers' criticism. However, the Italian sample did not differ in their emotional response or rating of their ability to perform the tasks after the criticism from the teacher or peers. In terms of motivation, it turned out that Japanese children had a similar level of motivation to keep trying after listening to the critique from both the teacher and peers. In contrast, Italian children were less motivated after receiving criticism from the teacher in comparison to the 'just failure' situation, while this difference was not apparent in the peer condition.

Thus, Japanese and Italian children differ in their sensitivity to criticism in unique ways. Among Japanese children, critique from the teacher lowers the perceived performance on the task more so than critique from their peers, whereas Italian children do not differentiate between their teacher's critique and their peers' criticism when it comes to their perceived performance. However, among Italian children, critique from the teacher lowers the motivation to complete the task more so than critique from their peers whereas Japanese children do not differentiate between their teacher's critique and their peers' criticism when it comes to their motivation to complete the task.

Continuing with this study (Mizokawa & Lecce, 2017) and considering the levels of ToM, it turned out that Japanese children had more positive emotions than Italian children regardless of the level of ToM. However, children with higher ToM in both countries rated their abilities to perform the maths and painting tasks lower than children with lower ToM levels. Overall, Japanese children were also more motivated to keep trying after receiving the critique than Italian children. When considering ToM level and motivation to keep trying, children with higher ToM were more motivated to persevere than children with lower ToM abilities. However, there were also cultural differences in this motivation. Italian children with higher ToM abilities were more motivated to persevere in comparison with those with lower ToM abilities. In contrast, Japanese children with low level of ToM were more motivated to keep trying in comparison to the Italian children with low level of ToM abilities. In general, the study has shown that there are no significant differences between children from two cultures in terms of sensitivity to criticism. However, Japanese children felt more positive emotions and rated their abilities lower after the teacher's critique in comparison to peers' critique. Moreover, Japanese children felt more positive emotions after criticism than Italian children. The results, similar to the previous ones, also showed a negative relationship between children's ToM level and rating of their ability to perform the tasks, namely the higher the ToM abilities the lower their perceived ability. Italian children with higher ToM were more motivated to persevere after the teacher's critique in comparison to Italian children with low ToM, but in the case of Japanese children the motivation after the teacher's critique was independent of their ToM level. The results, therefore, emphasise some undeniable cultural differences in upbringing and education between the countries. Children in Eastern cultures (broadly speaking) are more motivated to keep trying regardless of ToM level, regardless of who makes the critique, whereas in children Western cultures are more inclined to keep trying if they have a higher level of ToM following a critique from a teacher than a peer.

How to handle culture-specific differences in ToM and ability to perform a task:

Regardless of some cultural differences, paying attention to developing understanding of others and motivation among children, may help children to function better in everyday situations and handle feedback from teachers and peers better across cultures.

3.5.2 Academic achievement, criticism and theory of mind

Although two previously mentioned studies did not focus on academic achievement, the last set of works described in this review and published most recently go back to the idea of explaining the relationship between ToM and academic achievement in the context of sensitivity to criticism. The three-waves longitudinal study of Smogorzewska and colleagues (2022b) concerned 121 typically developing Polish children. The aim of the study was once again to analyse the relationship between ToM abilities, sensitivity to criticism and academic achievement, but with the addition of a new element to the model. The idea arose from the fact that sensitivity to criticism only partly explained the relationship between ToM and academic achievement by, presented in the studies of Lecce and colleagues (Hughes et al., 2014; Lecce et al., 2011). Therefore, it was assumed that besides sensitivity to criticism, school engagement in learning, in terms of behavioural, emotional and cognitive areas of students' functioning, would also explain the relationship between ToM and academic achievement (Fredricks et al., 2004). Based on past research (e.g. Pinxten et al., 2014), it was assumed that a higher level of motivation after the critique would be related to a higher level of general school engagement in students. Thus, it was assumed that a higher level of ToM strengthens children's motivation to keep trying after receiving the feedback from the teacher, and the motivation together with school engagement predict academic achievement of children. So, in this study (Smogorzewska et al., 2022a), children's ToM ability (average age at T1 = 7.4 years) was measured at T1 with ten stories from the Faux Pas Recognition Test (Baron-Cohen et al., 1999), five stories with and five without social *faux pas*. After 30 months, children's sensitivity to criticism was assessed (T2). This time, children listened to four stories concerning the teacher's criticism after a child made a mistake. The four stories considered language, maths, science and art tasks, respectively. These stories were prepared in accordance with the stories detailed in Heyman and colleagues (1992) and Mizokawa (2015). After listening to each story, children were asked questions about their emotional reaction to the critique and the level of motivation for improvement after receiving the critique. Children's level of school engagement was assessed by their teachers at T3. Additionally, at T1 and T3 (taking place ten months after T2 which in turn took place 30 months after T1), children's academic achievement in language and mathematics was assessed with tasks suitable to the age of children at both measurement times. The results showed that ToM was significantly correlated with motivation to improve their performance on the tasks after being criticised by the teacher, but not with emotional reaction after receiving the criticism. Therefore, in the model, motivation for improvement after receiving critique was used as a proxy measure of sensitivity to criticism. ToM abilities at T1 predicted children's motivation for improvement after critique with higher ToM at T1 corresponding with higher motivation for improvement at T2. Additionally, children's motivation for improvement at T2 predicted children's school engagement at T3. In turn, children's school engagement predicted their academic achievement both in language and maths at T3. Once again, the results showed only partial mediation of the relationship between ToM and academic achievement of children by sensitivity to criticism (understood as motivation to persevere) and school engagement. Therefore, Smogorzewska and colleagues (2022a) added a new element to the puzzle on the relationships among ToM, sensitivity to criticism and academic achievement, but the mystery was not solved completely.

3.5.3 Theory of mind, criticism and learning difficulties

The last study included in this review is somewhat different from the research presented so far. While all the previous studies concerned typically developing children, the last one focused on children with sensory impairments, i.e. deaf or hard-of-hearing (DHH) (Smogorzewska et al., 2022b). Although there is research showing some aspects of ToM development of children with sensory impairments, they are not as numerous as those conducted with typically developing children. Therefore, studies conducted with children with sensory impairments seem to be especially valuable in the context of everyday functioning of these groups of children. In the three-wave longitudinal study, 134 DHH children from hearing families (average age at T1=9.2 years) took part. The aim of this study was again to test the relationship between ToM, sensitivity to criticism and academic achievement. This time, however, a new element was added to the model, namely academic self-concept (ASC). It has been argued that children's sense of self can be a significant mediator, next to the sensitivity to criticism, in the relation between ToM and academic achievement. Research on ASC and academic achievement conducted with typically and atypically developing students has clearly shown that previous academic achievement influences further ASC of children, and their ASC affects later academic achievement, creating a reciprocal effect model (Marsh & Hau, 2003; Marsh et al., 2005; Szumski & Karwowski, 2015). Children's ASC is also co-created based on information children receive from 'significant others', such as teachers (Burnett, 2003; Parsons et al., 1982). Moreover, students who interpret criticism constructively may use the criticism to improve their achievement (Parsons et al., 1982). At the same time, the ability to understand the teacher's criticism, due to a better developed ToM, may influence ASC of students. Therefore, in the study the relationships among children's ToM, sensitivity to criticism, ASC, and academic achievement in language were assessed.

At T1, children's ToM was measured with the ToM scale (Peterson et al., 2005, 2012). It is important to mention that the development of ToM among DHH children from hearing families is significantly delayed compared with typically developing peers and those from families with a history of deafness (de Villiers & de Villiers, 2012; Peterson & Wellman, 2019; Smogorzewska et al., 2018). That is why in this study older children who were matched to the DHH children in terms of their developmental stage rather than their age were chosen instead of typically developing children for solving the tasks in the ToM scale. Language achievement at T1 and T3 (20 months after T1) was measured with tests suitable for the children's age and abilities. Sensitivity to criticism at T2 (ten months after T1) was measured with the same four stories as in the previous study (Smogorzewska et al., 2022a), and children answered the same two questions after listening to each story. ASC was also measured at T2 with the Self-Description Questionnaire I (Marsh, 1992), but only items concerning linguistic abilities were used because ASC is specific to each type of academic ability. The results showed that in the case of DHH children, emotional reaction to criticism, but not the motivation to persevere, was correlated with ToM suggesting that a better ToM development of DHH children corresponded with a stronger emotional reaction to critique. Therefore, emotional reaction was used as a proxy measure of sensitivity to criticism in the model. The model excellently fitted the data and showed that ToM of DHH children predicted a weaker emotional reaction to criticism – they were less sensitive to criticism, and had higher ASC in language ten months later (T2), as well as higher academic achievement in language 20 months later (T3) after controlling for language achievement at T1. Moreover, it has been shown that children who reacted less emotionally to a teacher's critique had significantly higher ASC in language. In turn, children who had higher ASC in language at T2 had higher academic achievement in language ten months later (T3). However, children's emotional reaction to critique at T2 was not associated with their achievement ten months later (T3). Furthermore, whereas the indirect path from ToM to ASC in language and achievement in language was significant, the paths through sensitivity to criticism were insignificant. Furthermore, in the case of this study, the direct link between previous ToM abilities and later academic achievement in language was the strongest. Therefore, it has been shown, that in the case of DHH children the concept of sensitivity to criticism is not helpful in explaining the relationship between ToM and academic achievement. Although the ASC adds a bit to the understanding of this relationship, the relationship between ToM and academic achievement is still not fully explained by sensitivity to criticism, hearing difficulties or ASC and, thus far, the research is still too little to solve the mystery.

How to help children handle criticism by improving ToM and academic self-concept:

For academic achievement of children, not only ToM and sensitivity to criticism are important, but also the engagement in learning and academic self-concept. Therefore, it is important to increase children's academic engagement by exposing them to interesting content, giving them opportunities to understand what are their strong and weak points, and how to improve the weak ones.

3.6 Final conclusions

The main aim of this chapter was to understand the relationship between ToM and sensitivity to criticism in the context of education. Therefore, sensitivity concerned children's reactions (emotions, rating of their ability to perform a task and motivation to persevere in improving their performance on a talk) to the teacher's critique. The literature reviewed has clearly shown that ToM, which is the ability to understand others, not only helps children to manage the teacher's critique, but also that children with better-developed ToM can use the critique to improve their academic achievement. Therefore, while in general experiencing criticism is neither nice nor easy, together with better-developed understanding of others, sensitivity to criticism can be beneficial for further functioning of the child in school. What is important, however, is that whereas sensitivity to criticism seems to be an important part of explanation of relationship between ToM and academic achievement for typically developing children, it does not work for children with DHH, even though DHH children with higher ToM are in general less sensitive to criticism. Also, in the case of typically children, sensitivity to criticism is clearly not the only element in explaining the relationship between previous ToM and further academic achievement. Either way, the findings are interesting and they give room for further discoveries.

Acknowledgements

The study has been financed by National Centre for Science (no. 2018/31/B/HS6/00520), Poland.

References

Ahnert, L., Harwardt-Heinecke, E., Kappler, G., Eckstein-Madry, T., & Milatz, A. (2012). Student–teacher relationships and classroom climate in first grade: How do they relate to students' stress regulation? *Attachment & Human Development*, *14*(3), 249–263. 10.1080/14616734.2012.673277

Alderman, M. K. (2004). *Motivation for achievement: Possibilities for teaching and learning* (2nd ed.). Lawrence Erlbaum Associates Publishers.

Astington, J. W., Pelletier, J., Homer, B. D., & Tamis-LeMonda, C. (2005). *Theory of mind, language, and learning in the early years: Developmental origins of school readiness* (1st ed., pp. 205–230). Psychology Press. 10.4324/9781315805634-12

Baillargeon, R. (2004). Infants' reasoning about hidden objects: Evidence for event-general and event-specific expectations. *Developmental Science*, *7*(4), 391–414. 10.1111/j.1467-7687.2004.00357.x

Baron-Cohen, S., O'Riordan, M., Stone, V., Jones, R., & Plaisted, K. (1999). Recognition of faux pas by normally developing children and children with Asperger syndrome or high-functioning autism. *Journal of Autism and Developmental Disorders*, *29*(5), 407–418. 10.1023/a:1023035012436

Białecka-Pikul, M., Kołodziejczyk, A., & Bosacki, S. (2017). Advanced theory of mind in adolescence: Do age, gender and friendship style play a role? *Journal of Adolescence*, *56*, 145–156. 10.1016/j.adolescence.2017.02.009

Blair, C., & Razza, R. P. (2007). Relating effortful control, executive function, and false belief understanding to emerging math and literacy ability in kindergarten. *Child Development*, *78*(2), 647–663. 10.1111/j.1467-8624.2007.01019.x

Bowlby, J. (1982). *Attachment and loss* (2nd ed.). Basic Books.

Burnett, P. C. (2003). The impact of teacher feedback on student self-talk and self-concept in reading and mathematics. *The Journal of Classroom Interaction*, *38*(1), 11–16.

Buyse, E., Verschueren, K., & Doumen, S. (2011). Preschoolers' attachment to mother and risk for adjustment problems in kindergarten: Can teachers make a difference? *Social Development (Oxford, England)*, *20*(1), 33–50. 10.1111/j.1467-9507.2009.00555.x

Caputi, M., Pantaleo, G., & Scaini, S. (2017). Do feelings of loneliness mediate the relationship between sociocognitive understanding and depressive symptoms during late childhood and early adolescence? *The Journal of Genetic Psychology*, *178*(4), 207–216. 10.1080/00221325.2017.1317629

Cornoldi, C., & Colpo, G. &. (1995). *Nuove prove di lettura MT [New MT tests of reading]*. Organizzazioni Speciali.

Cornoldi, C., Lucangeli, D., & Bellina, M. (2002). *AC-MT – Test di valutazione delle abilita` di calcolo [AC-MT – Test for the evaluation of calculation ability]*. Erickson.

Cutting, A. L., & Dunn, J. (2002). The cost of understanding other people: Social cognition predicts young children's sensitivity to criticism. *Journal of Child Psychology and Psychiatry*, *43*(7), 849–860. 10.1111/1469-7610.t01-1-00047

Davis, H. A. (2003). Conceptualizing the role and influence of student–teacher relationships on children's social and cognitive development. *Educational Psychologist*, *38*(4), 207–234. 10.1207/S15326985EP3804_2

de Villiers, P. A., & de Villiers, J. G. (2012). Deception dissociates from false belief reasoning in deaf children: Implications for the implicit versus explicit theory of mind distinction. *British Journal of Developmental Psychology*, *30*(1), 188–209. 10.1111/j.2044-835X.2011.02072.x

Devine, R. T., Grumley Traynor, I., Ronchi, L., & Lecce, S. (2024). Children in ethnically diverse classrooms and those with cross-ethnic friendships excel at understanding others' minds. *Child Development*, *95*(5), 1447–1461. 10.1111/cdev.14085

Devine, R. T., & Hughes, C. (2014). Relations between false belief understanding and executive function in early childhood: A meta-analysis. *Child Development*, *85*(5), 1777–1794. 10.1111/cdev.12237

Devine, R. T., & Hughes, C. (2018). Family correlates of false belief understanding in early childhood: A meta-analysis. *Child Development*, *89*(3), 971–987. 10.1111/cdev.12682

Dore, R. A., Amendum, S. J., Golinkoff, R. M., & Hirsh-Pasek, K. (2018). Theory of mind: A hidden factor in reading comprehension? *Educational Psychology Review*, *30*(3), 1067–1089. 10.1007/s10648-018-9443-9

Dunlosky, J., & Metcalfe, J. &. (2009). *Metacognition*. Sage.

Dunn, J. (1995). Children as psychologists: The later correlates of individual differences in understanding of emotions and other minds. *Cognition & Emotion*, *9*(2–3), 187–201. 10.1080/02699939508409008

Dunn, L. M., & Dunn, D. (1981). *Peabody picture vocabulary test-revised*. American Guidance Service.

Ebert, S. (2020). Theory of mind, language, and reading: Developmental relations from early childhood to early adolescence. *Journal of Experimental Child Psychology*, *191*, 104739. 10.1016/j.jecp.2019.104739

Fink, E., Begeer, S., Peterson, C. C., Slaughter, V., & de Rosnay, M. (2015). Friends, friendlessness, and the social consequences of gaining a theory of mind. *British Journal of Developmental Psychology*, *33*(1), 27–30. 10.1111/bjdp.12080

Florit, E., De Carli, P., Giunti, G., & Mason, L. (2020). Advanced theory of mind uniquely contributes to children's multiple-text comprehension. *Journal of Experimental Child Psychology*, *189*, 104708. 10.1016/j.jecp.2019.104708

Fredricks, J. A., Blumenfeld, P. C., & Paris, A. H. (2004). School engagement: Potential of the concept, state of the evidence. *Review of Educational Research*, *74*(1), 59–109. 10.3102/00346543074001059

Garner, P. W., & Waajid, B. (2008). The associations of emotion knowledge and teacher–child relationships to preschool children's school-related developmental competence. *Journal of Applied Developmental Psychology*, *29*(2), 89–100. 10.1016/j.appdev.2007.12.001

Gordis, F. W., Rosen, A. B., & Grand, S. &. (1989). Young children's understanding of simultaneous conflicting emotions. Paper presented at the *Biennial Meetings of the Society for Research in Child Development*. Kansas City, Missouri, April 27–30.

Gresham, F. M., & Elliott, S. N. &. (1990). *The Social Skills Rating System: Examiner's manual*. American Guidance Service.

Guajardo, N. R., & Cartwright, K. B. (2016). The contribution of theory of mind, counterfactual reasoning, and executive function to pre-readers' language comprehension and later reading awareness and comprehension in elementary school. *Journal of Experimental Child Psychology*, *144*, 27–45. 10.1016/j.jecp.2015.11.004

Hamre, B. K., & Pianta, R. C. (2001). Early teacher–child relationships and the trajectory of children's school outcomes through eighth grade. *Child Development*, *72*(2), 625–638. 10.1111/1467-8624.00301

Harris, P. L., Johnson, C. N., Hutton, D., Andrews, G., & Cooke, T. (1989). Young children's theory of mind and emotion. *Cognition and Emotion*, *3*(4), 379–400. 10.1080/02699938908412713

Hattie, J., & Timperley, H. (2007). The power of feedback. *Review of Educational Research*, *77*(1), 81–112. 10.3102/003465430298487

Heyman, G. D., Dweck, C. S., & Cain, K. M. (1992). Young Children's Vulnerability to Self-Blame and Helplessness: Relationship to beliefs about goodness. *Child Development*, *63*(2), 401–415. 10.1111/j.1467-8624.1992.tb01636.x

Hughes, C., Adlam, A., Happé, F., Jackson, J., Taylor, A., & Caspi, A. (2000). Good test—retest reliability for standard and advanced false-belief tasks across a wide range of abilities. *Journal of Child Psychology and Psychiatry*, *41*(4), 483–490. 10.1111/1469-7610.00633

Hughes, C., Devine, R. T., Ensor, R., Koyasu, M., Mizokawa, A., Lecce, S., & Meltzoff, A. N. (2014). Lost in translation? Comparing British, Japanese, and Italian children's theory-of-mind performance. *Child Development Research*, *2014*(2014), 1–10. 10.1155/2014/893492

Hyland, F., & Hyland, K. (2001). Sugaring the pill: Praise and criticism in written feedback. *Journal of Second Language Writing*, *10*(3), 185–212. 10.1016/S1060-3743(01)00038-8

Imuta, K., Henry, J. D., Slaughter, V., Selcuk, B., & Ruffman, T. (2016). Theory of mind and prosocial behavior in childhood: A meta-analytic review. *Developmental Psychology*, *52*(8), 1192–1205. 10.1037/dev0000140

Jónsson, Í. R., Smith, K., & Geirsdóttir, G. (2018). Shared language of feedback and assessment. Perception of teachers and students in three Icelandic secondary schools. *Studies in Educational Evaluation*, *56*, 52–58. 10.1016/j.stueduc.2017.11.003

Lecce, S., Bianco, F., & Hughes, C. (2021). Reading minds and reading texts: Evidence for independent and specific associations. *Cognitive Development*, *57*, 101010. 10.1016/j.cogdev.2021.101010

Lecce, S., Caputi, M., & Hughes, C. (2011). Does sensitivity to criticism mediate the relationship between theory of mind and academic achievement? *Journal of Experimental Child Psychology*, *110*(3), 313–331. 10.1016/j.jecp.2011.04.011

Lecce, S., Caputi, M., & Pagnin, A. (2014). Long-term effect of theory of mind on school achievement: The role of sensitivity to criticism. *European Journal of Developmental Psychology*, *11*(3), 305–318. 10.1080/17405629.2013.821944
Lecce, S., Caputi, M., Pagnin, A., & Banerjee, R. (2017). Theory of mind and school achievement: The mediating role of social competence. *Cognitive Development*, *44*, 85–97. 10.1016/j.cogdev.2017.08.010
Lecce, S., Ronchi, L., & Devine, R. T. (2024). The effect of peers' theory of mind on children's own theory of mind development: A longitudinal study in middle childhood and early adolescence. *Developmental Psychology*, *60*(7), 1269–1278. 10.1037/dev0001758
Liu, D., Wellman, H. M., Tardif, T., & Sabbagh, M. A. (2008). Theory of mind development in chinese children: a meta-analysis of false-belief understanding across cultures and languages. *Developmental Psychology*, *44*(2), 523–531. 10.1037/0012-1649.44.2.523
Lockl, K., Ebert, S., & Weinert, S. (2017). Predicting school achievement from early theory of mind: Differential effects on achievement tests and teacher ratings. *Learning and Individual Differences*, *53*, 93–102. 10.1016/j.lindif.2016.11.007
Magro, S. W., Hobbs, K. A., Li, P. H., Swenson, P., Riegelman, A., Rios, J. A., & Roisman, G. I. (2024). Meta-analytic associations between the student–teacher relationship scale and students' social competence with peers. *School Psychology Review*, *53*(5), 496–522. 10.1080/2372966X.2023.2258767
Marsh, H. W. (1992). Self Description Questionnaire (SDQ) I: A theoretical and empirical basis for the measurement of multiple dimensions of preadolescent self-concept. An interim test manual and research monograph. University of Western Sydney, Faculty of Education.
Marsh, H. W., & Hau, K. (2003). Big-fish-little-pond effect on academic self-concept: A cross-cultural (26-country) test of the negative effects of academically selective schools. *The American Psychologist*, *58*(5), 364–376. 10.1037/0003-066X.58.5.364
Marsh, H. W., Trautwein, U., Lüdtke, O., Köller, O., & Baumert, J. (2005). Academic self-concept, interest, grades and standardized test scores: Reciprocal effects models of causal ordering. *Child Development*, *76*(2), 397–416. 10.1111/j.1467-8624.2005.00853.x
Meltzoff, A. N. (2007). The 'like me' framework for recognizing and becoming an intentional agent. *Acta Psychologica*, *124*(1), 26–43. https://doi.org/10.1016/j.actpsy.2006.09.005
Miller, S. A. &. (2016). *Parenting and theory of mind*. Oxford University Press.
Milligan, K., Astington, J. W., & Dack, L. A. (2007). Language and theory of mind: Meta-analysis of the relation between language ability and false-belief understanding. *Child Development*, *78*(2), 622–646. 10.1111/j.1467-8624.2007.01018.x
Mizokawa, A. (2015). Theory of mind and sensitivity to teacher and peer criticism among japanese children. *Infant and Child Development*, *24*(2), 189–205. 10.1002/icd.1877
Mizokawa, A., & Lecce, S. (2017). Sensitivity to criticism and theory of mind: A cross cultural study on Japanese and Italian children. *European Journal of Developmental Psychology*, *14*(2), 159–171. 10.1080/17405629.2016.1180970
Moore, C. &. (2006). *The development of commonsense psychology*. Erlbaum.
Onishi, K. H., & Baillargeon, R. (2005). Do 15-month-old infants understand false beliefs? *Science*, *308*(5719), 255–258. 10.1126/science.1107621
Osterhaus, C., & Koerber, S. (2021). The development of advanced theory of mind in middle childhood: A longitudinal study from age 5 to 10 years. *Child Development*, *92*(5), 1872–1888. 10.1111/cdev.13627
Parsons, J. E., Kaczala, C. M., & Meece, J. L. (1982). Socialization of achievement attitudes and beliefs: Classroom influences. *Child Development*, *53*(2), 322–339. 10.2307/1128974

Peterson, C. C., & Wellman, H. M. (2019). Longitudinal theory of mind (ToM) development from preschool to adolescence with and without ToM delay. *Child Development*, *90*(6), 1917–1934. 10.1111/cdev.13064
Peterson, C. C., Wellman, H. M., & Liu, D. (2005). Steps in theory-of-mind development for children with deafness or autism. *Child Development*, *76*(2), 502–517. 10.1111/j.1467-8624.2005.00859.x
Peterson, C. C., Wellman, H. M., & Slaughter, V. (2012). The mind behind the message: Advancing theory-of-mind scales for typically developing children, and those with deafness, autism, or Asperger syndrome. *Child Development*, *83*(2), 469–485. 10.1111/j.1467-8624.2011.01728.x
Pinxten, M., Marsh, H. W., De Fraine, B., Van Den Noortgate, W., & Van Damme, J. (2014). Enjoying mathematics or feeling competent in mathematics? Reciprocal effects on mathematics achievement and perceived math effort expenditure. *British Journal of Educational Psychology*, *84*(1), 152–174. 10.1111/bjep.12028
Pons, F., & Harris, P. &. (2002). *Theory of mind test (TMT)*. Harvard University Press.
Pons, F., Harris, P. L., & de Rosnay, M. (2004). Emotion comprehension between 3 and 11 years: Developmental periods and hierarchical organization. *European Journal of Developmental Psychology*, *1*(2), 127–152. 10.1080/17405620344000022
Premack, D., & Woodruff, G. (1978). Does the chimpanzee have a theory of mind? *Behavioral and Brain Sciences*, *1*(4), 515–526. 10.1017/S0140525X00076512
Roebers, C. M., Krebs, S. S., & Roderer, T. (2014). Metacognitive monitoring and control in elementary school children: Their interrelations and their role for test performance. *Learning and Individual Differences*, *29*, 141–149. 10.1016/j.lindif.2012.12.003
Ruiz-Primo, M., & Li, M. (2013). Analyzing teachers' feedback practices in response to students' work in science classrooms. *Applied Measurement in Education*, *26*(3), 163–175. 10.1080/08957347.2013.793188
Schneider, W., Lockl, K., Bjork, R. A., & Dunlosky, J. (2008). *Procedural metacognition in children: evidence for developmental trends* (1st ed., pp. 391–409). Psychology Press.
Slaughter, V., Imuta, K., Peterson, C. C., & Henry, J. D. (2015). Meta-Analysis of Theory of Mind and Peer Popularity in the Preschool and Early School Years. *Child Development*, *86*(4), 1159–1174. 10.1111/cdev.12372
Smith, S., Dutcher, K., Askar, M., Talwar, V., & Bosacki, S. (2019). Emotional competencies in emerging adolescence: Relations between teacher ratings and student self-reports. *International Journal of Adolescence and Youth*, *24*(1), 19–28. 10.1080/02673843.2018.1455059
Smogorzewska, J., Szumski, G., & Grygiel, P. (n.d.) Greater diversity, faster change? The role of the educational setting in the development of advanced theory of mind among primary school children. Unpublished manuscript.
Smogorzewska, J., Szumski, G., Bosacki, S., Grygiel, P., & Karwowski, M. (2022a). School engagement, sensitivity to criticism and academic achievement in children: The predictive role of theory of mind. *Learning and Individual Differences*, *93*, 102111. 10.1016/j.lindif.2021.102111
Smogorzewska, J., Szumski, G., Bosacki, S., & Grygiel, P. (2022b). Just listen to your mind: Consequences of theory of mind development for deaf or hard-of-hearing children. *Research in Developmental Disabilities*, *127*, 104261. 10.1016/j.ridd.2022.104261
Smogorzewska, J., Szumski, G., & Grygiel, P. (2018). Same or different? Theory of mind among children with and without disabilities. *PloS One*, *13*(10), e0202553. 10.1371/journal.pone.0202553
Smogorzewska, J., Szumski, G., Grygiel, P., & Bosacki, S. (2025). Does emotional closeness with the teacher mediate the relationship between children's advanced theory of mind and social functioning at school? *Journal of Applied Developmental Psychology*, *98*, 101803. 10.1016/j.appdev.2025.101803

Sullivan, K., Zaitchik, D., & Tager-Flusberg, H. (1994). Preschoolers can attribute second-order beliefs. *Developmental Psychology*, *30*(3), 395–402. 10.1037/0012-1649.30.3.395

Szumski, G., & Karwowski, M. (2015). Emotional and social integration and the big-fish-little-pond effect among students with and without disabilities. *Learning and Individual Differences*, *43*, 63–74. 10.1016/j.lindif.2015.08.037

Thirion-Marissiaux, A., & Nader-Grosbois, N. (2008a). Theory of mind "beliefs", developmental characteristics and social understanding in children and adolescents with intellectual disabilities. *Research in Developmental Disabilities*, *29*(6), 547–566. 10.1016/j.ridd.2007.09.004

Thirion-Marissiaux, A., & Nader-Grosbois, N. (2008b). Theory of Mind "emotion", developmental characteristics and social understanding in children and adolescents with intellectual disabilities. *Research in Developmental Disabilities*, *29*(5), 414–430. 10.1016/j.ridd.2007.07.001

Trentacosta, C. J., & Izard, C. E. (2007). Kindergarten children's emotion competence as a predictor of their academic competence in first grade. *Emotion (Washington, DC)*, *7*(1), 77–88. 10.1037/1528-3542.7.1.77

Ueno, K., Nagoshi, N., & Konuki, S. (n.d.) *PVT-R manual*. Nihon Bunka Kagakusha.

Wellman, H. M. (2017). The development of theory of mind: Historical reflections. *Child Development Perspectives*, *11*(3), 207–214. 10.1111/cdep.12236

Wellman, H. M., Cross, D., & Watson, J. (2001). Meta-analysis of theory-of-mind development: The truth about false belief. *Child Development*, *72*(3), 655–684. 10.1111/1467-8624.00304

White, S., Hill, E., Happé, F., & Frith, U. (2009). Revisiting the strange stories: revealing mentalizing impairments in autism. *Child Development*, *80*(4), 1097–1117. 10.1111/j.1467-8624.2009.01319.x

Yirmiya, N., Erel, O., Shaked, M., & Solomonica-Levi, D. (1998). Meta-analyses comparing theory of mind abilities of individuals with autism, individuals with mental retardation, and normally developing individuals. *Psychological Bulletin*, *124*(3), 283–307. 10.1037/0033-2909.124.3.283

Yu, L., Li, L. M. W., & Tong, X. (2024). Understanding the link between theory of mind and loneliness among primary school students: A cross-lagged panel model analysis. *Journal of Experimental Child Psychology*, *242*, 105891. 10.1016/j.jecp.2024.105891

Chapter 4

Cultural variations in the perception of criticism

Alison M. Heru, Padmavati Ramachandran, Kanchana Mohan and Sandhya Shivakumar

Abstract

This chapter describes the cultural variations in the perception of criticism in families. For researchers and therapists, it is important to differentiate between the intent of criticism, the expression of criticism and the perception of criticism. Non-verbal criticism, such as a disapproving facial expression, is a subtle form of communication that may be difficult for researchers and clinicians to detect. The researcher and therapist must recognise their own cultural bias in their perceptions. Psychosocial constructs, such as expressed emotion (EE), are deeply influenced by the culture of the researcher, clinician, patient and their families. Family warmth, a positive component of the family environment, is emerging as an indicator of good outcome for a patient's illness. This chapter focuses on the cultural differences between individualistic and collectivistic societies, with three case examples illustrating how to assess and treat the nuances of criticism in families caught in cultural dilemmas.

4.1 Introduction

The word 'criticism' comes from the Greek word '*kritikos*', which means to judge or discern. Criticism is commonly defined as the act of forming a judgement about the positive or negative qualities of someone or something, but in common current usage the word 'criticism' is considered a negative appraisal. When criticism is pervasive, it leads to feelings of rejection and hurt (Neoh et al., 2024). In this chapter, we examine the variations in the perception of criticism that stem from differences in cultural values, particularly between individualistic and collectivistic societies. We examine how criticism is perceived using three family case studies that focus on questions of cultural and societal norms, and we show how to manage these conflicts using a problem-solving approach.

For researchers and therapists, it is important to identify three aspects of criticism, namely the intent of criticism, the expression of criticism and the perception of criticism. We begin the chapter by considering criticism in these aspects.

DOI: 10.4324/9781003388159-5

4.1.1 *Intent of criticism*

Regarding the intent of the criticism, it is important to identify if the communication is of the type called the double-bind, where a comment may appear pleasant on the surface, but is delivered with a critical feeling, resulting in the recipient being confused about the intent of the speaker. The double-bind was a classic early research finding that was thought to contribute to psychosis (Bateson et al., 1956; Koopmans, 1997). Although Bateson's double-bind theory has been discredited in the discussion of the relationship between schizophrenia and family interactions, his double-blind concept is still useful. For example, when a parent tells the child, 'I want you to be successful in this new culture, but you must adhere to the old culture's values', this creates a conflict for the child. This situation is not technically a double-bind in a Batesonian sense, unless there is a verbal and non-verbal contradictory component to the communication; however, it has been used by some researchers (Trovao, 2016). During acculturation, when cultural values of the 'old' country clash with the cultural values of the 'new' country, there are often high levels of expressed and perceived criticism. Thus, criticism may be direct or indirect, or may be delivered as a double-bind type of communication.

4.2 Cultural impact on expression and perception of criticism

It is important to clarify how culture affects the expression of emotions. There are universal features of emotional expression as well as considerable cultural variation among them. Cordaro and colleagues (2018) examined the expression of 22 emotions in five cultures and found clear patterns of emotional expression that apply across cultures, accounting for about 50% of the variance, and an additional 25% of variance due to cultural dialects (Cordaro et al., 2018). Thus, while the expression of emotions may be largely similar across cultures, there are dialectical differences in expression, and an assessment must be parsed using the cultural norms of the family.

A common tool used to measure criticalness in families is the Camberwell Family Interview (CFI; Leff & Vaughn, 1984), which measures the presence of hostility, critical comments and emotional over-involvement (EOI) (see Chapter 2). This tool was developed to predict the likelihood of relapse for patients with schizophrenia but it has become common practice to shorten it, and just use the number of critical comments as a predictor for relapse in many psychiatric conditions (Heru, 2021). However, when this tool is closely examined, profound cultural variation in both its use as an assessment tool and in its predictive ability emerge (Heru, 2021; O'Driscoll et al., 2019).

An interesting feature of the original research on the CFI was the conceptualisation of warmth as a protective family component. Warmth was defined as 'the expression of positive feeling', such as 'the tone of voice including a display of enthusiasm, positive changes in manner and tone versus flatness, or the presence of coldness', spontaneous expressions of warmth, expressions of sympathy, concern and empathy, especially when the relative was describing symptoms, and display of interest in the person and enthusiasm for their achievement (Leff & Vaughn, 1984, pp. 35–42). Evaluators were directed to pay attention to expressions of warmth about the patient. Warmth was measured on a six-point scale (0 = no warmth; 5 = high warmth). This concept has now seen a resurgence, and in several international studies individuals with psychosis are shown to have a better outcome in families with high warmth (Kopelowicz et al., 2015; López et al., 2009). In Mexican American families, the best predictors of good patient outcome were high warmth and moderate EOI (López et al., 2009). In families from Barcelona (n = 21 dyads), high warmth as measured by the CFI was correlated with fewer patient symptoms. In Puerto Rican children, high parental warmth was found to be protective against psychiatric disorders. In this study, the measurement of warmth included assessment of feelings of closeness, trust and anger towards the child. However, despite the increasing relevance of warmth as a predictor, its measurement still does not incorporate cultural/ethnic variation in the display of affection or the cultural variation in the expression of warmth. This resurgence in the use of warmth reflects the current trend in looking for positive factors that promote resilience, and a focus on strengths rather than deficits (Butterfield et al., 2021; López et al., 2009; Padilla-Walker et al., 2016).

Whilst criticism and warmth have predictive utility in patient outcomes in the research context, the fact that criticism and warmth are not fully recognised in the same way across cultures makes our clinical encounters fraught with opportunities for error. Criticism is often directed at individuals who are not complying with social norms, whether this is a collectivistic society or an individualistic society (Tirupati & Ramachandran, 2020), and it is important to tease out the basis for criticism, asking questions about culture and societal norms in order to fully understand the depth of the potential rift among family members. Regardless of culture, resilient families have common factors. A resilient family demonstrates coherence in family belief systems, organisational patterns, and communication for the purpose of problem-solving (Ritchie & Fitzpatrick, 1990). The family can be asked directly: 'Can the family adapt to the needs of its members?' 'Are the family beliefs focused on providing a healthy environment for each person?' 'Is the family able to communicate and solve problems together?'

When people from different cultures migrate and are embedded in a host country, they do not adopt all the characteristics of the host culture (Berry, 1997). Acculturation is a process that varies with each individual. People transitioning to the hosting culture will carry elements of their cultural heritage, such as affiliation to their family hierarchy and dynamics, gender role delineation, and concepts of individuality and independence, even though they may identify themselves with many other aspects of the host culture (Berry, 1997). This creates a tension between individualism and collectivism within each person, reflecting their desire to belong. Thoughts of rejection are heightened when host community members and immigrants adopt either a separation strategy or a marginalisation strategy over assimilation or integration strategies (Watt et al., 2025). Understanding our patients means deciphering how allegiances to the host culture and their own culture oppose each other and this cultural conflict impacts their sense of self and their family relationships (Foner, 1997). For example, in cultures with a collectivistic orientation, the families play a major and lifetime role in caring for its members, making decisions and acting in consideration of the welfare of all (Keil & Elizabeth, 2022), and in such situations the needs and priorities of individuals, especially women, may likely be superseded by the interests of the family as a whole.

The collectivistic values found across many Asian cultures are steeped in regional traditions and spiritual beliefs. Within this context, the role of criticism appears frequently in mythological and religious narratives. In Hindu thought, the family is often regarded as the foundation of *dharma* (duty) and *karma* (action), and collectivistic ideals such as respect for elders, interdependence, and shared moral development remain central (Sharma, 2000). In Buddhism, by contrast, scholars have observed a discourse in which familial ties are depicted as potential sources of attachment and suffering (Ohnuma, 2014). Clough (2001) discusses the ethics of family life in the *Theravāda Pāli* Canon, highlighting duties between husbands and wives, parents and children, as well as scriptural strategies for addressing familial discord. Buddhist stories frequently employ moral critique as a tool for ethical self-governance and transformation (Strong, 1983), conveying that criticism functions not as interpersonal antagonism but as a means of cultivating internal moral reflection (Appleton, 2011; Gethin, 1998).

Similarly, Hindu mythological narratives present criticism as a vehicle for moral inquiry and ethical development. Hiltebeitel (1999) observes that the Mahabharata depicts tensions between personal desire and moral responsibility, particularly in the relationships among Dhritarashtra, his son Duryodhana, and Bhishma – figures who embody competing loyalties and obligations. The primary tension is between Dhritarashtra and Duryodhana as the king is unable to restrain his son's *adharma*. His failure to morally guide Duryodhana may be illustrative of the consequences of weak kingship. There is also conflict between Duryodhana and Bhima – as he directly opposes Duryodhana's behaviour. Bhima exposes Duryodhana's jealousy, dishonesty and aggression, which thereby serves as a narrative mechanism through which Duryodhana's *adharma* is highlighted. Together, Dhritarashtra's inaction shows implicit narrative criticism, whereas Bhima's actions and words constitute explicit interpersonal criticism. Doniger (2011) further notes how mythical narratives use such familial and political tensions to illuminate broader ethical dilemmas. These examples show that criticism in both Buddhist and Hindu traditions is rooted in the pursuit of *dharma* and the cultivation of moral consciousness, rather than in opposition to family members themselves. Consequently, criticism becomes an integral cultural mechanism for awakening ethical awareness within family structures.

How to handle criticism alongside acculturation?

Discuss with family members about cultural values and sense of belonging to the host culture and own culture. This might involve developing strategies to assimilate with the other culture and perceive trust, curiosity and warmth towards the other culture.

How to handle criticism when it is seen as a moral obligation?

Family members can acknowledge that the criticism is not directed towards the person themselves, but towards their behaviour and to help the person navigate their own journey. They must also reassure the person to consider their own circumstances and give them independence to make their own decisions.

4.3 Criticism in the context of individualism and collectivism

The difference between individualistic and collectivistic systems helps explain the various attitudes, perceptions and behaviours in people of different cultures. Individualistic cultures favour self-reliance and members are more likely to use 'I' language, and put themselves forward individually rather than as members of a family (Lykes & Kemmelmeier, 2014; Park et al., 2012). In collectivist cultures, there is a prevailing ethos of social connectedness. In South Asian and East Asian societies such as India, Philippines or Japan, this ethos comprises feelings of belongingness, dependency, empathy and reciprocity (Aruta et al., 2021). Relationships with others are emphasised while personal autonomy, space and privacy are considered secondary. The lines of hierarchy and authority are clearly drawn, and the rules of conduct are aimed at creating and maintaining family harmony within the principle of 'collective responsibility' with greater readiness to cooperate with family members on decisions affecting almost all aspects of life including gender roles. In collectivist cultures, there is a power imbalance between men and women, with women having less independence and less authority imparted to them (Dutta et al., 2022). Women's roles are dominated by expectations of passivity, submission and dependence (Haj-Yahia & Sadan, 2008), which are very different from women in individualistic cultures where independence is often a defining character.

The right to express an opinion is one difference that may be easily misunderstood. People in individualistic cultures prioritise their personal autonomy and right to express their opinion as a fundamental right, whereas people in collectivistic cultures, such as India, value group harmony, and feel that direct and assertive communication is threatening (Park 2011). For instance, direct communication, such as explicit criticism using derogatory words, interferes with the need for social harmony in a collectivistic culture. Collectivistic cultures, such as the Thai culture, will deliver criticism indirectly, such as through subtle communication, suggestions, or body language to convey dissatisfaction and such communication may be missed by therapists based in individualist cultures (Aruta et al., 2021; Rojjanaprapayon, 1997). Families with more social contact can buffer criticism by offering different interpretations of the criticism, such as when other families scaffold each other when criticised (Guada et al., 2009). For instance, families with conversation-oriented communication patterns spend time discussing different topics and sharing activities with each other (Ritchie & Fitzpatrick, 1990), and when families have a consensual communication style, they are open to sharing new ideas. These types of families strive for conformity and openness (Ritchie & Fitzpatrick, 1990).

4.4 Role of gender

There is a hierarchy of expression of opinions in collectivistic cultures as explained above, where women are seen to be passive and submissive (Haj-Yahia & Sadan, 2008). Yet, research also suggests that there are gender differences in expression of criticism when family members take on caring roles such that women express more criticism and emotional over-involvement towards a patient with mental illness (Zanetti et al., 2019). When EE was measured in relatives of 94 patients with schizophrenia in Brazil, the family member was predominately female (71%) and middle-aged (mean age 56 years) (Zanetti et al., 2019). The relative (77%) expressed high EE, with 51% expressing criticism and 66% expressing EOI. Being a female relative, rather than a male relative, increased the likelihood of being emotionally over-involved to 88%. The authors explain that such heightened EOI of females, especially mothers, among Brazilian families is consistent with mothers spending more time with patients because of early childhood maternal attachment (Zanetti et al., 2019). Thus, being a female relative of the patient increased the likelihood of being critical to 99% and such high criticism may arise from the EOI and stress from the burden of care among female caregivers (Zanetti et al., 2019).

However, men more than women, were found to show a stronger association between perceived criticism at first year of marriage and depression one year later (Peterson-Post et al., 2014). In this study, 132 couples were assessed for marital adjustment and perceived criticism around the first year of marriage and their prediction of depression in the spouses was measured one year later, and five and ten years later (Peterson-Post et al., 2014). Depression was strongly associated with perceived criticism (Hooley & Teasdale, 1989). One can speculate that internalising the criticism may lead to learned helplessness, and therefore when men internalise the criticism, rather than reciprocate it or seek social support, they can feel depressed. When men perceive their female partner as demanding, they feel depressed (Uebelacker et al., 2003). Such gender differences can amplify the cultural differences in the impact of criticism.

This discrepancy between the rigid hierarchy of emotional expression in families in some collectivistic cultures and the EE from a female carer towards a patient with a serious mental illness suggests that the burden of care can change the communication style.

How to handle criticism in a collectivistic family setting?

Recognise that criticism can be expressed directly by expressing derogatory words. But criticism can also be expressed indirectly, e.g. by appearing to be pleasant on the surface, but is associated with a critical feeling and even displeasing body language.

Be open to different interpretations of the criticism to buffer its impact.

Acknowledge the gendered hierarchy within families with expressing views and give room for all family members to express their opinions.

Share the burden of care among members of the family with experiencing mental illness.

4.5 Impact of criticism on mental illness outcomes

Criticism can negatively impact mental health in several ways. Self-criticism can involve internalising expectations or standards and then finding fault with oneself, leading to feelings of low self-esteem, anxiety and depression. Self-critical people may have a higher risk of developing depression and other mental health disorders (McIntyre et al., 2018; Yamaguchi & Kim, 2013). The family's emotional climate from childhood throughout adulthood influences one's self-critical tendencies. Self-criticism can occur when children have experienced, then internalise, verbal abuse or criticism from their parents (Bleys et al., 2018). A longitudinal association has been observed between development of self-criticism and restrictive-rejecting behaviours of parents (Koestner et al., 1991). In adulthood, people with an avoidant personality are extremely sensitive to criticism and may avoid social interactions due to a fear of rejection (Premkumar et al., 2015). Therefore, family emotional climate should be considered in the development of illness.

4.5.1 *Case example one: critical comments between an interracial couple*

Joe and Esi want help with their relationship. The therapist asks: How does race impact your lives? Esi begins with a story about her ethics class, a story at sufficient distance from her domestic life.

'Me and a mulatto girl were in ethics class. We had a White professor. He seemed to think I had no education. If you are a woman of colour, you are automatically thought to have no education and that you don't know what you are talking about. He tried to shut me up. I know he thought from the tone of my voice that I was an angry Black woman, even although I am not Black and I am not angry! In this country, if you have any colour to your skin, you are called Black and relegated to a certain place: the bottom. I was excited about what he was teaching us, but when everyone looked at me with a certain gaze, like something bad was going to happen, all those White people, just looking, I sat back down.'

Her husband, who is White, reaches over and pats her hands.

'Esi, they are wrong. They shouldn't have treated you that way. White people can be insensitive.'

'But, Joe, you do the same to me.'

'What do you mean, Esi?' responded Joe, anxiously.

'Well, Joe, do you really want to hear how I felt last week after we came back from your sister's house?'

'Yes, Esi.'

'Remember when we went over, me and the kids sat with the other brown folks and you sat with your sister and her side of the family?'

'Yes, I remember. What is wrong with that?'

'Well, me and my coloured friends got loud and excited, and you shot me a look, like 'Pipe down over there.' Then, after we got home, the next day, your sister called you and said that I was too loud. Do you remember all that?'

'Yes, well you do get loud – especially when you are around your people.'

'My people! So why is it I have to fit in with your relatives and not the other way round? Why do I have to conform to the whiteness in your sister's world, not the other way round?'

'Well, we were in her house.'

'So if they came to our house and were too quiet, how would you feel if I called them up and said they needed to participate with more enthusiasm?'

'Esi, that's not fair, and you know it isn't.'

'So I check myself. It is the same all over, White people imposing their values and beliefs on me, on us. You can see their demeanour change, they pull back, sit up, back away, fidget, and won't look you in the eye. All these little tics that show that they are trying to get out of the situation. They are very critical.'

'Esi, I am sorry,' said Joe.

'You may be sorry but you are not willing to stand up for me against your sister and her White values, are you?'

'What do you want me to do?'

'I want you to call your sister out.'

'But she may not ever speak to me again!'

'OK, don't then,' and Esi looked down. She was finished talking.

'Keep talking this through,' the therapist instructs.

'Do you really want me to call my sister out, even if it means that she will not talk to me again?'

'That's your choice.'

'I don't know if I can do that.'

The therapist intervenes: 'What does that mean to you, Esi, that he doesn't know if he can do that?'

'It means he values his sister over me and our children. What do you think our daughter is learning?'

'That's not true, Esi.'

'Well, I check myself so that I can fit in with this White culture.'

Dr. Swarthmore realises the couple have to work this out if they are going to move forward.

'Esi and Joe, you are both caught in an important dilemma. Esi, you want more respect and less criticism from your husband and his family. Joe, you do not want to upset your family by confronting them. Is that right?'

'Yes,' they both say.

'Can you spend the next 10 minutes to work on this?'

'Ok, let's start. What skills do you have that can help you resolve this important issue?'

Dr Swarthmore frames the issue as one to be solved by the couple. The couple discuss that they are usually good at communication and solving problems. This problem is about whether or not Joe is more aligned with his White family than with Esi and their children.

Dr Swarthmore encourages them to think about this conflicting sense of commitment.

'How do you think you can educate yourselves about the issues at hand?'

Esi asks Joe to read a book about her culture of origin. Joe suggests that Esi think about what it might mean if his sister and their children were no longer part of their lives.

The therapist offers them a handout that includes such questions as 'How do I define myself racially?', 'When did I first become aware of race/skin colour in general, and mine in particular?', 'What messages have I learned about race/skin colour based on that first experience?', 'What direct and indirect messages have I received about race/skin colour?', 'What benefits do I gain because of my race/skin colour?', 'What do I lose because of my race/skin?'

This encounter was limited to 10 minutes, so the couple don't feel overwhelmed by their emotions. The goal is to focus on the strengths that they can bring to resolving the issue. The couple are thus empowered to solve their problem. There is no focus on criticism. Their problem is not construed as a problem of high EE or of criticism, but as a mutual problem to be solved.

How to resolve conflict in therapy?

Normalise conflict, approach as a problem to be solved, use history of family's prior success at problem-solving, positive hopeful stance, time limit discussions.

Consider education about family background and projection into future for the family's ethics and values.

4.5.2 *Case example two: interplay between criticism and serious mental illness*

At a time when research on treatment for serious mental illness appears to be focusing on the inclusion of persons with lived experience (Sunkel & Sartor, 2022), it is time to consider the criticism that persons with lived experience of psychosis are exposed to and how this could interfere with treatment processes that are planned. People with psychoses often report that they feel stressed when they interact with significant people in their lives. G, a 32-year-old woman, with a diagnosis of schizophrenia, relapsing course, on antipsychotics, regular psychiatric follow-up, lives with her aging parents, in a southern state of India. She is single after a divorce at age 25, largely due to the stigma of a diagnosis of schizophrenia and the need for medications. She is dependent on her parents and siblings for all aspects of existence. Over her lifetime, she has been exposed to many negative discriminatory comments from her immediate and extended family criticism, subtle or overt, was in the form of comments about her personal appearance, activities of daily living or socialisation. She has gradually begun to believe that these criticisms are true since she has a mental illness, although she has been clinically stable, with no psychotic symptoms. She says that her parents have consistently reiterated that she is useless and have expressed worry about her future.

A referral to a psychosocial rehabilitation programme in the city brought her into conversation with a case manager and a peer support volunteer at the facility. Using a needs-based approach, the treatment team, including a peer support volunteer, has charted out a collaborative plan that focused on creating a sense of personal identity and empowerment through decision-making tasks. She was encouraged to plan her day by herself, such as activities of daily living, and spending time outside her home, such as visits to the day rehabilitation facility and walking. These 'interventions' brought change. She realised that she needed to negotiate the criticisms 'meted' out to her by the family. However, conversations with her parents have not been productive, since they believe she can never be better – it is her fate! However, the case manager and the peer support volunteer have been very supportive and non-judgemental with M and she is now motivated to 'at least try' to become more functional.

The treatment team have continued to talk with the parents, hoping to make an impact on their views about their daughter's mental illness.

This case illustrates the traditional value placed on the woman as a subordinate and dutiful wife, who once tainted has no place in the traditional Indian world. The role of the therapist is to contrast this set of traditional values with more Western values that support growth, change and a sense of a future. Helping the patient see that her parents are operating on a set of traditional values that are not helpful to her rather than being critical of her herself, fostered a sense of who she might become if the values espoused by the treatment team are embraced.

4.5.3 *Case example three: criticism and parenting styles*

Cultural references to parenting styles and normalisation of criticism can be a barrier to care, especially when cultural practices are influenced by intergenerational beliefs. Literature on parenting styles has discussed the effects of criticism in depth (Martinez et al., 2020; Masud et al., 2019; Pong et al., 2010), showing that recurrent and persistent exposures to criticism especially in the early years of childhood can lead to self-critical tendencies, thereby increasing psychological vulnerability. Consequently, this can result in low self-esteem, depression and anxiety. In contrast, warm and positive child–parent interactions may be linked to more favourable psychological outcomes and increase resilience.

C is an 11-year-old boy living in North America, and is brought into a psychologist's practice by his mother, with a history of persistent fears that prevent him from engaging in any age-specific activities like sports, or visits to the homes of classmates. The recent life event at home resulted in his refusal to engage with a mandatory school activity that necessitated his being away from home overnight. When C' s father had a heart attack, his fears worsened and 'Will my father die?' questions gradually became 'When my father dies, what will I do?

His parents moved to the United States four years before C was born and more recently, about five years ago, his grandparents moved permanently to the USA from India. Overprotectiveness, seen in many Indian families, have prevented C from doing any activity at home for fear of harm. Several factors contribute to this style of parenting. Cultural values and practices, the role of discipline and authority, the deeply ingrained emphasis on the need to respect elders are some key factors that explain this style of parenting (Jambunathan & Counselman, 2002). A detailed history and examination revealed an authoritarian family environment. If C argues or starts crying, he is declared to be disobedient. The grandparents then refuse to speak with him as a 'punishment'.

Detailed mental status examination and psychometry result in a diagnosis of anxiety disorder. The psychologist has sessions with the young boy and his mother, but no progress is made since the family, especially the grandparents, refuse to believe that their parenting styles need to change, as these styles have been time-tested over generations.

This scenario raises child development concerns; the emotional impact of constraining the young boy in a 'free' culture is interfering with the emotional growth of the child and he is being held back in his adaptation to a new culture. This latter process is reported to be important for the physical, social and emotional well-being of immigrants (Clarke & Isphording, 2017; Martinez et al., 2020; Masud et al., 2019; Park, G. C., 2011; Pong et al., 2010; Reimers, 1983).

There is much literature on the benefit of elders in the rearing of children; however in this situation, the elders are preventing the child from normally developing in the 'new' culture. Transnational grand-parenting refers to situations where grandchildren are cared for by grandparents in the country of birth, distance grand-parenting, and when grandparents immigrate to live with their children and grandchildren to a new culture (Schuler et al., 2022). Maintaining links to the culture of origin, stories, language, value systems and ritualistic practices are important dimensions of cultural sustainability (Buttiler et al., 2023; Williams & Liu, 2023).

For C, the grandparents' reluctance to accept the need for change was apparent and C is caught between two cultures. This child's experience is clearly one of punishment, although there could be an element of a double-bind situation, which could be explored in future sessions. In such instances intergenerational and cross-cultural differences in parenting, the parents may need to take a stance against the grandparents' criticism while also allowing the grandparents to teach C about his culture.

4.6 Conclusion

Culture plays an important role in how the expression of criticism and warmth are intended, expressed and perceived. Culture also plays a role in how psychiatric disorder is construed. Most psychosocial concepts and constructs have been developed and applied in psychiatry and other medical disciplines without regard to sociocultural norms. Culture plays an important role in the diagnostic process, and cultural factors have a powerful impact on the development of psychopathology and on the severity of the presenting complaints (Alarcón, 2009). This can be seen in case one, where the couple are fighting over the basic concept of belonging. Broad categorisation of cultures as collectivistic and individualistic help to understand how criticism is expressed and perceived.

In current times, the word criticism is considered a negative appraisal that leads to feelings of rejection and hurt. In treatment situations for individuals from a culture with its focus on group harmony, direct expression of feedback feels more threatening than it would for an individual from an individualistic culture. On the other hand, individualistic cultures value personal autonomy and prioritise direct self-expression, viewing open communication as the fundamental right of an individual. Understanding these cultural differences is crucial for interpreting communication styles within families and larger communities, as they significantly influence social relationships and relationship satisfaction. In contrast to criticism, warmth is emerging as a protective factor associated with better outcomes for individuals with psychiatric conditions across various cultural contexts.

In the clinical setting, it is essential to consider the patient's cultural background, level of acculturation, family structure and dynamics, as these deeply influence the experience and response to criticism. Adaptation of family interventions also need to be culturally appropriate, balancing the need to adhere to the basic tenets of a treatment protocol with the need for the intervention to be culturally appropriate. For example, when family psycho-educational interventions were applied across cultures, there was no single 'universal' successful family psycho-educational intervention, and McFarlane noted that the American version of family psycho-educational may mesh better with certain cultures than with other cultures. The differences in efficacy of family psycho-educational lie in the quality of cultural adaptations, specific aspects of the studies' design or the cultural context (Swenson et al., 2016).

4.6.1 *Future directions*

Future research must deepen our understanding of the interplay of culture and gender in several areas. First, the involvement of extended family members is starkly different between collectivistic and individualistic cultures and should be considered as a routine part of an assessment. Current assessment tools can be adapted and tested to allow their participation. This is particularly important in Indian families, where extended family members deeply influence the values and beliefs of the nuclear family. Second, gender is an important consideration in the context of perception and response to criticism. Men and women likely express emotions, especially criticism, differently across cultures, aligned with the culture's gender norms and expectations (Zanetti et al., 2019). The role of women both as matriarchs and young mothers are changing and impact family size, both in individual and collective cultures (Peterson-Post et al., 2014). It would be interesting to examine how women from collectivist cultures manage the pressures of child rearing in individualist cultures. Lastly, families with mixed-race and mixed cultural backgrounds are becoming more common, and assessment tools can be created to include questions about navigating cultural difference. In each of these situations, including the assessment of warmth is in line with future research goals.

References

Alarcón, R. D. (2009). Culture, cultural factors and psychiatric diagnosis: Review and projections. *World Psychiatry*, *8*(3), 131–139. 10.1002/j.2051-5545.2009.tb00233.x

Appleton. (2011). In the footsteps of the Buddha? Women and the Bodhisatta Path in Theravāda Buddhism. *Journal of Feminist Studies in Religion*, *27*(1), 33. 10.2979/jfemistudreli.27.1.33

Aruta, J. J. B. R., Antazo, B. G., & Paceño, J. L. (2021). Self-stigma is associated with depression and anxiety in a collectivistic context: The adaptive cultural function of self-criticism. *The Journal of Psychology*, *155*(2), 238–256. 10.1080/00223980.2021.1876620

Bateson, G., Jackson, D. D., Haley, J., & Weakland, J. (1956). Toward a theory of schizophrenia. *Behavioral Science, 1*(4), 251–264. 10.1002/bs.3830010402

Berry, J. W. (1997). Immigration, acculturation, and adaptation. *Applied Psychology, 46*(1), 5–34. 10.1111/j.1464-0597.1997.tb01087.x

Bleys, D., Soenens, B., Claes, S., Vliegen, N., & Luyten, P. (2018). Parental psychological control, adolescent self-criticism, and adolescent depressive symptoms: A latent change modeling approach in Belgian adolescents. *Journal of Clinical Psychology, 74*(10), 1833–1853. 10.1002/jclp.22632

Butterfield, R. D., Silk, J. S., Lee, K. H., Siegle, G. S., Dahl, R. E., Forbes, E. E., Ryan, N. D., Hooley, J. M., & Ladouceur, C. D. (2021). Parents still matter! Parental warmth predicts adolescent brain function and anxiety and depressive symptoms 2 years later. *Development and Psychopathology, 33*(1), 226–239. 10.1017/S0954579419001718

Buttiler, M. B., Zhou, Q., & Uchikoshi, Y. (2023). Reasons for migration, parental acculturation, and language: The case of Chinese American and Mexican American parents and dual language learners. *Frontiers in Psychology, 14*, 1237143. 10.3389/fpsyg.2023.1237143

Clarke, A., & Isphording, I. E. (2017). Language barriers and immigrant health. *Health Economics, 26*(6), 765–778. 10.1002/hec.3358

Clough, B. (2001). Buddhism. In J. Neusner (Ed.), *The ethics of family life: What do we owe one another? Comparing religious traditions* (pp. 124–158). Wadsworth; Thomson Learning.

Cordaro, D. T., Sun, R., Keltner, D., Kamble, S., Huddar, N., & McNeil, G. (2018). Universals and cultural variations in 22 emotional expressions across five cultures. *Emotion (Washington, DC), 18*(1), 75–93. 10.1037/emo0000302

Doniger, W. (2011). *The implied spider: Politics and theology in myth*. Columbia University Press.

Dutta, N., Giddings, L., & Sobel, R. S. (2022). Does trust always help gender role attitudes? The role of individualism and collectivism. *Social Indicators Research, 159*(1), 379–408. 10.1007/s11205-021-02755-y

Foner, N. (1997). The immigrant family: Cultural legacies and cultural changes. *The International Migration Review, 31*(4), 961. 10.2307/2547420

Gethin, R. M. L. (1998). *The foundations of Buddhism* (1st ed.). Oxford University Press.

Guada, J., Brekke, J. S., Floyd, R., & Barbour, J. (2009). The relationships among perceived criticism, family contact, and consumer clinical and psychosocial functioning for African-American consumers with schizophrenia. *Community Mental Health Journal, 45*(2), 106–116. 10.1007/s10597-008-9165-4

Haj-Yahia, M., & Sadan, E. (2008). Issues in intervention with battered women in collectivist societies. *Journal of Marital and Family Therapy, 34*(1), 1–13. 10.1111/j.1752-0606.2008.00049.x

Heru, A. M. (2021). Cultural research deconstructs the psychosocial construct 'expressed emotion'. *British Journal of Psychiatry, 219*(4), 565–568. 10.1192/bjp.2020.148

Hiltebeitel, A. (1999). *Rethinking India's oral and classical epics: Draupadi among Rajputs, Muslims, and Dalits*. University of Chicago Press.

Hooley, J. M., & Teasdale, J. D. (1989). Predictors of relapse in unipolar depressives: expressed emotion, marital distress, and perceived criticism. *Journal of Abnormal Psychology, 98*(3), 229–235. 10.1037//0021-843x.98.3.229

Jambunathan, S., & Counselman, K. (2002). Parenting attitudes of Asian Indian mothers living in the United States and in India. *Early Child Development and Care, 172*(6), 657–662. https://doi.org/10.1080/03004430215102

Keil, M., & Elizabeth, V. (2022). The care of children when Pacific parents live apart: A case of mothers and othermothers caring together. *The Journal of Social Welfare & Family Law, 44*(3), 329–346. 10.1080/09649069.2022.2102763

Koestner, R., Zuroff, D. C., & Powers, T. A. (1991). Family origins of adolescent self-criticism and its continuity into adulthood. *Journal of Abnormal Psychology, 100*(2), 191–197. 10.1037/0021-843X.100.2.191
Koopmans, M. (1997). Schizophrenia and the family: Double bind theory revisited. https://goertzel.org/dynapsyc/1997/Koopmans.html
Kopelowicz, A., Zarate, R., Wallace, C. J., Liberman, R. P., Lopez, S. R., & Mintz, J. (2015). Using the theory of planned behavior to improve treatment adherence in Mexican Americans with schizophrenia. *Journal of Consulting and Clinical Psychology, 83*(5), 985–993. 10.1037/a0039346
Leff, J. P., & Vaughn, C. (1984). The expressed emotion scales. *Expressed emotion in families: Its significance for mental illness* (pp. 37–63). Guilford Press.
López, S. R., Ramírez García, J. I., Ullman, J. B., Kopelowicz, A., Jenkins, J., Breitborde, N. J., & Placencia, P. (2009). Cultural variability in the manifestation of expressed emotion. *Family Process, 48*(2), 179–194.
Lykes, V. A., & Kemmelmeier, M. (2014). What predicts loneliness? Cultural difference between individualistic and collectivistic societies in Europe. *Journal of Cross-Cultural Psychology, 45*(3), 468–490. 10.1177/0022022113509881
Martinez, I., Garcia, F., Veiga, F., Garcia, O. F., Rodrigues, Y., & Serra, E. (2020). Parenting styles, internalization of values and self-esteem: A cross-cultural study in Spain, Portugal and Brazil. *International Journal of Environmental Research and Public Health, 17*(7), 2370. 10.3390/ijerph17072370
Masud, H., Ahmad, M. S., Cho, K. W., & Fakhr, Z. (2019). Parenting styles and aggression among young adolescents: A systematic review of literature. *Community Mental Health Journal, 55*(6), 1015–1030. 10.1007/s10597-019-00400-0
McIntyre, R., Smith, P., & Rimes, K. A. (2018). The role of self-criticism in common mental health difficulties in students: A systematic review of prospective studies. *Mental Health & Prevention, 10*, 13–27. 10.1016/j.mhp.2018.02.003
Neoh, M. J. Y., Lieu, A. A., Perinelli, E., Balagtas, J. P. M., Nah, H., Ho, M. R., & Esposito, G. (2024). An intergenerational study of parental bonding on perceptions of parental and spousal criticism and marital relationship quality in Singapore. *Family Process, 63*(2), 947–966. 10.1111/famp.12942
O'Driscoll, C., Sener, S. B., Angmark, A., & Shaikh, M. (2019). Caregiving processes and expressed emotion in psychosis, a cross-cultural, meta-analytic review. *Schizophrenia Research, 208*, 8–15. 10.1016/j.schres.2019.03.020
Ohnuma, R. (2014). Buddhism and the family. *Oxford Bibliographies Online Datasets.*
Padilla-Walker, L., Nielson, M. G., & Day, R. D. (2016). The role of parental warmth and hostility on adolescents' prosocial behavior toward multiple targets. *Journal of Family Psychology, 30*(3), 331–340. 10.1037/fam0000157
Park, G. C. (2011). Becoming a 'model minority': Acquisition, construction and enactment of American identity for Korean Immigrant Students. *The Urban Review, 43*(5), 620–635. 10.1007/s11256-010-0164-8
Park, H. S., Levine, T. R., Weber, R., Lee, H. E., Terra, L. I., Botero, I. C., Bessarabova, E., Guan, X., Shearman, S. M., & Wilson, M. S. (2012). Individual and cultural variations in direct communication style. *International Journal of Intercultural Relations, 36*(2), 179–187. 10.1016/j.ijintrel.2011.12.010
Peterson-Post, K., Rhoades, G. K., Stanley, S. M., & Markman, H. J. (2014). Perceived criticism and marital adjustment predict depressive symptoms in a community sample. *Behavior Therapy, 45*(4), 564–575. 10.1016/j.beth.2014.03.002
Pong, S., Johnston, J., & Chen, V. (2010). Authoritarian parenting and asian adolescent school performance: Insights from the US and Taiwan. *International Journal of Behavioral Development, 34*(1), 62–72. 10.1177/0165025409345073

Premkumar, P., Onwumere, J., Albert, J., Kessel, D., Kumari, V., Kuipers, E., & Carretié, L. (2015). The relation between schizotypy and early attention to rejecting interactions: The influence of neuroticism. *The World Journal of Biological Psychiatry*, *16*(8), 587–601. 10.3109/15622975.2015.1073855

Reimers, C. W. (1983). Labor market discrimination against Hispanic and Black men. *The Review of Economics and Statistics*, *65*(4), 570–579. 10.2307/1935925

Ritchie, L. D., & Fitzpatrick, M. A. (1990). Family communication patterns: measuring intrapersonal perceptions of interpersonal relationships. *Communication Research*, *17*(4), 523–544. 10.1177/009365090017004007

Rojjanaprapayon, W. (1997). *Communication patterns of Thai people in a non-Thai context*. Purdue University.

Schuler, E., Schuler, F. d. M. G., & Dias, C. M. d. S. B. (2022). Transnational grandparenthood: A qualitative study on the relationship of grandparents and grandchildren in the migration context. *Interpersona: An International Journal on Personal Relationships*, *16*(2), 200–220. 10.5964/ijpr.6631

Sharma, A. (2000). *Classical Indian thought*. Oxford University Press.

Strong, J. S. (1983). *The legend of King Asoka; A study and translation of the Asokavadana*. Princeton University Press.

Sunkel, C., & Sartor, C. (2022). Perspectives: Involving persons with lived experience of mental health conditions in service delivery, development and leadership. *BJPsych Bulletin*, *46*(3), 160–164. 10.1192/bjb.2021.51

Swenson, S., Ho, G. W. K., Budhathoki, C., & Belcher, H., Tucker, S., & Miller, K., & Gross, D. (2016). Parents' use of praise and criticism in a sample of young children seeking mental health services. *Journal of Pediatric Health Care*, *30*(1), 49–56. https://doi.org/10.1016/j.pedhc.2015.09.010

Tirupati, S., & Ramachandran, P. (2020). Schizophrenia, recovery and the individual-cultural considerations. *Australasian Psychiatry: Bulletin of the Royal Australian and New Zealand College of Psychiatrists*, *28*(2), 190–192. 10.1177/1039856219889320

Trovao, S. S. (2016). Culture, ambivalence, and schismogenesis: Mothering double binds and gendered identities within Cape Verdean and Indian migrant families (Portugal). *Culture & Psychology*, *22*(2), 232–253. 10.1177/1354067X15606979

Uebelacker, L. A., Courtnage, E. S., & Whisman, M. A. (2003). Correlates of depression and marital dissatisfaction: Perceptions of marital communication style. *Journal of Social and Personal Relationships*, *20*(6), 757–769. 10.1177/0265407503206003

Watt, S. E., Alcott, Y. D., Feng, S., Keleher, A., & Littlewood, N. I. (2025). Don't you like us? Don't you want us? The influence of immigrants' acculturation strategies on cognitions of rejection in host community members. *International Journal of Intercultural Relations*, *108*, 102271. 10.1016/j.ijintrel.2025.102271

Williams, M. S., & Liu, C. (2023). Who am I and where do I belong? The impact of heritage cultural identity salience on immigrant workers acculturation strategies: who am I and where do I belong? The impact of heritage cultural identity salience on immigrant workers acculturation strategies. *Journal of International Migration and Integration*, *24*(2), 793–815. 10.1007/s12134-022-00978-7

Yamaguchi, A., & Kim, M. (2013). Effects of self-criticism and its relationship with depression across cultures. *International Journal of Psychological Studies*, *5*(1), 1.

Zanetti, A. C. G., Vedana, K. G. G., Pereira, C. C. M., de Azevedo Marques, J. M., da Silva, A., Heloisa Santana, Martin, I. d. S., Dantas, R. A. S., de Souza, J., Galera, S. A. F., & Gherardi-Donato, E. (2019). Expressed emotion and socio-demographic and clinical factors in families of Brazilian patients with schizophrenia. *International Journal of Social Psychiatry*, *65*(1), 56–63. 10.1177/0020764018815207

Chapter 5

Criticism as a conditional stimulus and its link to the brain reward system

Ahmad Zandbagleh and Preethi Premkumar

Abstract

This chapter reviews the neural mechanisms underlying the responses to criticism and praise, highlighting their roles as verbal social rewards and punishments. We first consider the septo-hippocampal network, which engages hippocampal, prefrontal and hypothalamic circuits in conflict detection and behavioural regulation as a means to theorise the possible neural circuits for perceiving and responding to criticism. In contrast, social reward processing, involves a broader cortico-striatal network of regions, including the striatum, orbitofrontal cortex, medial prefrontal cortex, amygdala and hippocampus. The chapter then conducts a selective review of neuroimaging studies on criticism in clinical and non-clinical populations. Empirical evidence from functional neuroimaging, electroencephalography, and brain stimulation studies demonstrates that responses to criticism and praise vary across mental disorders, developmental stages and interpersonal contexts. The dorsolateral prefrontal cortex consistently emerges as a key brain region of interest, particularly in relation to sustained attention, emotional regulation and vulnerability to perceived criticism. Findings also implicate the amygdala, anterior cingulate cortex, insula and posterior cingulate cortex, in the response to criticism. Finally, based on these findings, we have suggested some approaches for managing the impact of criticism. Overall, the neural response to criticism reflects complex interactions between brain regions responsible for cognitive control, salience, and emotional reactivity.

5.1 Introduction

Listening to conversations during social interaction engages the brain in many ways. Studying the brain's response to conversations during social interaction gives a deep insight into how the brain organises this information and the mental and cognitive faculties underlying this brain organisation. Undoubtedly, social interaction elicits responses in the receiver, such as thoughts, emotions and behaviours, and these processes are accompanied by activation of the

DOI: 10.4324/9781003388159-6

brain centres underlying these thoughts, emotions and behaviours. Responses may be both observable, such as reciprocating the speech, and unobservable, such as developing strategies to assimilate the communication. Deciphering the brain substrates for these responses varies by several factors, such as how the communication is delivered experimentally, how the brain response is measured and the individual differences in people based on their mental health, their age, gender and other demographic characteristics. Importantly, the brain response to criticism and praise can inform how people communicate and behave. This understanding can in turn inform interventions to minimise distress from criticism and even praise.

5.1.1 The septo-hippocampal network and the brain reward system

Criticism and praise are forms of positive and negative reinforcement. Arguably, therefore, the neural response to criticism and praise would engage the brain reward system. Indeed, self-criticism – the criticism of oneself – is related to the ability to evaluate the likelihood of receiving a reward in the form of the desire for gaining points when choosing one neutral stimulus (a geometric shape) over another neutral stimulus in a computerised gambling task (Duek et al., 2018). But self-criticism is not related to the likelihood of receiving a punishment in the form of losing points when choosing one neutral stimulus (a geometric shape) over another neutral stimulus in this computerised gambling task (Duek et al., 2018). One network that might form a part of the brain reward system is the septo-hippocampal network which is a reward system for behavioural inhibition (Gray, 1982). It is helpful to consider the components of this neural network before reviewing the literature on the brain response to criticism and praise. This septo-hippocampal network was put forward by Gray (1982). Here, the Behavioural Inhibition System, now referred to as the Goal Inhibition System (McNaughton, 2025), is 'concerned with detecting and resolving goal-conflicts and associated with the emotion of anxiety' (Corr, 2010). Gray argued that the septo-hippocampal system was the substrate of behaviours linked to responding to punishment (McNaughton, 2025). Grey (1982) hypothesised a network whereby the hippocampus responds to reinforcement and habituation; Grey proposed this network based on changes seen in Cornus Ammonu region 1 (CA1) which in turn triggers changes in the subicular cortex (Figure 5.1).

More broadly, McNaughton (2025) argued that the Goal Inhibition System engages a Decision Circuit where the conflict between attraction and repulsion is resolved. The **Decision Circuit** employs the orbitofrontal cortex and the cingulate cortex for planning or rumination, the hippocampus for risk aversion and the hypothalamus for risk assessment. The Goal Inhibition System is also thought to engage an **Arousal Circuit** based on the level of conflict created by the Goal Inhibition System and to produce an effortful goal-oriented response. This Arousal Circuit is also thought to employ the orbitofrontal cortex and

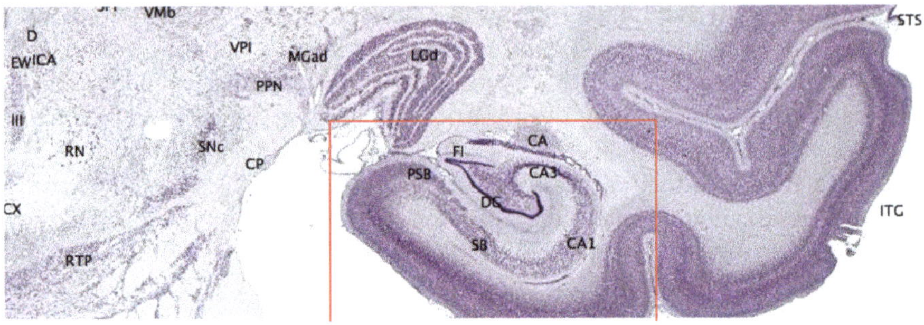

Figure 5.1 A coronal section through the left hippocampus (inside the square box) showing CA1, CA2, CA3, dentate gyrus (DG), subiculum (SB).

dorsolateral prefrontal cortex (DLPFC) for planning, while the hippocampus is engaged in risk aversion and the hypothalamus in risk assessment (McNaughton, 2025). Increased neural activity in the medial septum during reversal of learning a maze in rats suggests that the septum is also involved in decision flexibility (Bortz et al., 2019; Collins & Saunders, 2019). The septum in turn is connected to the subiculum as indicated by joint activation of these regions during reversal learning (Bortz et al., 2019; Collins & Saunders, 2019).

5.1.2 The social reward neural network

Neuroimaging research on social reward, including rejection and acceptance, suggests a wider cortical network than that assumed by the Goal Inhibition System (Fareri & Delgado, 2014; Premkumar, 2012). The motivation for social reward may be to fulfil social needs (Fareri & Delgado, 2014). The basal ganglia and prefrontal cortex (PFC) are attributed to social reward processing (Fareri & Delgado, 2014). The striatum forms part of the basal ganglia and includes the putamen, caudate nucleus and globus pallidus. The striatum is further divided into the dorsal striatum and ventral striatum. The dorsal striatum includes the caudate nucleus, putamen and globus pallidus (Figure 5.2), while the ventral striatum includes the nucleus accumbens and olfactory tubercle. The medial prefrontal cortex (mPFC) and ventromedial prefrontal cortex (vmPFC) are also affiliated with processing social reward (Fareri & Delgado, 2014). The reciprocal relay of dopaminergic neurotransmitters between the caudate nucleus and orbitofrontal cortex support reward learning (Fareri & Delgado, 2014). Thus, the striatum is intricately linked to the orbitofrontal cortex, vmPFC, amygdala and hippocampus through afferent (forward) pathways during reward learning and evaluation (Figure 5.3) (Fareri & Delgado, 2014). Overall, there appears to be some overlap between the brain regions purported to be involved in social

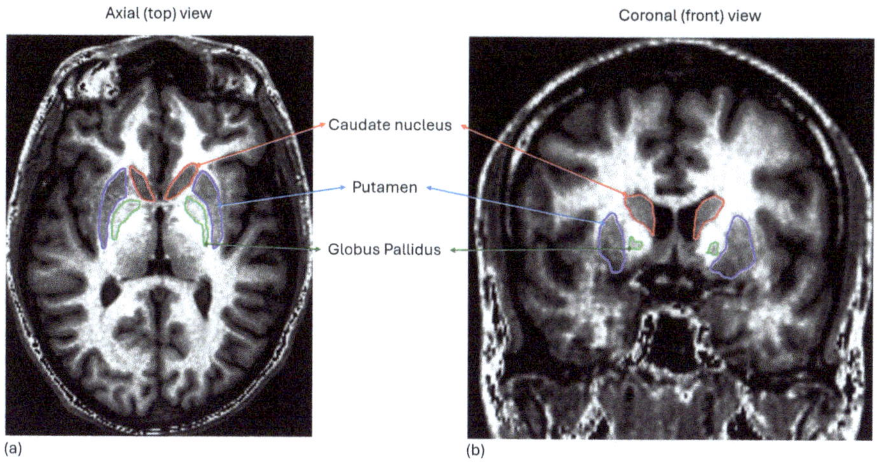

Figure 5.2 Brain scan showing the parts of the dorsal striatum, namely caudate nucleus (in red outline), putamen (blue outline) and globus pallidus (green outline), from (a) the axial view and (b) the coronal view.

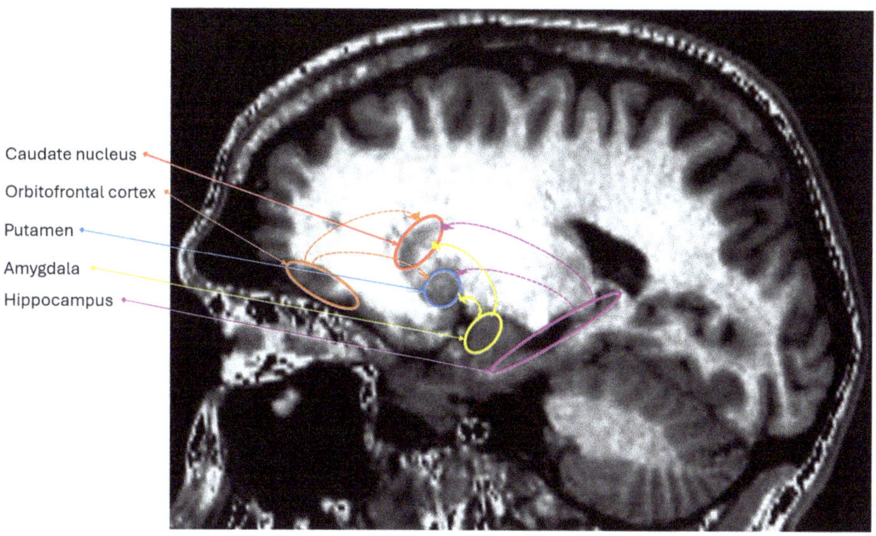

Figure 5.3 A sagittal slice of the brain showing the amygdala (yellow oval), caudate nucleus (red oval), hippocampus (purple oval), orbitofrontal cortex (brown oval) and putamen (blue oval). Arrows indicate the afferent pathways from the orbitofrontal cortex to the caudate nucleus and putamen and efferent pathways from the amygdala and hippocampus to the caudate nucleus and putamen according to Fareri & Delgado (2014).

reward and the septo-hippocampal complex involved in goal inhibition behaviour (McNaughton, 2025). But the relevance of these brain regions, such as the basal ganglia, mPFC, vmPFC, orbitofrontal cortex, amygdala and hippocampus, to criticism and praise deserves clarification.

5.2 A selective review of the brain's response to criticism and praise

The neural response to criticism and praise has been studied in patients with different types of mental disorder and in healthy individuals. The predominant method of neuroimaging is functional magnetic resonance imaging (fMRI), but other types of neuroimaging and brain stimulation methods have also examined the neural response to criticism, such as electroencephalography, transcranial direct current stimulation and functional near-infrared spectroscopy. The following selective review attempts to identify the core brain regions involved in the response to criticism and praise according to different types of mental disorder and healthy individuals. A literature search was conducted on EBSCOhost on 15 March 2025. The search terms were 'criticism' and 'neural' and the search was confined to literature in peer-reviewed journals. Thirty-eight studies were identified of which eight were excluded. The search excluded literature on measurement of physiological arousal, such as heart rate and skin conductance, and studies about self-criticism (Table 5.1).

Table 5.1 Excluded studies

Article title (citation)	*Reason for exclusion*
Neural Response to Self- and Other Referential Praise and Criticism in Generalized Social Phobia (Blair et al., 2008)	Participants read positive (e.g. You are beautiful), negative (e.g. You are ugly) and neutral (e.g. You are human) comments that could be either about the self or about somebody else (e.g. He is beautiful)
Exposure to Criticism Modulates Left but Not Right Amygdala Functional Connectivity in Healthy Adolescents: Individual Influences of Perceived and Self-Criticism (Bonduelle et al., 2021)	The stimuli were self-criticisms
Perceived patient–parent relationships and neural representation of parents in schizophrenia (Choi et al., 2013)	The stimuli were not audio-comments
Neural representation and clinically relevant moderators of individualised self-criticism in healthy subjects (Doerig et al., 2014)	The stimuli were self-criticisms
Having a word with yourself: Neural correlates of self-criticism and self-reassurance (Longe et al., 2010)	The stimuli were self-criticisms

(Continued)

Table 5.1 (Continued)

Article title (citation)	*Reason for exclusion*
The effect of criticism on functional brain connectivity and associations with neuroticism (Servaas et al., 2013)	The criticism involved statements asking the participant to lie down properly in the scanner, firstly in a neutral tone, 'It is important that you lie still' (neutral tone), then '[harrumph] Could you please lie still now for a moment?' (slightly agitated tone) and 'Lie still now please' (agitated tone). Excluded because the comments focus on one theme, are not about what the person does in terms of their relationship and are brief, ~3 seconds.
Affective and neural responses to parental criticism and praise in adolescents with depression (van Houtum et al., 2024)	The criticisms and praises were written and in the form a single modifiable word in the phrase. The words were personality traits
Affective and physiological reactivity to emotional comments in individuals at elevated risk for psychosis (Weintraub et al., 2019)	Explored the psychophysiological response to laboratory exposure to criticism and praise

5.2.1 The neural response to criticism and praise from a close relative using functional magnetic resonance imaging

Depression: Criticism and praise are verbal cues of social reward in contrast to rejection, acceptance and facial expressions which are non-verbal cues. Responding to criticism and praise requires listening to the spoken remark and then decoding the meaning of the remark. In an early brain imaging experiment, a standard example of a criticism that the relative was asked to provide was (Hooley et al., 2005, 2009, 2012):

> Jessica, one thing that bothers me about you is the style of clothing you wear. It seems like most of your wardrobe is old and shapeless and poorly fitting. The newer things you buy tend to be rather extreme in style, either wide-legged pants or tight skirts, neither of which is very flattering. I wish you'd spend a little more money on yourself and get some good advice on style. Better yet, I'd wish you'd take my advice on style.

The goal was to mimic criticism and praise spoken naturally in daily interaction as 'live' expressed emotion and assess their effect on mental health (Hooley et al., 2005). Mothers recorded four 30-second remarks similar to the example above, two of which were criticisms and two of which were praises (Hooley et al., 2005) (Table 5.2).

Table 5.2 Summary of studies on the neural response to criticism and brain regions activated or deactivated based on the blood oxygen level dependent (BOLD) response in clinical or sub-clinical populations

Citation	*Main participants*	*Study design and generating the criticism stimuli*	*Areas activated by main participants*	*Interpretation*
			DEPRESSION	
Hooley et al. (2005)	Seven participants with a former diagnosis of depression (mean age = 25.7 years, SD = 2.3) and 9 healthy controls (mean age = 23.9 years, SD = 2.6)	Mothers of main participants recorded two criticisms and two praises lasting 30 seconds each	Patients failed to activate the DLPFC during criticism compared to healthy controls even among those that reported a greater increase in negative mood following the criticism than the healthy controls. Patients and healthy controls equally activated the DLPFC while listening to praise. Correspondingly, there was an increase in positive mood following the praise.	Participants had been in remission for almost three years, but still showed diminished DLPFC activation. DLPFC is an area of vulnerability for depression and maternal criticism could be a social trigger for such brain vulnerability.
Hooley et al. (2009)	Twelve formerly depressed participants (mean age = 24.4 years, SD=3.0) and 11 healthy women (mean age = 24.3 years, SD=2.4)	Mothers of main participants recorded two criticisms, two praises and two neutral comments lasting 30 seconds each	Healthy women activated the DLPFC and ACC more than formerly depressed women during the comments, regardless of type of comment, while formerly depressed women activated the amygdala more than healthy women during maternal criticism. Besides the DLPFC and ACC, healthy participants also activated the putamen more during maternal criticism than formerly depressed women (Hooley et al., 2009). Both formerly depressed and healthy women reported increased positive mood following the praise and increased negative mood following criticism without differing in the level of change in mood.	Ruminating over the criticism was suggested as a possible explanation for the decreased brain activation in the DLPFC and ACC and increased activation of the amygdala in the formerly depressed women, although this did not explain the decreased activation of the DLPFC and ACC during neutral comments.

Hooley et al. (2012)	Thirty women (mean age = 25 years, SD = 3), some with current depression (n=10), others formerly diagnosed with depression (n=11) and yet others with no diagnosis of mental disorder (n=12). The participants with a former diagnosis of depression and the healthy participants were participants from the previous study (Hooley et al. 2009). Participants were grouped into high perceived criticism if they scored >4 on PCM (n=17) and low perceived criticism if they scored <4 on PCM (n=16)	Mothers of main participants recorded two criticisms and two praises lasting 30 seconds each	The high perceived criticism group activated the amygdala more, but activated the DLPFC less than the low perceived criticism group during maternal criticism. Continuous monitoring of the change in activation of the amygdala and DLPFC over the 30-second duration of the criticism and 10 seconds into the rest period after the criticism indicated that the amygdala continued to remain more active while the DLPFC remained less active in the high perceived criticism than the low perceived criticism group. Activation of the ACC did not differentiate between the two perceived criticism groups. The groups did not differ in how negatively they felt or upset they were by the criticism after leaving the scanner. Furthermore, scores on perceived criticism did not correspond with scores on depression.	DLPFC and amygdala are biomarkers of sensitivity to criticism. Failure of the activation of the ACC to differentiate the perceived criticism groups suggested that activation of the ACC was associated with depression rather than perceived criticism.

(*Continued*)

Table 5.2 (Continued)

Citation	*Main participants*	*Study design and generating the criticism stimuli*	*Areas activated by main participants*	*Interpretation*
Silk et al. (2017)	Twenty adolescents with depression and 28 health controls (mean age = 14.6 years, SD = 1.8)	Mothers of main participants recorded two criticisms, two praises and 2 neutral comments lasting 30 seconds each	Greater activation of the left parahippocampal gyrus during criticism than neutral comments in the depressed group than healthy controls. Less activation of the right vmPFC, right thalamus/caudate nucleus, right parahippocampal gyrus, right precuneus during praises than neutral comments in the depressed group.	Heightened activation of the parahippocampal gyrus and the role of the parahippocampal gyrus in encoding and memory recall suggests that the criticism may be more encoded than neutral comments. Diminished activation of the parahippocampal gyrus and thalamus during praise suggests that praise may be less salient and rewarding in adolescents with depression
Vandermeer et al. (2024)	Eighty-one children (mean age 11 years, SD = 0.8). No child had depression, but three children had high scores on the Children's Depression Inventory. Seven children had a lifetime history of anxiety disorder with co-morbid ADHD (n=3) and oppositional defiant disorder (n=1). Mothers of 26 children had a lifetime history of depression	Mothers provided two criticisms, two praises and two neutral comments lasting 30 seconds	No brain region differentiated between comment type in the children. Greater activity in left insula and left putamen during maternal criticism correlated with lower scores on the Children's Depression Inventory. Greater activity in the left inferior frontal gyrus during maternal praise was correlated with greater scores on the Children's Depression Inventory.	Thus, self-reported depression in children corresponds with diminished activation of insula and putamen in children. These results could suggest heighted salience of and reward-processing of criticism and early signs of disruption or resilience to maternal criticism. Activation of the inferior frontal gyrus during praise and its relation to self-reported depression can be attributed to greater self-referential processing of praise

PSYCHOSIS AND RISK FOR PSYCHOSIS				
Rylands et al. (2011)	Eleven patients with chronic schizophrenia who had relatives that were rated as high expressed emotion (mean age = 33 years, SD = 12.2)	A close relative and a stranger (as a control condition) provided criticisms and neutral comments. These comments were taken from the recording of the Camberwell Family Interview of the relative.	Patients activated the left inferior frontal gyrus and left temporal pole more during the relative's criticism than the relative's neutral comments. Left rostral ACC and left insula were least deactivated during relative's criticism compared to the relative's neutral comments.	Diminished deactivation of the left insula and rostral ACC during the relative's criticism compared to the relative's neutral comments suggested possible self-reflection during the criticism than neutral comment. The deactivation of the ACC during criticism in these patients concurs with the decreased activation observed in depressed patients (Hooley et al., 2009).
Premkumar et al. (2013)	Twelve participants with high schizotypy (mean age = 30, SD=10.6) and 11 participants with low schizotypy (mean age = 28.6, SD = 6.1)	A close relative provided five criticisms, five praises and five neutral comments lasting 30 seconds	No differences between groups in brain response to criticism. During praises, the low schizotypy group activated the left inferior frontal gyrus, left insula, left putamen, right lingual gyrus, right thalamus and right insula. During praises, the high schizotypy group deactivated the left inferior frontal gyrus, left insula, left putamen, right lingual gyrus, right thalamus and right insula.	Praise (or warmth) rather than criticism affects brain function in schizotypal individuals. The lower activation of the putamen and insula during praise in the high schizotypy group suggests that the schizotypal individuals were less rewarded by the praise. This diminished activation could also imply that the high schizotypy group was less convinced by the praise from their close relative than the low schizotypy group. Schizotypy is characterised by anhedonia which is a diminished ability to find pleasure in activities.

(*Continued*)

Table 5.2 (Continued)

Citation	*Main participants*	*Study design and generating the criticism stimuli*	*Areas activated by main participants*	*Interpretation*
Nook et al. (2018)	Twenty-one participants with familial high risk for schizophrenia, i.e. one or more relatives with a diagnosis of schizophrenia or schizophrenia-spectrum disorder (mean age = 27.3 years, SD = 3.9) and 20 individuals with no risk for schizophrenia (mean age = 26 years, SD = 3.9)	Participants listened to 20-second comments (four criticisms, four praises and four neutral conditions) in pseudorandomised order and rated each comment from 1 = very positive to 5 = very negative. The comments were delivered by a stranger. Participants maintained a daily diary for four weeks of their mood, symptoms and social conflict. Positive (e.g. cheerful or happy) and negative mood (e.g. anxious, sad) was rated from 1= 'not at all' to 5 'extremely'. Participants rated positive symptoms (e.g. 'I felt as if someone else could read my thoughts and feelings'), negative symptoms (e.g. 'I felt like I didn't care about anything') and disorganisation (e.g. 'I felt like my thoughts were jumbled') on 5-point scales (1 = not at all, 5 = extremely). Lastly, participants indicated if they experienced interpersonal conflict and how distressing those experiences were from 1 = not at all to 5 = extremely	Participants with familial high risk for schizophrenia had diminished activation of the left DLPFC, inferior parietal lobule and the bilateral middle temporal gyrus. This diminished activation appeared during criticism compared to neutral comments. Lower activity in the DLPFC during criticism, relative to neutral comments, was associated with more negative mood on days of social conflict in the group with familial high risk for schizophrenia. This association held true on the day before the social conflict and the day after the social conflict. There was no such association in the group with no familial high risk for schizophrenia. Lower activity in the DLPFC during criticism, relative to neutral comments, was also associated with more negative symptoms on days of social conflict in the group with familial high risk for schizophrenia. Likewise, lower activity in the DLPFC during criticism, relative to neutral comments, was also associated with more positive symptoms on days of social conflict. Lastly, the group with familial high risk for schizophrenia experienced more negative mood, negative symptoms and lower positive mood on days of distressing social conflict than the group without familial high risk for schizophrenia.	The activation of the DLPFC during criticism is a biomarker of vulnerability for distress from social conflict in individuals with familial high risk for schizophrenia. The findings suggest the key role of DLPFC in emotional regulation. Individuals' familial high risk for schizophrenia are also vulnerable to stress from interpersonal social conflict.

		ANXIETY		
Goldin et al. (2014)	59 patients with social anxiety disorder who either received CBT (n=31; mean age = 33.7, SD = 7.9) or were put on waitlist (n=28; mean age = 33.3, SD = 10.1)	Twelve-second video clips with actors verbalising and visually expressing criticism (e.g. 'You are a boring person') or praise (e.g., 'I feel really comfortable being with you'). Sixteen criticisms and sixteen praises were presented. The facial expression of actors matched the comment type, happy/ approving and angry/ disapproving facial expressions. Participants were trained to 'Just Watch' the video or to 'Reframe' by reappraising the situation in a way that reduces any negative response to the person delivering the social evaluation. Participants rated 'How negative do you feel?' from 1 (not at all) to 5 (very much) after each comment. Participants assigned to CBT received 16 CBT sessions over four months.	Patients who received CBT had greater improvement in social anxiety after therapy than the waitlist group. They also rated less negative emotion after the criticisms and praises than the waitlist group. When participants just watched the criticism, the CBT group activated, while the waitlist group deactivated the right superior frontal gyrus and right inferior parietal lobule. The CBT group also deactivated, while the waitlist group activated the left superior temporal gyrus. When participants just watched the praises, the CBT group activated the right superior frontal gyrus, inferior parietal lobule, superior frontal gyrus and the middle occipital gyrus more than the waitlist group. When reappraising criticism, the CBT group activated, while the waitlist group deactivated the right superior/middle frontal gyrus and the right middle occipital gyrus.	The activation of the right superior frontal gyrus and right inferior parietal lobule by the CBT group when just watching the praise and criticism suggested greater mentalising and monitoring and greater visual attention, since the inferior parietal lobule is implicated face processing. Likewise, the increased activation of the superior frontal gyrus during reappraisal of criticism suggests greater monitoring, mentalising, introspection and self-referential evaluation and reflection.

(*Continued*)

Table 5.2 (Continued)

Citation	*Main participants*	*Study design and generating the criticism stimuli*	*Areas activated by main participants*	*Interpretation*
Birk et al. (2019)	56 participants (30 male, 35 diagnosed with SAD, mean age = 32.74, SD = 8.67; 21 healthy controls, mean age = 32.57, SD = 9.88). Participants were screened for comorbidities and excluded for ongoing pharmacotherapy, psychotherapy, past CBT, history of medical or neurological disorders, or met diagnostic criteria for any psychiatric condition other than generalised anxiety disorder, agoraphobia without panic attacks, specific phobia, panic disorder, or dysthymia.	Stimuli consisted of: 12-second video clips of actors displaying either social criticism (angry/disapproving expression) or social praise (happy/approving expression). Each trial began with a 1.5-second cue ('Just Watch' or 'Reframe'), followed by a 4.5-second neutral facial wait, and a 7.5-second spoken evaluation (e.g., 'You're pathetic' or 'You're amazing'). Control task involved counting asterisks (non-emotional baseline). Participants rated (1–5 scale) their negative affect after each trial (3-second). The study focused on neural responses during 'Just Watch' conditions for criticism and praise, compared to a non-social asterisk-counting control.	Whole-brain analysis: No significant associations between BOLD responses and FNE, FPE, social anxiety or depression in patients. However, in healthy controls, higher FNE was associated with reduced activation in the left dACC during criticism vs. praise contrast in healthy controls. ROI analysis: FNE was positively correlated with increased activation in: Right amygdala during criticism vs control; Left and right anterior insula during praise vs control; Social anxiety symptoms were positively associated with: Left amygdala and left anterior insula during criticism vs. control; Left and right anterior insula during praise vs control; FPE and depressive symptoms showed no significant association with neural responses in any condition.	FNE, more than FPE, appears to play a critical role in heightened neural reactivity to social evaluation, particularly in emotional-processing regions such as the amygdala and insula. The study found that social anxiety symptoms were linked to increased neural sensitivity to both criticism and praise. Reduced activation in the ACC among healthy individuals with high FNE may reflect disengagement or attentional control mechanisms. The lack of neural effects related to FPE could be due to the general and non-personal nature of the praise stimuli used in the experiment.

Sequeira et al. (2019)	Thirty-eight youth (ages 11–17, M = 13.52, SD = 1.34; 20 females, 94.7% white) with a history of anxiety disorders (GAD, SAD or separation anxiety disorder).	During fMRI scanning, participants listened to two 30-second audio clips each of parental criticism, praise, and neutral comments, recorded by their primary caregiver (typically the biological mother). Clips were preceded by a training session. Neutral clips were always presented first, and the order of praise and criticism clips was counterbalanced. Maternal acceptance and peer victimisation were assessed through self-report. Depressive symptoms were measured one year later using the Mood and Feelings Questionnaire. Although participants listened to all three types of audio during the scan, the study analysed only the neural responses to praise vs neutral comments.	Activation to parental praise (vs. neutral) was measured in key reward-related regions. A significant three-way interaction in the bilateral caudate nucleus showed that greater caudate nucleus activation predicted higher depressive symptoms one year later, but only for youth with low maternal acceptance and high peer victimisation.	Findings suggest that adolescents with heightened caudate activation to parental praise may be more sensitive to social contexts, particularly when facing peer victimisation and low maternal acceptance. This supports the neurobiological susceptibility to social context model. Activation of the caudate nucleus may reflect a social prediction error or a history of negative social experiences, contributing to increased risk for depression.

(*Continued*)

Table 5.2 (Continued)

Citation	*Main participants*	*Study design and generating the criticism stimuli*	*Areas activated by main participants*	*Interpretation*
Butterfield et al. (2021)	Thirty adolescents (mean age at baseline = 11.1, SD = 0.3) with a history of anxiety disorder who were followed up two years after therapy	Mothers of most main participants, except for one main participant whose father was the primary caregiver, provided two criticisms, two praises and two neutral comments lasting 30 seconds. Adolescent participants were randomised to 16 weekly sessions of CBT (n=19) or child-centred therapy (11). Adolescent participants underwent brain scans at two-year follow-up. Parental warmth as rated by the main adolescent participants was correlated with the neural response to parental comments while controlling for treatment type and parental warmth at two-year follow-up because adolescents receiving child-centred therapy had higher anxiety than adolescents receiving CBT. Also, adolescent-rated parental warm post-treatment did not correlate with parental warmth at two-year follow-up suggesting variability in adolescents' perception of parental warmth	Lower activation of the left amygdala, bilateral insula and sgACC during parental criticism, which are areas associated with social evaluation, correlated with parental warmth post-treatment. Lower activation of ACC and right VLPFC, which are emotion-regulatory network regions, during parental criticism also correlated with parental warmth post-treatment.	Warmth denotes acceptance, love, approachability, and attention. The correspondence between parental warmth and lower activation of brain regions involved in social evaluation and emotional regulation during parental criticism suggests that warmth can protect against the adverse neural effects of criticism in adolescents. It also suggests that parenting styles two years earlier continue to correspond with how anxious adolescents internalise aversive social interaction and pathological states.

Note: ACC: anterior cingulate cortex; ADHD: attention deficit hyperactivity disorder. CBT: cognitive behavioural therapy; DLPFC: dorsolateral prefrontal cortex; FPE: fear of positive evaluation; GAD: generalised anxiety disorder; pcm: perceived criticism measure; SAD: social anxiety disorder; SD: standard deviation.

Participants were patients with a former diagnosis (not currently diagnosed) of depression because of the well-evidenced relationship between perceived criticism and the relapse of depression. The DLPFC was considered the epicentre of diminished emotional reactivity in patients with depression due to the DLPFC's role in sustained attention. Notwithstanding the small sample (seven individuals with a former diagnosis of depression and nine healthy controls), patients failed to activate the DLPFC during criticism compared to healthy controls even among those who reported an increase in negative mood following the criticism (Hooley et al., 2005). In contrast, patients and healthy controls equally activated the DLPFC during praise. Correspondingly, there was an increase in positive mood following the praise. The findings suggested that the DLPFC was a brain area of vulnerability for social distress in patients with depression because of its role in emotional reactivity.

A subsequent study of a larger sample of women (n=23; 12 formerly depressed participants and 11 healthy women) (Hooley et al., 2009) replicated the activation of the DLPFC. The anterior cingulate cortex (ACC) was proposed as a further region of interest because of its link to remission from depression and likewise the amygdala because of its hyperactivity in people who are depressed. Healthy women activated the DLPFC and ACC more than formerly depressed women during both criticism and praise, while formerly depressed women activated the amygdala more than healthy women during maternal criticism. Besides the DLPFC and ACC, healthy participants activated the putamen more than formerly depressed women during maternal criticism (Hooley et al., 2009). Both formerly depressed women and healthy women reported increased positive mood following the praise, but increased negative mood following criticism. Depressed and healthy women did not differ in change in mood. Ruminating over the criticism was used to explain the decrease in brain activation of the DLPFC and ACC and increased activation of the amygdala in the formerly depressed women.

Sensitivity to criticism could be enough to trigger emotional dysregulation and relapse in patients with depression (Hooley et al., 2012). Thus, Hooley et al. (2012) hypothesised that greater perceived criticism would be associated with heightened activation of the amygdala, but with decreased activation of the DLPFC regardless of level of depression. In this study, a further group of patients with current depression (n=10) participated alongside the 11 women formerly diagnosed with depression and 12 healthy women who took part in the previous study (Hooley et al., 2009). Participants rated the Perceived Criticism Measure of their mother on a single item, 'How critical is your relative of you?', rating their response from 0 to 10. Participants were categorised into high (n=17) and low perceived criticism (n=16) based on those who scored above and below the median of four on Perceived Criticism Measure, respectively. As hypothesised, the high perceived criticism group activated the amygdala more, but activated the DLPFC less than the low perceived criticism group during maternal criticism. The high perceived criticism group continued to activate the amygdala 10 seconds into the rest period after the 30-second criticism more than the low perceived criticism group. The groups did not differ in the activation of ACC during criticism. Furthermore, scores on perceived criticism did not correspond with scores on depression. The study reinforces the crucial role of the DLPFC and amygdala as biomarkers of sensitivity to criticism.

However, these possible biomarkers of sensitivity to criticism do not extend to adolescents and children (Silk et al., 2018; Vandermeer et al., 2024). Adolescents with a history of depression activated the left parahippocampal gyrus during maternal criticism more than healthy adolescents (Silk et al., 2018) which suggested stronger encoding of criticism. In contrast, they activated the right parahippocampal gyrus, vmPFC, thalamus/caudate nucleus and precuneus less than healthy adolescents during praise which suggested less salience of and reward from praise. Among healthy children and children with various mental disorders, greater activation of the insula and putamen correlated with level of depression (Vandermeer, et al., 2024). This activation suggested that heightened salience and reward processing of criticism is associated with depression in children.

How to handle low mood during criticism:

Since criticism engages brain reward centres, engaging in positive behaviours that engage the reward centre is meaningful.

1) Engage in behavioural activation (exercise, hobbies after criticism, listening to calming music, to diffuse the impact of criticism): Rewarding behaviours activate the striatal reward circuits (e.g. putamen, insula), helping elevate mood after critical experiences.
2) Recall praise to enhance positive affect: Praising stimuli (like compliments) engage reward-related brain regions such as the putamen. Engaging with memories of praise strengthens these circuits to counterbalance criticism.

The psychosis continuum: Expressed emotion (EE) is a predictor of relapse in chronic and first-episode psychosis (Alvarez-Jimenez et al., 2012; Bebbington & Kuipers, 1994; Kuipers et al., 2006). Schizophrenia is a severe form of psychosis, and it alters brain function extensively, but certain brain regions, such as the PFC and basal ganglia, are more impacted at the chronic stage partly due to antipsychotic medication (Premkumar et al., 2006). A study (Rylands et al., 2011) hypothesised that brain regions involved in processing aversive social information would be activated in patients with schizophrenia, namely the amygdala, ACC and mPFC, bearing some parallels with the biomarkers of criticism in depression (Hooley et al., 2012). Participants were 11 patients with schizophrenia living in the community who had a close relative who rated high on EE as criticism. The criticism, e.g. 'He's so lazy', and neutral comments, e.g. 'He is right-handed', from the key relative were extracted from the Camberwell Family Interview. The comment was delivered by a relative or a stranger, resulting in four types of comments, a criticism and neutral comment by a close relative and a criticism and neutral comment by a stranger. The relative's criticism, compared to other types of comments, activated the left inferior frontal gyrus and left temporal pole the most and deactivated the left insula and rostral ACC the least (Rylands et al., 2011). The authors interpreted the diminished deactivation of the left insula and rostral ACC during the relative's criticism as self-reflection during the criticism than neutral comment. The deactivation of the ACC and insula during criticism in these patients (Rylands et al., 2011) concurs with the decreased activation observed in depressed patients (Hooley et al., 2009), but contradicts the association between insula activation and depression in children (Vandermeer et al., 2024). But the suggestion that the DLPFC and amygdala are biomarkers of perceived criticism (Hooley et al., 2012) was not upheld by Rylands et al. (2011).

Conflictual communication between adolescents at risk for psychosis and their carer increases the severity of psychosis-like symptoms in adolescents at risk for psychosis (O'Brien et al., 2009). Thus, individuals with familial risk for psychosis activated the DLPFC less during criticism than neutral comments (Nook et al., 2018). This lower activation of the DLPFC was associated with lower mood and more positive and negative symptoms on days that participants encountered social conflict. These findings reinforce the role of the DLPFC in emotional regulation and as a biomarker of social conflict in both depression and vulnerability for psychosis. Premkumar et al. (2013) also tested the propensity for criticism to differentiate activity in these brain regions in schizotypy, a non-clinical expression of schizophrenia suggesting some signs of vulnerability for psychosis. Schizotypal traits are a cluster of personality styles that resemble psychosis-like experiences and reflect vulnerability for psychosis in the non-clinical population (Cochrane et al., 2010; Thomas et al., 2019). Participants were those with high and low schizotypy based on those scoring 7 and above on the unusual experiences subscale of the short form of the Oxford-Liverpool Inventory of Feelings and Experiences (Mason et al., 2005) (high schizotypy) and 2 and below on the unusual experiences subscale (low schizotypy). A close relative recorded themselves expressing criticism, praise and neutral comments about the main participant. Criticism did not differentiate between the high and low schizotypy groups in brain activity. However, criticism activated the left superior and middle frontal gyri and bilateral posterior cingulate cortex (PCC) across the whole sample. The superior and middle frontal gyri are associated with emotion regulation and this function possibly explained why criticism engaged these regions, whereas the posterior cingulate gyrus is associated with thinking about oneself during emotional situations. Thus, emotional regulation may be optimal during criticism in those within the normal range of the psychosis continuum. Furthermore, the high schizotypy group activated the putamen, insula, middle frontal cortex and lingual gyrus during praise less than the low schizotypy group. The lower activation of the putamen and insula during praise in the high schizotypy group suggests that the schizotypal individuals were less rewarded by the praise (Premkumar et al., 2013). This diminished activation could also imply that the individuals in the high schizotypy group were less convinced by the praise from their close relative than those in the low schizotypy group.

The studies on the neural response to criticism from a relative or stranger in individuals along the psychosis continuum indicate that patients with frank psychosis fail to activate the ACC and insula, while those at familial risk for schizophrenia under-activate the DLPFC. In contrast, individuals with high schizotypal traits do not differ from individuals with low schizotypal traits in brain activity.

Anxiety: Four studies examined individuals with anxiety of which two studies recruited participants who were adults (Birk et al., 2019; Goldin et al., 2014) and two studies recruited participants who were adolescents (Birk et al., 2019; Butterfield et al., 2021; Goldin et al., 2014; Sequeira et al., 2019). Adult patients activated the superior frontal gyrus during criticism in one study (Goldin et al., 2014). Greater activation of the dACC was associated with greater fear of negative evaluation, and greater activation of the insula and amygdala was associated with greater social anxiety in another study (Birk et al., 2019), and these associations were present across both patients with social anxiety disorder (SAD) and healthy individuals. Thus, key brain areas implicated in mentalising and self-reflection (superior frontal gyrus), emotional attention (dACC), salience (insula) and fear (amygdala) during criticism are associated with social anxiety.

These areas are also implicated in adolescents with anxiety (Butterfield et al., 2021) where parental warmth two years ago is associated with lower activation of the insula, amygdala, subgenual anterior cingulate cortex (sgACC) and right ventrolateral prefrontal cortex (VLPFC) during criticism. Another study (Sequeira et al., 2019) found that higher activation of caudate nucleus during praise was associated with higher depression a year later in youth with anxiety, lower maternal acceptance and more peer victimisation. Heightened reward sensitivity to praise in anxious youth may be indicative of subsequent depression and poorer social functioning.

Healthy individuals: Four studies examined the brain's response to criticism and/praise in young adults (Eckstein et al., 2023; Gao et al., 2018; Kim, et al., 2020a; Kim, et al., 2020b; Miedl et al., 2016) and four in adolescents (Chen et al., 2024; James et al., 2023; Lee et al., 2015; Mohamed Ali et al., 2023) (Table 5.3). In healthy adults, criticism activated the mPFC more than praise, but praise activated the amygdala more than criticism (Gao et al., 2018). Also,

Table 5.3 Summary of studies on the neural response to criticism and brain regions activated or deactivated based on the blood oxygen level dependent (BOLD) response in the healthy population

Citation	*Main participants*	*Study design and generating the criticism stimuli*	*Areas activated by main participants*	*Interpretation*
Lee et al. (2015)	Thirty-two healthy adolescents (22 women, aged 9–17 years; mean age = 14.3, SD = 2)	Mothers provided audio-recordings of two criticisms, two praises and two neutral comments lasting 30 seconds each. The comments of each type were presented in a block together in the scanner	Increased activity was observed in the left putamen and left insula during criticism. Decreased activity was observed in the bilateral DLPFC, caudal ACC, bilateral temporal-parietal junction extending to the inferior parietal lobe and precuneus during criticism. Parental warmth was negatively correlated with activity in left temporal-parietal junction extending to the inferior parietal lobe, and precuneus during criticism.	Putamen and insula are areas associated with emotion and reward, while the DLPFC and caudal ACC are associated with cognitive control. The temporal parietal junction extending to the inferior parietal lobe and precuneus are part of the social cognitive processing network. The increased activation of the affective network suggests that maternal criticism may elicit sustained emotional reactivity in children. The diminished activation of the cognitive control network may suggest poorer attention and problem-solving and finding alternative solutions.

(*Continued*)

Table 5.3 (Continued)

Citation	*Main participants*	*Study design and generating the criticism stimuli*	*Areas activated by main participants*	*Interpretation*
Miedl et al. (2016)	37 healthy participants (21 female; mean age = 24.76 years, SD = 4.19); all right-handed except one male. Participants reported no history of mental or neurological illnesses, were not taking any prescription medications aside from oral contraceptives, and had no current issues with alcohol or drug dependence.	Participants viewed a total of 90 short video clips from a validated set of naturalistic, social-evaluative stimuli (known as E.Vids), consisting of 30 negative, 30 neutral, and 30 positive statements delivered directly to the viewer. Each 3-second clip featured an actor delivering a sentence in a realistic and emotionally expressive tone. Each participant saw 6 different posers, each delivering 5 sentences (out of 8 possible sentences) in only one emotional category to avoid mixed-valence confusion. Participants rated arousal and unpleasantness after each video block. Trait measures (BFNE-R and FPES) were also collected to assess individual differences in sensitivity to social evaluation.	During social evaluation, main participants showed activation in the mPFC, rACC and temporal regions for both praise and criticism. Criticism additionally activated the anterior insula, posterior insula, amygdala and thalamus. Praise did not activate the insula or thalamus significantly, but showed amygdala activation only in the ROI analysis. Posterior insula activity during praise increased with higher FPES.	Negative social evaluations (criticism) activated core emotion-processing brain regions – including the amygdala and insula – in all participants, suggesting a universal neural sensitivity to criticism. In contrast, positive evaluations (praise) primarily activated mentalising and self-referential regions like mPFC and rACC, with amygdala activation observed but insula involvement absent. Notably, individuals with high fear of positive evaluation showed increased posterior insula activation in response to praise, indicating that, for some, even positive feedback can trigger discomfort. Thus, while criticism elicits consistent neural distress, praise produces variable responses depending on individual vulnerability. These findings highlight a neural vulnerability factor in social-interaction-related psychopathologies.

Gao et al. (2018)	Thirty healthy Chinese participants (15 males; age range = 20–25; mean age = 22.73 years, SD = 1.57; right-handed) All had no vision problems or language disabilities, and reported no history of neurological or psychiatric disorders.	Stimuli included 36 emotionally neutral faces and 144 standardised verbal comments categorised as: Criticising-others, Praising-others, Criticising-objects, Praising-objects. Each face was paired with four comments (all of one type or a mix of two praises and two criticisms). The comments were validated in a pre-study (n = 30) to ensure that the praise and criticism differ in valence alone, but not in arousal, likelihood, or comprehension. Each trial presented two face–comment pairs (5 s each), followed by a 10 s face-only interval, then two more face–comment pairs. Participants then rated the likeability of the person on an 8-point scale, with the scale shown for 10 s.	Criticism (vs praise) increased activation in the dorsal mPFC, while praise elicited greater activation in the right amygdala. Comments about others (vs objects) increased activation in the left pSTS and PCC/precuneus. A valence × target interaction was observed in the mPFC, showing the strongest activation for criticism targeted to others. Functional connectivity among the mPFC, pSTS, PCC/precuneus and right amygdala with the left TPJ, bilateral caudate and PCC/precuneus was enhanced during social praise but reduced during social criticism, especially when targeting others.	The study demonstrates that the brain integrates valenced social information (praise and criticism) via interaction between the mentalising network (mPFC, TPJ, PCC, pSTS) and affective learning network (amygdala, caudate). Criticism enhances mPFC activation and weakens network connectivity, potentially encoding social threat and avoidance. Praise enhances amygdala activation and strengthens connectivity, reinforcing social reward and approach behaviour. These patterns correlate with likeability ratings: people who criticise others are rated as less likeable. The TPJ emerges as a key hub mediating social emotional inference. No gender differences were found in behavioural or neural responses.

(Continued)

Table 5.3 (Continued)

Citation	*Main participants*	*Study design and generating the criticism stimuli*	*Areas activated by main participants*	*Interpretation*
Kim et al. (2020a, 2020b)	40 participants (mean age = 22 years, SD = 0.49; 27 female)	Participants engaged alternatively in self-criticism and self-reassurance while viewing 60 written statements (30 emotional, 30 neutral) describing personal mistakes, setbacks, or failures. Eight blocks of trials, counterbalanced for order of self-criticism vs. self-reassurance. Each trial: 6s stimulus presentation + 3s rating of intensity of self-criticism/self-reassurance. They rated (1–4 scale) the intensity of their self-critical or self-reassuring responses on each trial inside an fMRI scanner.	In one study (Kim, et al., 2020b), the left calcarine gyrus, left ACC, left anterior insula, and left amygdala were activated more during self-criticism than self-reassurance, while both conditions equally activated the bilateral lingual gyrus, left mPFC, and left PCC. Furthermore, a network correlation analysis showed significant involvement of the lingual gyrus in visual mental imagery, which was correlated with amygdala activity, reflecting its role in processing threat and fear during self-criticism (Kim, et al., 2020a). Additionally, secure attachment was positively correlated with lingual gyrus activation, whereas avoidant attachment was negatively correlated with lingual gyrus activation during self-criticism (Kim, et al., 2020a). Amygdala activation moderated this relationship.	Securely attached individuals showed greater lingual gyrus activation under high threat, while avoidantly attached individuals showed less activation. Attachment styles may influence visual mental imagery and threat processing during self-criticism, with implications for mental health. Attachment mechanisms may influence threat responses and mental imagery during self-criticism, with significant clinical and social implications.

Eckstein et al. (2023)	Eighty-six healthy individuals (43 heterosexual romantic couples), mean age = 24.4 years (SD = 2.8), exclusively dating for ≥6 months, highly satisfied with their relationship, right-handed, no history of mental disorders.	A hyperscanning fMRI setup was used with two synchronised 3T MRI scanners, allowing simultaneous scanning of both partners. Each participant prepared up to 18 partner-initiated compliments and 18 self-compliments prior to scanning, based on 23 relational/personality domains (e.g., trust, humour). Paradigms included (1) sending a compliment to partner, (2) receiving one from partner, and (3) viewing self-compliments (control). 15 trials per condition. Each trial had two 10-second phases: waiting, and message viewing, with jittered intervals. Real-time live video of the partner was shown during all tasks to simulate natural interaction.	SFG, SMA, IFG, DLPFC, insula, vmPFC, cerebellum, and temporal gyri were activated while receiving compliments (partner or self). Stronger activation in the insula, superior temporal cortex, and amygdala while receiving partner-initiated compliments than receiving self-compliments Greater activation in the vmPFC, ACC, and IFG while receiving self-compliments than partner-initiated compliments. Results on brain activation while sending compliments are omitted.	Receiving partner and self-compliments both led to increased activity in regions including the IFG, DLPFC, vmPFC, insula and temporal gyri. Compared to self-compliments, receiving partner compliments resulted in stronger activation of the insula, superior temporal cortex and amygdala. In contrast, receiving self-compliments elicited greater activity in the vmPFC, ACC, and IFG. These results suggest that verbal expressions of appreciation within romantic relationships engage brain regions involved in reward, social cognition and affective processing, providing a potential neurobiological mechanism for the stabilising effects of positive couple interaction.

(*Continued*)

Table 5.3 (Continued)

Citation	*Main participants*	*Study design and generating the criticism stimuli*	*Areas activated by main participants*	*Interpretation*
James et al. (2023)	Forty-four youth aged 11–16 years (mean age = 13.31 years, SD = 1.33; 57% female; 95.5% White) with a history of anxiety disorders, most previously treated with psychotherapy; At the time of the study, 13 participants still met criteria for an anxiety disorder, and others had additional comorbidities (e.g., depressive disorder NOS (n=1), Tourette's disorder (n=2), ADHD (n=2)).	Parents (95.5% mothers) recorded two 30-second critical, two 30-second praising, and two 30-second neutral audio clips. During fMRI, adolescents listened to these clips while rating their emotional intensity. Emotional experience was also tracked in daily life using a 10-day EMA protocol.	Higher activation in the sgACC during parental criticism (v neutral statements) was observed. Higher sgACC activation during criticism was significantly associated with less happiness during positive interpersonal situations. No significant association between activation of the amygdala or anterior insula and daily happiness. Supplemental analyses showed activation in left PFC regions (dACC, DLPFC, aPFC) also negatively correlated with daily happiness in positive interpersonal situations.	Adolescents who showed higher sgACC reactivity to parental criticism reported lower happiness during positive interpersonal situations in daily life, particularly with peers. This suggests that heightened neural sensitivity to parental criticism may undermine positive social experiences, potentially increasing risk for depression. (The activation of sgACC may reflect a mechanism of over-regulation, which could increase depression risk.)

Mohamed Ali et al. (2023)	Eighty-one community-dwelling youths (mean age = 11.1, *SD* = 0.63 years, 44% girls) drawn from a larger longitudinal community sample, including 26 at high risk for depression due to maternal history of recurrent major depression or single major depressive episode with anxiety disorder and 55 low-risk children (no maternal psychiatric history). Participants were predominantly White, from middle-class, well-educated parents, with most coming from two-parent homes.	Longitudinal design (approximately 8 years apart). At age 3, irritability was measured observationally using the Lab-TAB. At age 11, participants reported perceived maternal care, and listened to their mothers' prerecorded feedback during fMRI scanning. Mothers recorded two criticisms, two praises, and two neutral statements (30 seconds each) using a standardised sentence stem.	Irritability at age 3 was negatively associated with neural reactivity to maternal criticism in a cluster in the right DLPFC at age 11, especially among adolescents who reported higher levels of good maternal parenting. Among youth reporting higher maternal care, irritability was significantly associated with decreased DLPFC activation during maternal criticism, suggesting a reduced neural response to negative maternal feedback. There was no significant neural activation in response to maternal praise in any of the ROIs or in exploratory whole-brain analyses.	Reduced DLPFC activation in response to maternal criticism among irritable youth who perceived high maternal care may reflect disengagement from negative feedback in a supportive caregiving context, potentially buffering against psychopathology risk. In contrast, no brain region was activated during praise, suggesting distinct pathways may shape responses to social rewards (like parental praise) versus non-social rewards (such as monetary incentives) in the context of irritability. The lack of significant findings for maternal praise suggests that irritability may selectively alter processing of negative, rather than positive, interpersonal feedback.

(*Continued*)

Table 5.3 (Continued)

Citation	*Main participants*	*Study design and generating the criticism stimuli*	*Areas activated by main participants*	*Interpretation*
Chen et al. (2024)	64 healthy adolescents (42 girls, 22 boys), aged 14–17 years (Mean = 16.53, SD = 1.03). Individuals with mood or psychotic disorders, current psychotropic medication, high suicide risk, neurological issues, or MRI contraindications were excluded.	Participants listened to 30-second self-referential auditory segments of negative (critical), positive (praising), and neutral comments delivered by a female voice actor, mimicking a maternal tone, during fMRI. Comments were standardised and not individualised and participants asked to imagine the speaker as someone close to them. Presentation order: 2 neutral → 2 praising → 2 neutral → 2 critical comments.	Left pgACC, Left DLPFC, Right precuneus; Criticism decreased excitatory connectivity from precuneusto DLPFC. Both praise and criticism increased inhibitory connectivity from DLPFC to pgACC.	Adolescents showed increased mood disturbance and rumination after criticism. Criticism weakened excitatory precuneus-to-DLPFC connectivity, a typical pattern of emotional-cognitive processing. Those with higher perceived criticism showed less inhibition of this connection, indicating greater engagement of the Central Executive Network to regulate self-referential negative input. Strengthened inhibitory DLPFC-to-pgACC connectivity during both praise and criticism suggests active cognitive control over emotional responses. Findings offer potential biomarkers for vulnerability to mood disorders during adolescence.

Note: ACC: anterior cingulate cortex; ADHD: attention deficit hyperactivity disorder; aPFC: anterior prefrontal cortex; BFNE-R: brief fear of negative evaluation – revised; BOLD: blood-oxygen-level dependent; CBT: cognitive behavioural therapy; CEN: Central Executive network; dACC: dorsal anterior cingulate cortex; DLPFC: dorsolateral prefrontal cortex; VLPFC: ventrolateral prefrontal cortex; EMA: ecological momentary assessment; fMRI: functional magnetic resonance imaging; FNE: fear of negative evaluation; FPES: fear of positive evaluation scale; GAD: generalised anxiety disorder; IFG: inferior frontal gyrus; Lab-TAB: laboratory temperament assessment battery; mPFC: medial prefrontal cortex; NOS: not otherwise specified; pgACC: pregenual anterior cingulate cortex; PCC: posterior cingulate cortex; PCM: perceived criticism measure consisting of a single item 'How critical is your relative of you?', on a scale of 0 to 10; preCUN: precuneus; pSTS: posterior superior temporal sulcus; ROI: region of interest; rACC: rostral anterior cingulate cortex; SAD: social anxiety disorder; SD: standard deviation; sgACC: subgenual anterior cingulate cortex; SMA: supplementary motor area; SFG: superior frontal gyrus; TPJ: temporoparietal junction; vmPFC: ventromedial prefrontal cortex.

connectivity between mPFC, posterior superior temporal sulcus (pSTS), PCC/precuneus, and right amygdala with the left TPJ, bilateral caudate, and PCC/precuneus was greater during praise than criticism (Gao et al., 2018). During social evaluation, main participants showed activation in the mPFC, rostral ACC, and temporal regions for both praise and criticism. Criticism additionally activated the anterior/posterior insula, amygdala, and thalamus (Miedl et al., 2016). Activation of these regions suggested that there is more emotional reactivity and salience during criticism, but more mentalising during praise (Miedl et al., 2016). Activity of the posterior insula during praise increased with higher fear of positive evaluation, suggesting that heightened salience towards praise can denote fear of positive evaluation (Miedl et al., 2016). Self-criticism activated the left calcarine gyrus, left ACC, left anterior insula and left amygdala more than self-reassurance, but both self-criticism and self-reassurance activated the bilateral lingual gyrus, left mPFC and left PCC equally (Kim, et al., 2020b). Greater activation of the lingual gyrus, a region implicated with mentalising ability and mental imagery, during self-criticism was associated with secure attachment (Kim, et al., 2020a). Thus, self-directed criticism may engage brain regions for mental imagery especially when individuals are securely attached (Kim, et al., 2020a). Receiving compliments, whether from oneself or a romantic partner, increased activity in regions including the inferior frontal gyrus, DLPFC, vmPFC, insula and temporal gyri (Eckstein et al., 2023). Receiving compliments from the partner activated the insula, superior temporal cortex and amygdala more than self-compliments. These results suggest that brain regions involved in gauging salience, emotional reactivity and emotional and non-emotional decision-making are linked to appreciation within romantic relationships. In summary, criticism activates some of the core brain regions associated with emotional reactivity, decision-making and regulation in healthy adults, namely the ACC, insula and amygdala. Equally, praise or self-reassurance activated the mPFC, DLPFC and inferior frontal gyrus, suggesting better mental imagery, decision-making and salience during praise.

Increased activity of the putamen and insula, but decreased activity in DLPFC and dACC during maternal criticism in adolescents suggests heightened reward sensitivity and emotional reactivity, but diminished sustained emotional attention and regulation (Lee et al., 2015). Criticism activated the sgACC more than neutral comments in adolescents (James et al., 2023). Activation of sgACC, DLPFC and dACC was associated with less happiness during daily positive interactions among adolescents. Reduced DLPFC activation in response to maternal criticism among irritable youth who perceived high maternal care (and some of whom were at risk for depression) may reflect disengagement from negative feedback in a supportive caregiving context, potentially buffering against psychopathology risk (Mohamed Ali et al., 2023). In adolescents, criticism diminished the connectivity between precuneus and

DLPFC (Chen et al., 2024). Thus, in adolescents than in adults, studies are more consistent in finding decreased activity of DLPFC and dACC during criticism, with happiness and maternal security buffering the neural response.

Overall, differences in regions of brain activation between studies may be due to differences in the experimental paradigms, with some involving videos of an actor overlapping with a written comment (Gao et al., 2018; Miedl et al., 2016), others applying cognitive techniques during the exposure to criticism (Kim, et al., 2020a; Kim, et al., 2020b) and one listening to just praises (Eckstein et al., 2023). Studies in adolescents typically involves listening to criticism from their mother (James et al., 2023; Lee et al., 2015; Mohamed Ali et al., 2023) or an actor (Chen et al., 2024).

How to offset criticism by warmth:

Studies suggest that a high level of criticism increases the brain response for emotional attention whereas warmth, kindness and understanding reduce the level of brain activation. Practice calm breathing to reduce social-evaluative fear. Greater dACC and amygdala activation during criticism is tied to fear of negative evaluation in social anxiety. Breathing exercises can calm hyperreactivity in these circuits. In adolescents, the lower activation of the DLPFC during criticism, may suggest disengagement from criticism. Therefore, adolescents could learn to buffer criticism with happy thoughts.

5.2.2 *Electroencephalography*

Brain electrical signals that appear during exposure to external stimuli signify time-locked responses to these stimuli. Electroencephalography (EEG) is more precise about the timing of brain responses than fMRI due to the higher sampling rate. Therefore, studying the event-related brain electrical signals using EEG can determine the level of emotional arousal, awareness of and sustained attention to stimuli (Premkumar et al., 2019). Listening to criticism and praise corresponded with increased continuous occipital alpha activity and continuous frontal theta activity, and this response corresponded with a greater level of schizotypal traits (Premkumar et al., 2019) (Table 5.4). Heightened occipital alpha activity denotes reduced awareness of stimuli, whereas heighted theta activity denotes greater emotional arousal. Lower occipital alpha and frontal theta activity corresponded with less perceived emotional support in individuals with a high level of schizotypal traits. The findings suggested that diminished arousal, but increased awareness of criticism and praise corresponds with less emotional support from a close relative in individuals with

Table 5.4 Summary of studies on the neural response to criticism and brain signals based on EEG in sub-clinical populations

Citation	*Main participants*	*Study design and generating the criticism stimuli*	*Areas activated by main participants*	*Interpretation*
Premkumar et al. (2019)	Thirty-two participants (mean age = 26.6 years, SD = 7.4; 52.4% female) from the general population with a full range of positive schizotypy (O-LIFE); a high schizotypy subgroup (n = 22) completed the LEE scale (perceived lack of emotional support).	Participants listened to 40 criticisms, 40 praises, and 40 neutral comments (5–10 seconds each) previously standardised to resemble EE-like statements and delivered by strangers in a male and female voice. Participants rated the self-relevance of each comment on an 11-point Likert scale. EEG spectral power analysis determined the brain responses to criticism and praise.	–Lower frontal theta power (F3/FC3, F4/FC4) and lower occipital alpha power (P3/PO3, P4/PO4) during criticism and praise were associated with greater perceived lack of emotional support in high schizotypy individuals. –In the full sample, greater frontal theta power during criticism and praise correlated with higher total schizotypy scores. –Frontal theta and occipital alpha responses were dissociable, relating to emotional arousal and emotional attention, respectively.	People with high schizotypy who perceived low emotional support showed reduced emotional arousal (lower frontal theta) but increased emotional attention (lower occipital alpha) to both criticism and praise. This suggests blunted affective response, but heightened awareness of social-emotional cues. The study supports the dissociation of neural systems involved in processing emotional stimuli and highlights a potential neural basis for social distress in schizotypy.

(*Continued*)

Table 5.4 (Continued)

Citation	*Main participants*	*Study design and generating the criticism stimuli*	*Areas activated by main participants*	*Interpretation*
Zandbagleh et al. (2022)	Twenty-nine participants from the general community were included in the EEG analysis: 19 high schizotypy (mean age = 24.79, SD = 8.12) and 10 low schizotypy (mean age = 22.6, SD = 3.31), identified using the SPQ.	Participants listened to auditory comments (praise, criticism, neutral) delivered by strangers in a male and female voice, followed by a screen showing either a standard word ('normal' in 75% of trials) or a mood-congruent deviant word (e.g. 'happy' after praise, 'rage' after criticism in 25% of trials). Participants responded with a key press to indicate whether the target word matched the mood of the comment.	P3a activity was analysed over frontal regions (F3, F4), associated with automatic attention and anterior cortex involvement. P3b (a late P300 component) was analysed over parietal regions (P3, P4) and this response is linked to sustained attention and posterior cortex activation. high schizotypy individuals showed significantly greater P3b response (amplitude and latency) during criticism and praise trials than low schizotypy individuals, indicating enhanced recruitment of parietal regions (posterior cortices). Absence of differences in P3a (an early P300 component) between groups suggested minimal frontal (anterior) differentiation.	Individuals with high schizotypy exhibited stronger and delayed P3b responses to emotionally salient target words following criticism and praise than individuals with low schizotypy, suggesting greater cognitive and attentional engagement with socially affective stimuli, especially criticism. These findings highlight the sensitivity of high schizotypy individuals to family-related emotional content and support the role of posterior brain regions in processing social stress.

Rösler et al. (2024)	Thirty-four right-handed Dutch participants (mean age = 23.48, SD = 4.17; 27 females); EEG data from 21 participants.	Participants completed a donation task where they allocated money between themselves and charities. Written positive and negative feedback (trait words as moral evaluations, e.g. 'cooperative', 'uncooperative') denoted praise and criticism. Feedback was construed as being delivered by senders who could be framed as ingroup or outgroup based on the participant's social values. Senders' intentions were communicated in three ways: not communicated (control), communicated as intending to help (e.g. 'I want to help you by reminding you that you said it is important for you to donate to charities', or communicated as signalling moral superiority, e.g. 'I seem to be a better person than you are.' Feedback following selfish decisions was considered 'criticism', while feedback following altruistic decisions were positive. EEG was recorded while participants received these written feedback messages.	The study primarily analyzed ERP components: -P200: amplitudes decreased when feedback was delivered with helpful intentions than with moral superiority or no intention, observed at frontocentral and centroparietal electrodes Fz, FCz, Cz, and CPz. -P300 and early LPP: amplitudes unexpectedly increased when feedback conveyed moral superiority than when feedback was helpful or not communicated; amplitudes were observed at centroparietal electrodes Pz, CPz, and Cz.	Communicating helpful intentions following selfish decisions reduced early attentional vigilance toward moral criticism (as shown by reduced P200 amplitudes), suggesting lower perceived threat to criticism. Conversely, morally superior feedback following selfish decisions elicited greater attentional engagement (increased P300 and LPP), indicating enhanced processing of socially threatening cues. The study concludes that expressing helpful motives can mitigate defensive neural responses to moral criticism.

(Continued)

Table 5.4 (Continued)

Citation	*Main participants*	*Study design and generating the criticism stimuli*	*Areas activated by main participants*	*Interpretation*
James et al. (2021)	202 children (age range 7–11 years, mean age = 9.71 years, SD = 1.38; 52% male; 72.8% Caucasian, 13.9% were African American, 0.5% were Asian or Pacific Islander, and 11.9% were biracial) and their mothers. Mothers were assessed for EE-criticism using the Five Minute Speech Sample. 51 mothers were classified as critical, and 151 as non-critical.	Correlational, cross-sectional EEG study. Mothers provided a Five Minute Speech Sample, which was coded for EE-criticism. Children then completed the 'Doors Task' (a guessing game with monetary rewards/losses) while EEG was recorded. Neural responses to gains and losses were measured through ERPs, focusing on the RewP component.	Children of highly critical mothers showed blunted RewP amplitudes in frontocentral regions (peak at FC2, ~320 ms post-stimulus) during both gain and loss feedback compared to children of non-critical mothers. Raw data also showed reduced activity at FCz. Findings were independent of both maternal and child internalising psychopathology.	Children exposed to maternal criticism exhibited reduced neural reactivity to both reward and loss, suggesting a general dampening of sensitivity to environmental feedback. This blunted reactivity may indicate disruptions in reinforcement learning and emotional processing in late childhood, potentially increasing vulnerability to future psychopathology such as depression. The effects were present even when accounting for current depression and anxiety symptoms in both mothers and children.

Note: EE: expressed emotion; EEG: electroencephalography; ERP: event-related potential; LEE: level of expressed emotion; LPP: late positive potential; O-LIFE: Oxford–Liverpool Inventory of Feelings and Experiences; RewP: reward positivity; SD: standard deviation; SPQ: schizotypal personality questionnaire.

schizotypal traits. When these comments were followed by mood congruent emotional words, e.g. criticism followed by the word 'rage' and praise followed by the word 'surprise', greater late P300 amplitudes during these emotional words was observed in high, than low, schizotypy individuals. This finding suggested that individuals with high schizotypal traits have sustained attention to both criticism and praise (Zandbagleh et al., 2022). This response may arise because of a heightened sensitivity to criticism and praise in individuals with high schizotypy.

The neural response to criticism was also studied in healthy individuals during emotional decision-making tasks, such as donating to a charity (Rösler et al., 2024) or guessing the reward value behind two doors (James et al., 2021). Reprimands following lower charitable giving increased the amplitude of attention-related brain potential in healthy adults (Rösler et al., 2024). By contrast, children of critical mothers showed diminished amplitude of attention-related brain potential following both monetary gains and losses when guessing the reward value behind two doors (James et al., 2021).

These studies show that criticism and praise increase attention and alertness in high schizotypal and healthy adults. In contrast, in children, maternal criticism can diminish children's appraisal of reward.

How to divert attention from criticism:

Balance attention to praise and criticism: High schizotypy individuals show sustained attention to both criticism and praise, which can prolong rumination. Practising 'attentional shifting' (e.g. deliberately focusing on neutral or positive cues in the environment) may prevent getting stuck on negative feedback.

5.2.3 Other neuroimaging methods

A randomised, sham-controlled cross-over study (Dedoncker et al., 2019) investigated whether a single session of prefrontal transcranial direct current stimulation (tDCS) modulates mood and neural connectivity in response to criticism depending on level of perceived criticism. Forty-one healthy right-handed young females (age range 20–29, mean age = 22.9 years, standard deviation (SD) = 2.61) received both active and sham tDCS, with the anodal electrode placed over the left DLPFC and the cathodal electrode placed over the right supraorbital area. Prior to stimulation, baseline resting-state fMRI and mood ratings using visual analogue scales were assessed (T1), followed by a second assessment immediately after stimulation (T2) and a final assessment after participants listened to standardised 30-second self-referential comments (critical, praising and neutral) delivered in a fixed order inside the magnetic resonance imaging scanner (T3). Functional connectivity analyses revealed that in high perceived criticism individuals, active tDCS significantly reduced connectivity between the left dACC and the right DLPFC following criticism, compared to low perceived criticism individuals. Additionally, tDCS modulated connectivity between the left DLPFC and the left posterior insula, with high perceived criticism participants showing reduced connectivity after active stimulation. These findings suggest that prefrontal tDCS can attenuate medial prefrontal connectivity in response to criticism in individuals with higher perceived criticism, providing evidence for the potential utility of tDCS in modulating neural circuits related to emotional regulation.

Functional near-infrared spectroscopy (fNIRS) measures the haemodynamics of the brain following exposure to an event. Neoh and colleagues (2022) investigated how the type of person delivering criticism (romantic partners, friends, or parents) influences PFC activity. The study involved 49 healthy undergraduates (mean age = 21.65, SD=1.49 years; 25 females) who read vignettes depicting critical interactions from a third-person perspective. Each vignette was randomly assigned to describe a different relationship context, and participants rated the justification and impact of the criticism after each vignette. fNIRS was used to measure hemodynamic changes in the PFC during exposure to these stimuli. A significant interaction emerged between relationship type and maternal perceived criticism ratings in the DLPFC, specifically the left middle frontal gyrus (BA46L). Individuals with high perceived criticism from their mothers showed increased DLPFC activation in response to criticism from romantic partners and parents, but decreased activation in response to criticism from friends. This suggests that neural processing of criticism is moderated by one's interpersonal history, particularly parental relationships, and that high perceived criticism individuals may exert more cognitive control when processing criticism from more emotionally salient sources. These findings highlight the importance of the identity of the critic and their relational context when evaluating neural responses to social criticism.

5.3 Summary

The chapter began with the premise that brain areas for social reward will be implicated in the response to criticism. These constituted the DLPFC, dACC, amydala, hippocampus, striatum, orbitofrontal cortex and mPFC. The overriding brain region implicated across studies using different types of neuroimaging techniques is the DLPFC which is involved in sustained attention. Connectivity between the DLPFC and insula is heightened in individuals with high perceived criticism which transcranial direct stimulation disrupts (Dedoncker et al., 2019). And DLPFC is activated during criticism in individuals with high maternal perceived criticism as measured by fMRI (Hooley et al., 2012) and near infrared spectroscopy (Neoh et al., 2022). Yet, the brain response to criticism goes beyond the brain's social reward system to include the insula (salience) in anxious adolescents (Butterfield et al., 2021) and posterior cingulate in healthy individuals (Premkumar et al., 2013).

In addition, the brain activation sites differ by type of mental disorder, age group and the manner of exposure to criticism. Studies of patients with depression implicate the ACC, insula, amygdala, mPFC and DLPFC. Studies of individuals along the psychosis continuum implicate the DLPFC, ACC and insula. Studies of adults and adolescents with anxiety implicate brain regions involved in emotional attention (dACC), salience (insula), fear (amygdala) and mentalising and self-reflection (superior frontal gyrus) during criticism. It appears that the brain response to criticism in adolescents is offset by praise and parental warmth as there is overlap in brain activation of both types of comments (Butterfield et al., 2021). Those with secure attachment mentalise criticism better (Kim, et al., 2020a). Addressing the functions that underlie these brain regions, such as diverting attention and engaging in positive activities, such as taking deep breaths, doing exercise and exposure to positive communication, such as warmth from a friend, could be strategies to handle criticism.

References

Alvarez-Jimenez, M., Priede, A., Hetrick, S. E., Bendall, S., Killackey, E., Parker, A. G., McGorry, P. D., & Gleeson, J. F. (2012). Risk factors for relapse following treatment for first episode psychosis: A systematic review and meta-analysis of longitudinal studies. *Schizophrenia Research, 139*(1), 116–128. 10.1016/j.schres.2012.05.007

Bebbington, P., & Kuipers, L. (1994). The predictive utility of expressed emotion in schizophrenia: an aggregate analysis. *Psychological Medicine, 24*(3), 707–718. 10.1017/S0033291700027860

Birk, S. L., Horenstein, A., Weeks, J., Olino, T., Heimberg, R., Goldin, P. R., & Gross, J. J. (2019). Neural responses to social evaluation: The role of fear of positive and negative evaluation. *Journal of Anxiety Disorders, 67*, 102114. 10.1016/j.janxdis.2019.102114

Blair, K., Geraci, M., Devido, J., McCaffrey, D., Chen, G., Vythilingam, M., Ng, P., Hollon, N., Jones, M., Blair, R. J. R., & Pine, D. S. (2008). Neural response to self- and other referential praise and criticism in generalized social phobia. *Archives of General Psychiatry, 65*(10), 1176–1184. 10.1001/archpsyc.65.10.1176

Bonduelle, S. L. B., Chen, Q., Wu, G., Braet, C., De Raedt, R., & Baeken, C. (2021). Exposure to criticism modulates left but not right amygdala functional connectivity in healthy adolescents: individual influences of perceived and self-criticism. *Frontiers in Psychiatry, 12*, 673805. 10.3389/fpsyt.2021.673805

Bortz, D. M., Gazo, K. L., & Grace, A. A. (2019). The medial septum enhances reversal learning via opposing actions on ventral tegmental area and substantia nigra dopamine neurons. *Neuropsychopharmacology (New York, NY), 44*(13), 2186–2194. 10.1038/s41386-019-0453-1

Butterfield, R. D., Silk, J. S., Lee, K. H., Siegle, G. S., Dahl, R. E., Forbes, E. E., Ryan, N. D., Hooley, J. M., & Ladouceur, C. D. (2021). Parents still matter! Parental warmth predicts adolescent brain function and anxiety and depressive symptoms 2 years later. *Development and Psychopathology, 33*(1), 226–239. 10.1017/S0954579419001718

Chen, Q., Bonduelle, S. L. B., Wu, G., Vanderhasselt, M., De Raedt, R., & Baeken, C. (2024). Unraveling how the adolescent brain deals with criticism using dynamic causal modeling. *NeuroImage (Orlando, Fla.)*, *286*, 120510. 10.1016/j.neuroimage.2024.120510

Choi, S., Lee, S., Park, H., Chun, J. W., Kang, J. I., & Kim, J. (2013). Perceived patient–parent relationships and neural representation of parents in schizophrenia. *European Archives of Psychiatry and Clinical Neuroscience*, *263*(3), 259–269. 10.1007/s00406-012-0334-7

Cochrane, M., Petch, I., & Pickering, A. D. (2010). Do measures of schizotypal personality provide non-clinical analogues of schizophrenic symptomatology? *Psychiatry Research*, *176*(2), 150–154. 10.1016/j.psychres.2009.01.031

Collins, A. L., & Saunders, B. T. (2019). Brain reward network effects underlie septo-hippocampal control of flexible decision making. *Neuropsychopharmacology (New York, NY)*, *44*(13), 2153–2154. 10.1038/s41386-019-0487-4

Corr, P. J. (2010). The psychoticism–psychopathy continuum: A neuropsychological model of core deficits. *Personality and Individual Differences*, *48*(6), 695–703. 10.1016/j.paid.2009.12.023

Dedoncker, J., Vanderhasselt, M., Remue, J., De Witte, S., Wu, G., Hooley, J. M., De Raedt, R., & Baeken, C. (2019). Prefrontal TDCS attenuates medial prefrontal connectivity upon being criticized in individuals scoring high on perceived criticism. *Brain Imaging and Behavior*, *13*(4), 1060–1070. 10.1007/s11682-018-9927-8

Doerig, N., Schlumpf, Y., Spinelli, S., Späti, J., Brakowski, J., Quednow, B. B., Seifritz, E., & Grosse Holtforth, M. (2014). Neural representation and clinically relevant moderators of individualised self-criticism in healthy subjects. *Social Cognitive and Affective Neuroscience*, *9*(9), 1333–1340. 10.1093/scan/nst123

Duek, O., Shahar, G., Osher, Y., & Kofman, O. (2018). Role of self-criticism in reward and punishment probabilistic learning. *Personality and Individual Differences*, *134*, 155–163. 10.1016/j.paid.2018.06.007

Eckstein, M., Stößel, G., Gerchen, M. F., Bilek, E., Kirsch, P., & Ditzen, B. (2023). Neural responses to instructed positive couple interaction: an fMRI study on compliment sharing. *Social Cognitive and Affective Neuroscience*, *18*(1) 10.1093/scan/nsad005

Fareri, D. S., & Delgado, M. R. (2014). Social rewards and social networks in the human brain. *The Neuroscientist*, *20*(4), 387–402. 10.1177/1073858414521869

Gao, S., Geng, Y., Li, J., Zhou, Y., & Yao, S. (2018). Encoding praise and criticism during social evaluation alters interactive responses in the mentalizing and affective learning networks. *Frontiers in Neuroscience*, *12*, 611. 10.3389/fnins.2018.00611

Goldin, P. R., Ziv, M., Jazaieri, H., Weeks, J., Heimberg, R. G., & Gross, J. J. (2014). Impact of cognitive-behavioral therapy for social anxiety disorder on the neural bases of emotional reactivity to and regulation of social evaluation. *Behaviour Research and Therapy*, *62*, 97–106. 10.1016/j.brat.2014.08.005

Gray, J. A. (1982). Précis of The neuropsychology of anxiety: An enquiry into the functions of the septo-hippocampal system. *The Behavioral and Brain Sciences*, *5*(3), 469–484. 10.1017/S0140525X00013066

Hooley, J. M., Gruber, S. A., Parker, H. A., Guillaumot, J., Rogowska, J., & Yurgelun-Todd, D. (2009). Cortico-limbic response to personally challenging emotional stimuli after complete recovery from depression. *Psychiatry Research: Neuroimaging*, *171*(2), 106–119. 10.1016/j.pscychresns.2008.04.001

Hooley, J. M., Gruber, S. A., Scott, L. A., Hiller, J. B., & Yurgelun-Todd, D. (2005). Activation in dorsolateral prefrontal cortex in response to maternal criticism and praise in recovered depressed and healthy control participants. *Biological Psychiatry*, *57*(7), 809–812. 10.1016/j.biopsych.2005.01.012

Hooley, J. M., Siegle, G., & Gruber, S. A. (2012). Affective and neural reactivity to criticism in individuals high and low on perceived criticism. *PloS One*, *7*(9), e44412. 10.1371/journal.pone.0044412

James, K. M., Foster, C. E., Tsypes, A., Owens, M., & Gibb, B. E. (2021). Maternal criticism and children's neural responses to reward and loss. *Journal of Experimental Child Psychology*, *211*, 105226. 10.1016/j.jecp.2021.105226

James, K. M., Sequeira, S. L., Dahl, R. E., Forbes, E. E., Ryan, N. D., Hooley, J., Ladouceur, C. D., & Silk, J. S. (2023). Adolescents' neural reactivity to parental criticism is associated with diminished happiness during daily interpersonal situations. *Social Cognitive and Affective Neuroscience*, *18*(1) 10.1093/scan/nsad020

Kim, J. J., Kent, K. M., Cunnington, R., Gilbert, P., & Kirby, J. N. (2020a). Attachment styles modulate neural markers of threat and imagery when engaging in self-criticism. *Scientific Reports*, *10*(1), 13776. 10.1038/s41598-020-70772-x

Kim, J. J., Parker, S. L., Doty, J. R., Cunnington, R., Gilbert, P., & Kirby, J. N. (2020b). Neurophysiological and behavioural markers of compassion. *Scientific Reports*, *10*(1), 6789. 10.1038/s41598-020-63846-3

Kuipers, E., Bebbington, P., Dunn, G., Fowler, D., Freeman, D., Watson, P., Hardy, A., & Garety, P. (2006). Influence of carer expressed emotion and affect on relapse in non-affective psychosis. *British Journal of Psychiatry*, *188*(2), 173–179. 10.1192/bjp.bp.104.007294

Lee, K. H., Siegle, G. J., Dahl, R. E., Hooley, J. M., & Silk, J. S. (2015). Neural responses to maternal criticism in healthy youth. *Social Cognitive and Affective Neuroscience*, *10*(7), 902–912. 10.1093/scan/nsu133

Longe, O., Maratos, F. A., Gilbert, P., Evans, G., Volker, F., Rockliff, H., & Rippon, G. (2010). Having a word with yourself: Neural correlates of self-criticism and self-reassurance. *NeuroImage (Orlando, Fla.)*, *49*(2), 1849–1856. 10.1016/j.neuroimage.2009.09.019

Mason, O., Linney, Y., & Claridge, G. (2005). Short scales for measuring schizotypy. *Schizophrenia Research*, *78*(2), 293–296. 10.1016/j.schres.2005.06.020

McNaughton, N. (2025). The legacies of the neuropsychology of anxiety for reinforcement sensitivity theory. *Motivation Science*, *11*(1), 1–17. 10.1037/mot0000353

Miedl, S. F., Blechert, J., Klackl, J., Wiggert, N., Reichenberger, J., Derntl, B., & Wilhelm, F. H. (2016). Criticism hurts everybody, praise only some: Common and specific neural responses to approving and disapproving social-evaluative videos. *NeuroImage (Orlando, Fla.)*, *132*, 138–147. 10.1016/j.neuroimage.2016.02.027

Mohamed Ali, O., Vandermeer, M. R. J., Liu, P., Joanisse, M. F., Barch, D. M., & Hayden, E. P. (2023). Associations between childhood irritability and neural reactivity to maternal feedback in adolescence. *Biological Psychology*, *182*, 108645. 10.1016/j.biopsycho.2023.108645

Neoh, M. J. Y., Teng, J. H., Lee, A., Setoh, P., Mulatti, C., & Esposito, G. (2022). Negative emotional reactions to criticism: Perceived criticism and source affects extent of hurt and relational distancing. *PloS One*, *17*(8), e0271869. 10.1371/journal.pone.0271869

Nook, E. C., Dodell-Feder, D., Germine, L. T., Hooley, J. M., DeLisi, L. E., & Hooker, C. I. (2018). Weak dorsolateral prefrontal response to social criticism predicts worsened mood and symptoms following social conflict in people at familial risk for schizophrenia. *NeuroImage Clinical*, *18*, 40–50. 10.1016/j.nicl.2018.01.004

O'Brien, M. P., Zinberg, J. L., Ho, L., Rudd, A., Kopelowicz, A., Daley, M., Bearden, C. E., & Cannon, T. D. (2009). Family problem solving interactions and 6-month symptomatic and functional outcomes in youth at ultra-high risk for psychosis and with recent onset psychotic symptoms: A longitudinal study. *Schizophrenia Research*, *107*(2), 198–205. 10.1016/j.schres.2008.10.008

Premkumar, P. (2012). Are you being rejected or excluded? Insights from neuroimaging studies using different rejection paradigms. *Clinical Psychopharmacology and Neuroscience: The Official Scientific Journal of the Korean College of Neuropsychopharmacology*, *10*(3), 144–154. 10.9758/cpn.2012.10.3.144

Premkumar, P., Kumari, V., Corr, P. J. J., & Sharma, T. (2006). Frontal lobe volumes in schizophrenia: Effects of stage and duration of illness. *Journal of Psychiatric Research*, *40*(7), 627–637. 10.1016/j.jpsychires.2006.05.009

Premkumar, P., Santo, M. G. E., Onwumere, J., Schürmann, M., Kumari, V., Blanco, S., Baker, J., & Kuipers, E. (2019). Neural responses to criticism and praise vary with schizotypy and perceived emotional support. *International Journal of Psychophysiology*, *145*, 109–118. 10.1016/j.ijpsycho.2019.05.008

Premkumar, P., Williams, S. C., Lythgoe, D., Andrew, C., Kuipers, E., & Kumari, V. (2013). Neural processing of criticism and positive comments from relatives in individuals with schizotypal personality traits. *The World Journal of Biological Psychiatry: The Official Journal of the World Federation of Societies of Biological Psychiatry*, *14*(1), 57–70. 10.3109/15622975.2011.604101 [doi]

Rösler, I. K., van Nunspeet, F., & Ellemers, N. (2024). Beneficial effects of communicating intentions when delivering moral criticism: Cognitive and neural responses. *Cognitive, Affective, & Behavioral Neuroscience*, *24*(3), 421–439. 10.3758/s13415-024-01164-1

Rylands, A. J., McKie, S., Elliott, R., Deakin, J. F. W., & Tarrier, N. (2011). A functional magnetic resonance imaging paradigm of expressed emotion in schizophrenia. *The Journal of Nervous and Mental Disease*, *199*(1), 25–29. 10.1097/NMD.0b013e3182043b87

Sequeira, S. L., Butterfield, R. D., Silk, J. S., Forbes, E. E., & Ladouceur, C. D. (2019). Neural activation to parental praise interacts with social context to predict adolescent depressive symptoms. *Frontiers in Behavioral Neuroscience*, *13*, 222. 10.3389/fnbeh.2019.00222

Servaas, M. N., Riese, H., Renken, R. J., Marsman, J. C., Lambregs, J., Ormel, J., & Aleman, A. (2013). The effect of criticism on functional brain connectivity and associations with neuroticism. *PloS One*, *8*(7), e69606. 10.1371/journal.pone.0069606

Silk, J. S., Lee, K. H., Elliott, R. D., Hooley, J. M., Dahl, R. E., Barber, A., & Siegle, G. J. (2017). 'Mom – I don't want to hear it': Brain response to maternal praise and criticism in adolescents with major depressive disorder. *Social Cognitive and Affective Neuroscience*, *12*(5), 729–738. 10.1093/scan/nsx014

Silk, J. S., Tan, P. Z., Ladouceur, C. D., Meller, S., Siegle, G. J., McMakin, D. L., Forbes, E. E., Dahl, R. E., Kendall, P. C., Mannarino, A., & Ryan, N. D. (2018). A randomized clinical trial comparing individual cognitive behavioral therapy and child-centered therapy for child anxiety disorders. *Journal of Clinical Child and Adolescent Psychology*, *47*(4), 542–554. 10.1080/15374416.2016.1138408

Thomas, E. H. X., Rossell, S. L., Tan, E. J., Neill, E., Van Rheenen, T. E., Carruthers, S. P., Sumner, P. J., Louise, S., Bozaoglu, K., & Gurvich, C. (2019). Do schizotypy dimensions reflect the symptoms of schizophrenia? *Australian and New Zealand Journal of Psychiatry*, *53*(3), 236–247. 10.1177/0004867418769746

van Houtum, L. A. E. M., Wever, M. C. M., van Schie, C. C., Janssen, L. H. C., Wentholt, W. G. M., Tollenaar, M. S., Will, G., & Elzinga, B. M. (2024). Sticky criticism? Affective and neural responses to parental criticism and praise in adolescents with depression. *Psychological Medicine*, *54*(3), 507–516. 10.1017/S0033291723002131

Vandermeer, M. R. J., Liu, P., Mohamed Ali, O., Daoust, A. R., Joanisse, M. F., Barch, D. M., & Hayden, E. P. (2024). Children's neural reactivity to maternal praise and criticism: Associations with early depressive symptoms and maternal depression. *Development and Psychopathology*, *36*(1), 12–27. 10.1017/S0954579422000840

Weintraub, M. J., Weisman de Mamani, A., Villano, W. J., Evans, T. C., Millman, Z. B., Hooley, J. M., & Timpano, K. R. (2019). Affective and physiological reactivity to emotional comments in individuals at elevated risk for psychosis. *Schizophrenia Research*, *206*, 428–435. 10.1016/j.schres.2018.10.006

Zandbagleh, A., Mirzakuchaki, S., Daliri, M. R., Premkumar, P., Carretié, L., & Sanei, S. (2022). Tensor factorization approach for ERP-based assessment of schizotypy in a novel auditory oddball task on perceived family stress. *Journal of Neural Engineering*, *19*(6), 66028. 10.1088/1741-2552/aca69f

Chapter 6

Treatment approaches for reducing criticism and expressed emotion in families with serious mental illness

Amy Weisman de Mamani and Preethi Premkumar

Abstract

This chapter examines strategies designed to reduce criticism and high levels of expressed emotion (EE) in families of individuals with serious mental illness (SMI). Although multiple approaches have been developed to address these interpersonal risk factors, we will focus on those that have received substantial empirical support. We begin by presenting a cognitive model of caregiving appraisal and a model of family intervention (FI) related to such appraisal. First, we review early behavioural family therapy (BFT) models and their immediate derivative, family focused therapy (FFT), which were among the first interventions to systematically target EE. Next, we discuss culturally informed therapy for schizophrenia (CIT-S), an adaptation that builds upon these foundational approaches while integrating cultural values and beliefs. Finally, we explore multi-family group interventions, which leverage peer support and shared learning to reduce criticism and improve family functioning. Within each section, we will describe the mechanisms through which these approaches address EE and criticism most directly. We also present a hypothetical clinical case example to illustrate how the concepts reviewed in this chapter may be applied in family therapy.

6.1 Family intervention and a cognitive model of caregiving for psychosis

Brown and colleagues (1962, 1966, 1972) identified a clear link between expressed emotion (EE) and relapse in patients with schizophrenia. Since then, various models of family intervention (FI) have arisen (Kuipers, 2006). This section reviews literature on a cognitive model of FI that focuses on the appraisals of caregivers and a cognitive model of intervention (Kuipers et al., 2010). Psychoeducation and problem-solving skills seem to be the common thread running through different forms of FI (Yesufu-Udechuku Amina et al., 2015). Yet, the style of improving family dynamics varies by the model of FI.

DOI: 10.4324/9781003388159-7

Directly following the seminal studies by Brown and colleagues (1962, 1966, 1972) and the formulation of the concept of EE, a social intervention was developed to address high EE and it involved psychoeducation (Leff et al., 1982, 1985). Here, psychoeducation involved learning about the aetiology, symptoms, course, and treatment and management of schizophrenia. Two to four psychoeducation sessions were delivered to families during home visits. In addition, high and low EE relatives of patients were brought together to discuss coping strategies and to try out new ways of handling the problems at home. Furthermore, the clinician visited the patient and their carer in their home to engage them in improving the dynamics of their interaction by finding new ways of interpreting events and to adopt other types of behavioural intervention. Twenty-four patients living with a high EE relative were randomly allocated to either the social intervention mentioned above or routine care and were assessed for psychiatric symptoms at baseline, at the time of discharge from hospital and nine months after discharge. Nine per cent (1 out of 12) of patients who received the social intervention relapsed nine months after discharge, whereas 50% of patients (6 out of 12) who received routine care relapsed (Leff et al., 1982). The number of criticisms during the Camberwell Family interview also decreased from 16 on average to 7 on average in the high EE relatives who received the social intervention, compared to the reduction from 12 on average to 10 on average in the group that received routine care. The benefits of the social intervention were maintained at two-year follow-up (Leff et al., 1985). The findings of this early social model suggested that addressing EE can reduce the risk of relapse, but it did not explain the mechanism by which this happens.

A meta-analysis of randomised controlled trials of FI compared to other interventions, such as treatment as usual (TAU), for schizophrenia included 15 studies (Pilling et al., 2002). Randomised controlled trials are the highest quality of evidence for determining the effectiveness of interventions because they assume that any difference between two interventions is based on chance (National Institute of Health and Care Excellence, 2002). The meta-analysis found that relapse rate over four years was lower for FI (38%; 144 out of 381 patients) than any other treatment (54%; 206 out of 384 patients). This difference between FI and any other treatment equated to FI reducing the relative risk of relapse by 13% compared to any other intervention, and reducing the number of patients needed to treat and prevent relapse to eight. In addition, offering FI in a single-family format, rather than multiple family-group format, maintained an advantage over any other treatment in reducing the risk of readmission by 49% and lowering the number of patients needed to treat and prevent relapse to n=3. The meta-analysis also found that FI, when delivered in a single-family format, rather than in a multiple family group format, reduced the burden of care compared to TAU. These findings substantiate the recommendation for FI as a primary intervention for psychosis (National Institute for Health and Care Excellence, 2014). More recently, a meta-analysis of 90 randomised controlled trials of FI compared to other interventions for schizophrenia also found that FI reduced the risk of relapse compared to TAU 12 months after treatment (Rodolico et al., 2022).

In light of the emerging collective evidence favouring FI over TAU for psychosis, Kuipers and colleagues (2002) designed a FI involving improving communication, offering discussion of up-to-date information about psychosis, problem-solving, reducing criticism and conflict, improving activity, and the emotional processing of grief, loss and anger. Delivered to family members who spent at least 10 hours a week with patients with non-affective psychosis over nine sessions and usually in the family's home (Garety et al., 2008), the intervention revolved around the problems that the family identified. It also emphasised relapse prevention by educating families on detecting early signs of relapse. Eight-three patients were randomly allocated to FI plus TAU (n=28), TAU alone (28) or cognitive behavioural therapy (CBT) plus TAU (n=27). Outcomes that would determine the efficacy of the intervention included remission and relapse, months since remission and relapse, symptom severity and EE, and they were assessed at end of treatment, i.e. 12 months after baseline and at 12-month follow-up, i.e. 24 months after baseline. Relapse and remission were determined by raters assessing the case notes written by the clinician managing the patient and these reports were made monthly (Garety et al., 2008). At the 12-month end-of-treatment time point, 33% (9 out of 27) of patients remitted in the FI group compared to 50% (14 out of 28) in the CBT group and 48% (13 out 27) in the TAU group, and these differences were not statistically significant. The three groups (FI, CBT and TAU) did not differ in the number of months since remission or relapse or in symptom improvement. However, when combining the two groups that received an intervention (i.e. FI or CBT) with TAU, overall symptoms, negative symptoms and social functioning were better in the groups that received either intervention than the group that received TAU alone. Additionally, carers of patients that received FI expressed fewer criticisms after the intervention. The reasons for the limited effectiveness of FI on its own over TAU were suggested to be due to poor statistical power, the low level of relapse across all groups and the FI not being directed specifically at carers with high EE; i.e. the families may have been low EE to begin with.

One cognitive explanation of high EE and mechanism of FI is how the carer appraises mental disorder and caregiving. Carer appraisal of the caring role as burdensome is associated with high EE, as reviewed in Chapter 2 (Kuipers et al., 2007; Onwumere et al., 2016, 2018, 2020). Carer appraisal involves evaluation of the behaviour of the patient and evaluation of the illness, and this appraisal can trigger cognitive and affective responses in the carer that can impact their engagement with services and with the patient (Kuipers et al., 2010). Greater burden is also perceived when carers spend more time with patients with schizophrenia (Scazufca & Kuipers, 1996). Thus, high EE carers of patients with first-episode psychosis perceived the caring role as difficult and felt more loss than low EE carers (Raune et al., 2004). High EE carers also applied more avoidant coping, such as behavioural disengagement and denial (Raune et al., 2004). The stress of caring is understandable given the carers' poor quality of life and isolation (Onwumere et al., 2016), but helping carers to understand the nature of symptoms and find positive coping strategies is key to FI (Kuipers, 2006). This can include improving carer self-esteem and using more problem-focused, rather than emotional, coping strategies.

Kuipers and colleagues (2010) suggest that having a positive relationship with the patient to begin with can maintain a low EE style of caring where the carer seeks positive help from others and is not isolated. In such cases, the carer maintains their wider interests beyond the patient and the caring is just one of many roles of the carer. In such cases, information about the illness and ongoing support with emotional problems can sustain the caring role. High EOI carers tend to be parents and they maintain that they must do all they can to protect their child (Kuipers et al., 2010). In such cases, FI must foster independence of the carer and allow them to pursue their own interests beyond the caring role. Where carers are critical and hostile, this dynamic may precede illness onset and delay help-seeking. Carers are likely to be anxious and depressed. If they are to continue to be in a caring role, then psychoeducation about the illness would be beneficial and ease the carer's control over the patient's welfare. Thus, changing carer appraisal of the illness from a pessimistic outlook to an optimistic one can change the burden of care.

How to address maladaptive carer appraisals of serious mental illness:

Carers must maintain a balance between caring and pursuing their own interests.

Carers must understand the nature of the patient's symptoms by seeking information from trusted sources, such as the National Health Service.

Carers must have proactive problem-orientated coping strategies, such as reaching out to others for positive help and resolving conflict with the patient, rather than avoidant and emotional coping strategies, such as feelings of loss and denial.

6.2 Behavioural family therapy (BFT) and family focused therapy (FFT)

Falloon and colleagues (1984) developed behavioural family therapy (BFT) in the late 1970s and early 1980s, and BFT was a landmark intervention designed to address one of the most robust predictors of relapse in schizophrenia, namely high EE. Early research demonstrated that patients returning to high-EE households were significantly more likely to relapse than those in low-EE environments (Brown et al., 1972). Falloon and colleagues (1984) innovation was to utilise these findings to motivate the development of a structured, skills-based programme that directly targeted criticism and interpersonal stress within families.

Grounded in the vulnerability-stress model, BFT conceptualised schizophrenia as the result of an interaction between biological predisposition and environmental stressors, with family dynamics playing a central role (Falloon et al., 1984). The therapy aimed to reduce interpersonal stress by equipping families with practical tools to manage symptoms and prevent crises. Psychoeducation was the first step: relatives learned that schizophrenia was a medical condition rather than a character flaw, thus reframing blame and reducing the impulse toward critical remarks. This shift in attribution was essential for lowering hostility and fostering empathy.

Communication training formed the core of BFT's strategy to reduce criticism. Families practiced speaking in clear, calm and supportive ways, replacing negative comments with constructive statements. Role-playing exercises allowed relatives to rehearse common conflicting scenarios, while therapists provided corrective feedback to reinforce adaptive patterns. Homework assignments extended these skills into daily life, encouraging family members to monitor their tone and language during stressful interactions. By systematically reinforcing positive communication and discouraging hostile exchanges, BFT sought to transform the emotional climate of the home.

Problem-solving training complemented these efforts by offering families a structured approach to managing challenges. Instead of reacting with frustration or blame, relatives learned to define problems, generate solutions, and implement plans collaboratively. This method reduced emotional reactivity and minimised opportunities for criticism during crises. Over the course of nine to twelve months, families engaged in regular sessions that combined these techniques with behavioural reinforcement, creating predictable and supportive environments for recovery (Falloon, 1988).

The impact of BFT was profound. Controlled trials demonstrated that when combined with pharmacotherapy, BFT reduced relapse rates substantially compared to standard care (e.g. Falloon et al., 1985). These findings established as evidence-based practice and they influenced treatment guidelines worldwide. By focusing on reducing criticism and high EE through structured communication and problem-solving, Falloon's work shifted the paradigm of schizophrenia care, positioning families as active partners in treatment rather than passive observers.

Several derivative models emerged to refine and expand strategies for reducing criticism and high EE by building on the principles of BFT. Among these, family focused therapy (FFT) stands out as one of the most widely studied and applied approaches, particularly in the treatment of bipolar disorder. FFT retains the core elements of psychoeducation, communication training and problem-solving introduced by Falloon and colleagues (1984), but integrates additional components to address mood regulation and relapse prevention in a broader range of serious mental illnesses.

Similar to BFT, FFT typically begins with an intensive psychoeducational phase, helping families to understand the biological and psychosocial underpinnings of the illness and the role of EE in symptom exacerbation (Miklowitz & Goldstein, 1997). This knowledge reframes illness-related behaviours as symptoms rather than personal failings, reducing blame and criticism. The second phase emphasises communication enhancement training, where families learn and practise skills such as expressing positive feelings, making constructive requests and negotiating disagreements without hostility. Role-playing and therapist feedback are central to this process, ensuring that families replace critical or accusatory statements with supportive, solution-focused dialogue. Finally, FFT incorporates structured problem-solving sessions to help families collaboratively address stressors that could trigger episodes, thereby reducing emotional volatility and opportunities for criticism.

As with BFT, empirical evidence supports FFT's effectiveness in lowering EE and improving clinical outcomes in mood disorders. Randomised controlled trials have shown that FFT, when combined with pharmacotherapy, significantly reduces relapse rates and improves medication adherence compared to standard care (Miklowitz et al., 2000; Rea et al., 2003). These findings underscore the enduring influence of Falloon's original framework while highlighting the adaptability of family-based interventions across diagnostic categories.

6.3 Culturally informed therapy for schizophrenia (CIT-S)

CIT-S was developed by Weisman de Mamani and colleagues (2014, 2021, 2023), and it extends the principles of earlier family-based interventions by incorporating cultural values, spiritual beliefs and family traditions into treatment. This approach recognises that criticism and high EE often arise when family members interpret symptoms through a lens of personal responsibility or moral failure. By reframing these interpretations within culturally meaningful frameworks, CIT-S helps families reduce blame and hostility while strengthening cohesion and support.

Unlike traditional BFT/FFT models that begin with psychoeducation, CIT-S starts with a collectivism module, which emphasises family unity, interdependence and shared responsibility. This initial focus sets the tone for collaboration and reduces individual blame, creating a supportive environment from the outset. Families are encouraged to draw on cultural narratives that highlight compassion and communal values, which helps counteract critical attributions and high EE attitudes, and promotes understanding.

CIT-S (Weisman de Mamani et al., 2021) then addresses psychoeducation, similar to BFT and FFT, but explores cultural views of healing and stigma around mental illness. This process not only reduces critical attributions, but also promotes empathy by aligning illness explanations with the family's worldview. Another key component of CIT-S (Weisman de Mamani et al., 2021) is the integration of spiritual practices, such as prayer or mindfulness, when these are consistent with the family's beliefs. These practices serve as stress-reduction tools and provide alternative coping strategies that replace emotionally charged high-EE exchanges with collaborative problem-solving.

The final two modules of CIT-S are communication training and problem solving, and they are similar to those in BFT and FFT but include cultural adaptations that make them more effective for diverse families. CIT-S emphasises culturally congruent language and respect-based interaction patterns, which help reduce harsh or judgemental tones that often fuel high EE. In these modules, therapists guide families to align communication strategies with their core values and to 'pick their battles wisely'. This means learning to distinguish between issues that truly matter and those that can be set aside to preserve harmony. For example, consider a spouse who, after becoming ill, resists leaving the house but agrees to attend church, a practice that holds deep cultural and spiritual significance for the family, yet insists on wearing jeans instead of more formal attire. Rather than escalating conflict over clothing, the therapist helps the family recognise the greater value in supporting church attendance and social engagement. By reframing priorities and respecting cultural norms, this approach reduces unnecessary criticism, fosters flexibility, and strengthens collaboration, ultimately lowering EE.

Empirical studies have shown that CIT-S improves patient outcomes, including symptom severity and quality of life, compared to standard psychoeducation (Weisman de Mamani et al., 2014, 2023). By embedding cultural and spiritual resources into therapy, CIT-S offers a nuanced pathway for reducing criticism and fostering a supportive family environment. Importantly, research indicates that increases in family cohesion serve as a key mechanism of change. Brown and Weisman de Mamani (2018) found that CIT-S significantly enhanced family cohesion, which in turn mediated reductions in emotional distress among patients and relatives. This suggests that strengthening family bonds, through culturally congruent communication and value-based problem solving, is central to lowering EE and improving overall wellbeing.

6.4 Multi-family group therapy (MFGT)

Multi-family group therapy (MFGT) was pioneered by McFarlane and colleagues (1995), and it represents another evidence-based approach for reducing high EE in families of individuals with schizophrenia and other serious mental illnesses. Unlike single-FIs, MFGT brings together multiple families in a shared therapeutic setting, creating a community of support and learning. This structure helps normalise experiences, reduces isolation and diminishes the sense of blame that often fuels criticism and hostility within families (McFarlane, 2002).

The mechanism by which MFGT lowers EE is multifaceted. First, psychoeducation is delivered in a group format, allowing families to hear diverse perspectives and recognise that illness-related behaviours are symptoms rather than personal failings. This collective reframing reduces critical attributions and fosters empathy. Second, the group setting provides opportunities for modelling and reinforcement of adaptive communication. Families observe others practising constructive dialogue and problem-solving, which helps them internalise non-critical interaction patterns. Over time, these skills generalise to the home environment, reducing negative emotional exchanges (McFarlane, 2002; McFarlane et al., 1995).

Another key feature of MFGT is its emphasis on collaborative problem-solving across families. By working together on common challenges, such as medication adherence or managing stress, participants in the group learn structured strategies that replace reactive, blame-oriented responses with proactive solutions. The supportive network created within the group also buffers stress, making it less likely that relatives will resort to criticism during crises. Empirical studies have demonstrated that MFGT significantly reduces relapse rates and improves family functioning, with reductions in EE serving as a primary mediator of these outcomes (McFarlane, 2002; McFarlane et al., 1995). By combining psychoeducation, skill-building and peer support, MFGT offers a powerful intervention for transforming high-EE environments into collaborative, low-stress systems of care.

6.5 Case example

In the following section, we illustrate how family therapy techniques can be applied in a clinical setting. To do this, we integrate strategies from BFT, FFT and CIT-S to demonstrate their combined impact on reducing criticism and high EE. This integration is presented through a hypothetical case example of the Rivera family, which highlights how these approaches work together to foster collaboration, improve communication, and strengthen cultural and relational bonds.

6.5.1 Background

Marisol Rivera is a 27-year-old Mexican American woman living with her parents, Elena and Roberto, and her younger brother, Diego, in Homestead, Florida. The Riveras immigrated from Michoacán when Marisol was eight, joining extended family already established in the area. Their home is warm, lively, and often filled with relatives dropping by unannounced. The family identifies as culturally Catholic, though they attend church only on holidays. Their spirituality is expressed more through family rituals, lighting candles for deceased relatives, keeping a small altar with photos of grandparents and offering quiet moments of reflection during difficult times.

Marisol was diagnosed with schizophrenia at age 24 after a period of escalating stress. She had been working full-time at a bakery while taking night classes at a community college. During finals week, she began sleeping very little, convinced that classmates were whispering about her. She later reported hearing a woman's voice calling her name at night, sometimes urging her to 'stay alert'. Her family initially attributed these experiences to exhaustion or 'nervios', a common cultural idiom for stress.

The situation escalated when Marisol left home one evening and was found hours later sitting on a curb outside a closed supermarket, speaking softly to someone who wasn't there. After a brief hospitalisation, she began medication and outpatient treatment. Her symptoms improved, but the family struggled to adjust to the new reality.

6.5.2 *Family dynamics and sources of criticism*

The Riveras are a close-knit family with strong interdependence. Elena, the mother, is nurturing but anxious. She often hovers over Marisol, asking repeatedly whether she has taken her medication, eaten enough or slept well. Her worry frequently turns into criticism: 'You need to try harder', 'You can't keep forgetting things', 'Other people work and study without these problems'. She believes she is motivating her daughter, but Marisol experiences these comments as painful reminders of her limitations.

Roberto, the father, is quieter but firm. He works long hours in construction and sees himself as the family's stabilising force. He loves Marisol deeply but struggles to understand her illness. He interprets her withdrawal as laziness and her cognitive difficulties as lack of discipline. When frustrated, he raises his voice, insisting that she 'snap out of it' or 'stop letting the illness win'.

Diego, age 19, is protective of his sister but is often caught in the middle. He tries to defuse arguments but sometimes joins in the criticism when overwhelmed. He misses the version of Marisol who used to help him with homework, drive him to soccer practice and joke around with him.

The family's high EE, particularly criticism and over-involvement, creates a tense environment that exacerbates Marisol's symptoms. She becomes quieter, more withdrawn and more fearful of disappointing her family. Her therapist recommends family-based work to help reduce criticism, improve communication and create a more supportive environment.

6.5.3 *Beginning therapy*

The first session opens with a brief moment of silence, a practice the therapist introduces as a way to 'set intentions for the hour'. The Riveras appreciate this gentle ritual, which feels familiar to their cultural traditions without being overtly religious. The therapist invites each family member to share what they hope will change.

Marisol says she wants 'peace at home'. Elena wants her daughter to 'be responsible again'. Roberto wants to 'understand what's happening'. Diego simply wants 'less fighting'. The therapist listens carefully, validating each perspective while highlighting the shared desire for harmony. The family is surprised to hear how similar their goals sound when spoken aloud.

6.5.4 *Understanding the illness together*

In early sessions, the therapist helps the family understand the symptoms that Marisol experiences, her difficulty concentrating, her tendency to misinterpret social cues and her occasional fearfulness. The therapist explains these symptoms in simple, non-judgemental language, emphasising that they are part of the illness rather than personal failings.

Elena begins to cry when she realises that Marisol's forgetfulness is not intentional. Roberto looks down, visibly uncomfortable, as he hears how stress and criticism can worsen symptoms. Diego nods, saying he had suspected this but didn't know how to explain it to their parents.

The therapist gently redirects the conversation towards what the family *can* do to help. They discuss how tone of voice, pacing and clarity can make communication easier for Marisol. The therapist models speaking slowly, using short sentences and checking for understanding without sounding patronising. The family practises these skills in session. At first, Roberto feels awkward, but when Marisol smiles and says, 'That helps', he softens.

6.5.5 *Addressing criticism and emotional climate*

As therapy progresses, the therapist helps the Riveras identify moments when criticism arises. Elena admits that she often scolds Marisol when she is scared. 'If I don't push her, she won't get better', she says. The therapist validates her fear but reframes the idea of 'pushing', suggesting that encouragement and structure may be more effective than criticism.

Roberto acknowledges that he raises his voice when he feels helpless. 'I don't know how to fix this', he says. The therapist normalises his frustration and helps him explore alternative ways of expressing concern.

The family practises replacing critical statements with supportive ones. For example:

- Instead of 'You always forget things,' Elena tries, 'Let's write this down together so it's easier to remember.'
- Instead of 'Why aren't you trying harder?' Roberto says, 'How can I help make this task easier for you?'
- Diego learns to step in early when tension rises, using humour or gentle redirection.

The therapist reinforces every small success, helping the family notice how Marisol responds when the emotional climate is calmer.

How to replace critical statements with supportive ones in therapy:

- Write down the alternative style of communication; e.g. instead of 'Why aren't you trying harder?' say, 'How can I help make this task easier for you?'
- Scaffold the steps needed to change the difficult situation by joint action, 'How can I understand the situation differently so that we can resolve it together more easily next time?'

6.5.6 *Strengthening family bonds*

The therapist encourages the Riveras to reconnect with activities they once enjoyed together. They begin taking short evening walks, cooking meals as a family and visiting Marisol's aunt on Sundays. These shared experiences help rebuild trust and reduce the focus on Marisol's symptoms. The therapist also invites the family to reflect on their cultural strengths, loyalty, warmth and collective responsibility. These values become a foundation for their progress. The family begins to see themselves not as a group struggling with illness but as a team working together.

6.5.7 *Moments of tension and growth*

Not every session is smooth. One afternoon, Marisol arrives visibly upset after an argument with her mother. Elena had scolded her for leaving a pot on the stove unattended, raising her voice and saying, 'You can't keep making these mistakes. You're going to hurt someone.' Marisol shut down immediately, retreating to her room for the rest of the day.

In session, the therapist invites each person to describe what happened from their perspective. Elena explains that she panicked; her own mother once started a kitchen fire, and the memory still frightens her. Roberto says he came home to find the house tense and didn't know how to help. Diego admits he tried to distract Marisol but felt helpless.

The therapist slows the conversation, helping the family identify the emotions beneath their reactions. Elena realises that her criticism came from fear, not anger. Marisol shares that she already felt embarrassed, and the scolding made her feel 'like a child'. Roberto acknowledges that he tends to withdraw when overwhelmed, which leaves Elena feeling alone in managing the household.

The therapist guides the family through a structured communication exercise. Each person practises expressing concerns using calm tone, short statements and a focus on specific behaviours rather than character judgements. They rehearse the stove incident:

- Elena practises saying, ‘I got scared when I saw the pot. Can we think of a way to help you remember when something is cooking?’
- Marisol practises responding with, ‘I didn’t mean to forget. I want to find a way to avoid that happening again.’

The therapist highlights how this exchange feels different, less charged, more collaborative. The family agrees.

How to diffuse tension in a crisis:

- Partake in finding a solution by taking ownership instead of expecting one person to take responsibility. Practise saying, ‘Can we think of a way to remember when the stove is on?’ or ‘Can we take turns in who keeps an eye on the stove?’

6.5.8 *Building practical skills*

Over the next several sessions, the therapist helps the Riveras develop concrete strategies to reduce stress and prevent misunderstandings at home. They create a shared household plan that includes:

- A whiteboard in the kitchen where Marisol writes down tasks she starts
- A family agreement to check in calmly rather than criticise
- A routine of short evening walks to decompress together
- A signal word (‘pause’) that anyone can use when conversations become heated.

How to generalise the practice of constructive communication strategies:

- Create a writing space, such as a magnetic whiteboard on the fridge, for the changes each person could make.
- Develop a habit of speaking calmly and taking ownership of making changes in sensitive situations.
- Plan shared outdoor activities, such as going for walks.

The therapist also helps Marisol identify early signs of stress such as tightness in her chest, difficulty focusing or hearing faint whispers. The family practises responding supportively when these signs appear. Instead of panicking or scolding, they offer grounding strategies: sitting together, dimming lights or taking a brief walk outside. These small adjustments begin to shift the emotional climate at home. Marisol reports fewer moments of feeling overwhelmed, and her family notices she is more engaged and willing to participate in daily activities.

6.5.9 *Cultural strengths and family identity*

The therapist encourages the Riveras to reflect on the cultural values that have sustained them through past challenges. Elena speaks about the importance of '*sacar adelante a la familia*', lifting the family up together. Roberto recalls how his own father taught him that strength includes patience. Diego mentions that their extended family often rallies around one another during difficult times.

The therapist helps them to see how these values can support Marisol's recovery. Instead of interpreting her symptoms as personal shortcomings, they begin to view their role as one of collective support. The family starts incorporating small cultural rituals into their routine. For example, they light a candle for calm before difficult conversations, sharing a quiet moment of gratitude before meals, and visiting Marisol's grandmother on Sundays. These practices help the family reconnect with a sense of unity and purpose.

6.5.10 *A turning point*

A notable shift occurs when Marisol volunteers to help her aunt at a weekend market. Previously, she avoided unfamiliar environments, fearing she might misinterpret people's expressions or conversations. But with her family's encouragement and the communication tools they've practised, she feels more confident. After the event, she proudly tells the therapist that she managed the cash box for an hour and chatted with customers. Elena beams with pride. Roberto says he hadn't seen her that animated in years. Diego jokes that she's now the 'market queen'. The therapist uses this moment to reinforce the family's progress. They reflect on how reduced criticism, clearer communication and a calmer home environment have contributed to Marisol's increased confidence.

6.5.11 *Preparing for future challenges*

As therapy nears its end, the therapist helps the Riveras anticipate future stressors. They discuss how to respond if Marisol becomes overwhelmed, forgets tasks or misinterprets social cues. The family practices supportive responses, emphasising patience and collaboration.

They also identify warning signs that may indicate that Marisol needs additional support, such as changes in sleep, increased withdrawal or heightened suspicion. The therapist encourages them to approach these signs with curiosity rather than fear or blame.

The family creates a written plan outlining:

- How to communicate concerns
- When to contact Marisol's psychiatrist
- How to reduce household stress during difficult periods
- Ways to maintain their own wellbeing

The therapist praises their commitment, noting that their willingness to work together has already transformed their home environment.

6.5.12 *End of treatment*

By the end of treatment, the Riveras have developed a more compassionate and supportive way of interacting with one another. Criticism has decreased significantly, replaced by collaborative problem-solving and clearer communication. Marisol reports feeling safer and more understood at home, which has helped reduce her stress and improve her daily functioning. Elena expresses gratitude for learning how to support her daughter without overwhelming her. Roberto says he feels more connected to his family and more confident in his ability to help. Diego notes that the house feels 'lighter', with fewer arguments and more shared laughter.

The therapist ends the final session with a brief moment of reflection, inviting the family to acknowledge how far they've come. The Riveras leave with renewed confidence in their ability to navigate challenges together, grounded in their cultural strengths, improved communication and a shared commitment to supporting Marisol's recovery.

How to lower expressed emotion, your perception of expressed emotion in others and develop supportive communication styles:

Practise how to provide constructive criticism, rather than hostile criticism:

- Write down a typical criticism.
- Make it constructive. Here's an example of a criticism: 'You spend too much time watching television. We don't get enough time to talk to each other.' Change it to a constructive criticism: 'We could

watch the television. Let's also try to spend more time doing other things like reading together and chatting to each other.'

Listening to criticism can be challenging at times, especially when it is not accompanied by guidance on how to grow from the criticism. Share your learning from the feedback with that person. Ask the person who criticised you to suggest how they might respond in that situation and what might be a good way to address the criticism.
Change the amount of cohesiveness:

- Rate on a scale of 1 to 10 how clear the boundaries are between family members.
- Define boundaries and sharing time and space together. Are all family members involved in making decisions about family activities?

6.6 Directions for future research

The National Institute for Health and Care Excellence in the UK recommends that FI be a primary intervention for schizophrenia (National Institute for Health and Care Excellence, 2014), and this applies even to early interventions for psychosis where FI significantly reduces relapse compared to standard care (Bird et al., 2010). FI is cost-effective. Yet, the reality is that FI is rarely delivered (Onwumere et al., 2016). The gap between recommendation and delivery arises from limited resources and specialist training. One step for future improvement of psychoeducation is to present a range of explanations of symptoms, such as social, biological and cognitive. This is important because if the goal of FI is to alleviate distress from family EE, such as criticism and overprotection, then helping the family to understand the symptoms of mental distress from different perspectives can have a positive outcome.

For example, hearing voices (also known as auditory hallucinations) is a psychological phenomenon characterised by perceiving voices in one's mind as distinct from one's own thoughts, such that they are beyond the person's control and appear to come from an external source (American Psychiatric Association, 2015). One explanation of hearing voices is that the voices relate to how the person thinks about their social relationships (Hayward, 2003). Furthermore, the voices can be critical, rejecting, controlling and threatening (Berry et al., 2012). For instance, the power struggles in voices can resemble the differences in power between the voice hearer's many social relationships

(Birchwood et al., 2000). Therefore, relating to the voices in a dominant way, such as in terms of the voices gaining advantage over others, has been found to be related to voice-hearers gaining advantage over others in their relationships (Hayward, 2003). In addition, relating to the voices closely, such as clinging to the voices, has been found to be related to closeness to others in the relationships of voice hearers (Hayward, 2003). These findings reinforce the value of understanding primary symptoms of serious mental illness, such as hearing voices, as existing through relationships with significant others and wider social networks. Drawing such an association between symptoms of serious mental illness and the goals of psychological intervention can also help families understand the need to engage in FI. Incorporating such social models of psychiatric symptoms into psychoeducation are directions for further development of FI.

6.7 Conclusion

To summarise, BFT, FFT, CIT-S and MFT are different systemic approaches to reducing high EE towards patients with a serious mental illness. Psychoeducation about the nature of the symptoms can help family members foresee the recurrence of symptoms after a period of remission and take steps to avert the frank onset of symptoms. Key to psychoeducation is taking away the blame of the event from each member of the family and offering a medical explanation. CIT-S emphasises the collectivistic beliefs of family unity, interdependence and shared responsibility, and leverages them to reinforce support, cohesion and collective problem-solving. Again, such steps can reduce hostility and emotional over-involvement, and reduce stigma. Addressing the cognitive appraisal of illness and the caring role through caregiver-focused intervention can alleviate the burden of care. Developing practical steps, such as speaking calmly, keeping reminders of reframing feedback in a constructive way, organising shared family events such as going for walks and family members taking ownership in facilitating change, can sustain the benefits of family-based interventions.

References

American Psychiatric Association. (2015). *Schizophrenia spectrum and other psychotic disorders: DSM-5® selections* (1st ed.). American Psychiatric Publishing.

Berry, K., Wearden, A., Barrowclough, C., Oakland, L., & Bradley, J. (2012). An investigation of adult attachment and the nature of relationships with voices. *British Journal of Clinical Psychology*, *51*(3), 280–291. 10.1111/j.2044-8260.2011.02027.x

Birchwood, M., Meaden, A., Trower, P., Gilbert, P., & Plaistow, J. (2000). The power and omnipotence of voices: Subordination and entrapment by voices and significant others. *Psychological Medicine*, *30*(2), 337–344.

Bird, V., Premkumar, P., Kendall, T., Whittington, C., Mitchell, J., & Kuipers, E. (2010). Early intervention services, cognitive-behavioural therapy and family intervention in early psychosis: systematic review. *The British Journal of Psychiatry: The Journal of Mental Science*, *197*(5), 350–356. 10.1192/bjp.bp.109.074526 [doi]

Brown, C. A., & Weisman de Mamani, A. (2018). The mediating effect of family cohesion in reducing patient symptoms and family distress in a culturally informed family therapy for schizophrenia: A parallel-process latent-growth model. *Journal of Consulting and Clinical Psychology*, *86*(1), 1–14. 10.1037/ccp0000257

Brown, G. W., Birley, J. L. T., & Wing, J. K. (1972). Influence of family life on the course of schizophrenic disorders: A replication. *British Journal of Psychiatry*, *121*(562), 241–258. 10.1192/bjp.121.3.241

Brown, G. W., Bone, M., Dalison, B., & Wing, J. K. (1966). *Schizophrenia and social care: A Comparative follow-up study of 339 schizophrenic patients*. London: Oxford University Press. 10.1016/S0033-3506(66)80062-8

Brown, G. W., Monck, E. M., Carstairs, G. M., & Wing, J. K. (1962). Influence of family life on the course of schizophrenic illness. *British Journal of Preventive & Social Medicine*, *16*(2), 55–68. 10.1136/jech.16.2.55

Falloon, I. R., Boyd, J. L., McGill, C. W., Williamson, M., Razani, J., Moss, H. B., Gilderman, A. M., & Simpson, G. M. (1985). Family management in the prevention of morbidity of schizophrenia. Clinical outcome of a two-year longitudinal study. *Archives of General Psychiatry*, *42*(9), 887–896. 10.1001/archpsyc.1985.01790320059008

Falloon, I. R. H. (1988). *Handbook of behavioural family therapy*. Routledge.

Falloon, I. R. H., Boyd, J. L., & McGill, C. W. (1984). *Family care of schizophrenia: A problem-solving approach to the treatment of mental illness*. Guilford Press.

Garety, P. A., Fowler, D. G., Freeman, D., Bebbington, P., Dunn, G., & Kuipers, E. (2008). Cognitive-behavioural therapy and family intervention for relapse prevention and symptom reduction in psychosis: Randomised controlled trial. *British Journal of Psychiatry*, *192*(6), 412–423. 10.1192/bjp.bp.107.043570

Hayward, M. (2003). Interpersonal relating and voice hearing: To what extent does relating to the voice reflect social relating? *Psychology and Psychotherapy*, *76*(4), 369–383. 10.1348/147608303770584737

Kuipers, E. (2006). Family interventions in schizophrenia: evidence for efficacy and proposed mechanisms of change. *Journal of Family Therapy*, *28*(1), 73–80. 10.1111/j.1467-6427.2006.00338.x

Kuipers, E., Leff, J. P., & Lam, D. (2002). *Family work for schizophrenia: A practical guide* (2nd ed.). Gaskell.

Kuipers, E., Onwumere, J., & Bebbington, P. (2010). Cognitive model of caregiving in psychosis. *British Journal of Psychiatry*, *196*(4), 259–265. 10.1192/bjp.bp.109.070466

Kuipers, E., Watson, P., Onwumere, J., Bebbington, P., Dunn, G., Weinman, J., Fowler, D., Freeman, D., Hardy, A., & Garety, P. (2007). Discrepant illness perceptions, affect and expressed emotion in people with psychosis and their carers. *Social Psychiatry and Psychiatric Epidemiology*, *42*(4), 277–283. 10.1007/s00127-007-0165-4

Leff, J., Kuipers, L., Berkowitz, R., Eberlein-Vries, R., & Sturgeon, D. (1982). A controlled trial of social intervention in the families of schizophrenic patients. *British Journal of Psychiatry*, *141*(2), 121–134. 10.1192/bjp.141.2.121

Leff, J., Kuipers, L., Berkowitz, R., & Sturgeon, D. (1985). A controlled trial of social intervention in the families of schizophrenic patients: Two year follow-up. *British Journal of Psychiatry*, *146*(6), 594–600. 10.1192/bjp.146.6.594

McFarlane, W. R. (2002). *Multifamily groups in the treatment of severe psychiatric disorders*. Guilford Press.

McFarlane, W. R., Lukens, E., Link, B., Dushay, R., Deakins, S. A., Newmark, M., Dunne, E. J., Horen, B., & Toran, J. (1995). Multiple-family groups and psychoeducation in the treatment of schizophrenia. *Archives of General Psychiatry*, *52*(8), 679–687. 10.1001/archpsyc.1995.03950200069016

Miklowitz, D. J., & Goldstein, M. J. (1997). *Bipolar disorder: A family-focused treatment approach*. Guilford Press.
Miklowitz, D. J., Simoneau, T. L., George, E. L., Richards, J. A., Kalbag, A., Sachs-Ericsson, N., & Suddath, R. (2000). Family-focused treatment of bipolar disorder: 1-year effects of a psychoeducational program in conjunction with pharmacotherapy. *Biological Psychiatry (1969)*, *48*(6), 582–592. 10.1016/S0006-3223(00)00931-8
National Institute for Health and Care Excellence. (2014). *CG178: Psychosis and schizophrenia in adults: prevention and management*. National Institute for Health and Care Excellence. https://www.nice.org.uk/Guidance/CG178
National Institute of Health and Care Excellence. (2002). *NICE real-world evidence framework*. National Institute of Health and Care Excellence. https://www.nice.org.uk/corporate/ecd9/chapter/introduction-to-real-world-evidence-in-nice-decision-making
Onwumere, J., Bonetto, C., Lasalvia, A., Miglietta, E., Veronese, A., Bellini, F., Imbesi, M., Bebbington, P., Kuipers, E., & Ruggeri, M. (2020). Predictors and moderators of burden of care and emotional distress in first-episode psychosis caregivers: results from the GET UP pragmatic cluster randomised controlled trial. *Epidemiology and Psychiatric Sciences*, *29*, e27. 10.1017/S2045796019000155
Onwumere, J., Grice, S., & Kuipers, E. (2016). Delivering cognitive-behavioural family interventions for schizophrenia. *Australian Psychologist*, *51*(1), 52–61. 10.1111/ap.12179
Onwumere, J., Sirykaite, S., Schulz, J., Man, E., James, G., Afsharzadegan, R., Khan, S., Harvey, R., Souray, J., & Raune, D. (2018). Understanding the experience of 'burnout' in first-episode psychosis carers. *Comprehensive Psychiatry*, *83*, 19–24. 10.1016/j.comppsych.2018.02.003
Pilling, S., Bebbington, P., Kuipers, E., Garety, P., Geddes, J., Orbach, G., & Morgan, C. (2002). Psychological treatments in schizophrenia: I. Meta-analysis of family intervention and cognitive behaviour therapy. *Psychological Medicine*, *32*(5), 763–782. 10.1017/S0033291702005895
Raune, D., Kuipers, E., & Bebbington, P. E. (2004). Expressed emotion at first-episode psychosis: investigating a carer appraisal model. *British Journal of Psychiatry*, *184*(4), 321–326. 10.1192/bjp.184.4.321
Rea, M. M., Tompson, M. C., Miklowitz, D. J., Goldstein, M. J., Hwang, S., & Mintz, J. (2003). Family-focused treatment versus individual treatment for bipolar disorder: Results of a randomized clinical trial. *Journal of Consulting and Clinical Psychology*, *71*(3), 482–492. 10.1037/0022-006X.71.3.482
Rodolico, A., Bighelli, I., Avanzato, C., Concerto, C., Cutrufelli, P., Mineo, L., Schneider-Thoma, J., Siafis, S., Signorelli, M. S., Wu, H., Wang, D., Furukawa, T. A., Pitschel-Walz, G., Aguglia, E., & Leucht, S. (2022). Family interventions for relapse prevention in schizophrenia: a systematic review and network meta-analysis. *The Lancet Psychiatry*, *9*(3), 211–221. 10.1016/S2215-0366(21)00437-5
Scazufca, M., & Kuipers, E. (1996). Links between expressed emotion and burden of care in relatives of patients with schizophrenia. *British Journal of Psychiatry*, *168*(5), 580–587. 10.1192/bjp.168.5.580
Weisman de Mamani, A., Lopez, D., McLaughlin, M. M., Ahmad, S. S., & Altamirano, O. (2023). A pilot study to assess the feasibility and efficacy of a transdiagnostic, religiously/spiritually-integrated, culturally informed therapy. *Spirituality in Clinical Practice* (Washington, D.C.), *10*(3), 233–244. 10.1037/scp0000308
Weisman de Mamani, A., McLaughlin, M., Altamirano, O., Lopez, D., & Ahmad, S. S. (2021). *Culturally informed therapy for schizophrenia: A family-focused cognitive behavioral approach*. Oxford University Press.

Weisman de Mamani, A., Weintraub, M. J., Gurak, K., & Maura, J. (2014). A randomized clinical trial to test the efficacy of a family-focused, culturally informed therapy for schizophrenia. *Journal of Family Psychology*, *28*(6), 800–810. 10.1037/fam0000021

Yesufu-Udechuku, A., Harrison, B., Mayo-Wilson, E., Young, N., Woodhams, P., Shiers, D., Kuipers, E., & Kendall, T. (2015). Interventions to improve the experience of caring for people with severe mental illness: systematic review and meta-analysis. *British Journal of Psychiatry*, *206*(4), 268–274. 10.1192/bjp.bp.114.147561

Chapter 7

Depict VR

A virtual-reality intervention for hearing voices and addressing perceived criticism in close relationships

Dominic Rees-Roberts, Jennifer Nicholls, Mark Hayward and Preethi Premkumar

Abstract

Digital mental health interventions (DMHIs) are expanding with the growth of digital technologies and the growing prevalence of mental health problems. We review the benefits of and barriers to implementing DMHIs. And we consider the aesthetic and functional criteria when designing meaningful virtual-reality (VR) interventions for mental health. We then spotlight Depict VR as a VR application for addressing hearing voices in connection with perceived criticism. Depict VR aims to allow young people to build their relationship with a trusted confidante. Preliminary evidence suggests that young people value Depict VR as a two-person VR intervention. Furthermore, clinicians in the Child and Adolescent Mental Health services regard Depict VR as a tool to facilitate therapeutic engagement with young people. The path to commercialisation and implementation in community settings of Depict VR are envisioned.

7.1 Introduction

Digital mental health interventions (DMHIs) are proliferating alongside the rapid advancement of digital technology (Hollis et al., 2017; Philippe et al., 2022; Wies et al., 2021). The explosion of DMHIs coincides with the growing prevalence of mental health problems in young people (Hollis et al., 2017). One in five young people experience mental disorders globally (World Health Organization, 2001). DMHIs take many forms, including smartphone applications, internet-based interventions, VR-based interventions and computer-based psychological therapy (Hollis et al., 2017; Wies et al., 2021). A plethora of smartphone interventions exist (>2,200), but only a small number are based on therapeutic principles and evidence clinical efficacy (Philippe et al., 2022). Internet-based interventions are also varied, and include psychoeducation, self-help therapy, journaling, assessments, reminders to take medication, motivational interventions and web-based peer support (Philippe et al., 2022).

DOI: 10.4324/9781003388159-8

DMHIs are more accessible than face-to-face interventions with a therapist, thus reducing the treatment gap and affordability, and balancing the power dynamics between patients and their therapist (Philippe et al., 2022; Wies et al., 2021). DMHIs offer young people autonomy, empowerment and an ability to implement coping strategies outside the therapeutic setting (Wies et al., 2021). In turn, young people value the privacy of DMHIs, since young people in the United Kingdom do not trust that their general practitioner will handle the young person's mental health concerns confidentially, and young people fear that their parents will find out (Dare et al., 2023; Leavey et al., 2011). Furthermore, young people in industrialised societies are digital natives and are accustomed to digital assessment of mental health and the internet as a source of information (Wies et al., 2021). However, DMHIs exclude cultures that lack the socio-economic resources to offer these services, especially in remote areas and in low-to-middle-income countries where internet access is poor (Wies et al., 2021).

When considering DMHIs for older adults, in contrast to young people, older patients with mental health problems prefer contact with the healthcare professional side-by-side with the DMHI (Philippe et al., 2022). Specifically, patients with schizophrenia are guarded and feel uncomfortable about DMHIs because they feel monitored. A small proportion of patients experience side-effects, such as headache (8%) and panic (7%) (Freeman et al., 2023). Nonetheless, VR-based interventions for symptoms of psychosis, such as paranoia and agoraphobia, have improved persecutory delusions, avoidance of crowds and distress (Freeman et al., 2016; Freeman, et al., 2022).

7.2 How to design an effective VR-based intervention

As with designing a face-to-face psychological therapy, designing a VR-based intervention is based on theoretical assumptions about improving specific psychological problems or symptoms. Using graded exposure therapy in a VR-based intervention relies on changing behaviours and confronting feared situations and is helpful in treating anxiety disorders (Knowles & Tolin, 2022). One technique used in graded exposure therapy is fear extinction (Knowles & Tolin, 2022). The key assumption underlying fear extinction is that the fear is a conditioned response (CR) to a neutral stimulus, and this scientific understanding of fear is based on the principles of classical conditioning as put forward by Ivan Pavlov (1927, cited in Lieberman, 2012a). Imagine a scenario where an electric spark sets a rug on fire in your living room. This natural event of the fire would be an unconditioned stimulus (US) according to the theory of classical conditioning. And consider that this outbreak of fire makes you fearful and disorganised. Then, the fear and disorganisation would be the unconditioned response (UR) to the US according to the theory of classical conditioning. Also imagine that your partner tells you, 'You need to handle electrical equipment carefully', when the rug catches fire. The theory of classical conditioning states that pairing the incident of the fire (US) with your partner passing this remark (conditioned stimulus; CS) causes you to associate your partner's remark with the rug catching fire. Thus, your partner telling you to handle electrical equipment carefully, which was previously a neutral stimulus, now becomes a source of fear and disorganisation because they were paired with the US (e.g. the outbreak of fire). Because you associated this remark (which was previously a neutral stimulus) with the US, the neutral stimulus becomes a CS and it produces fear and disorganisation. Then, fear and disorganisation become the CR to the CS which is your partner telling you to handle electrical equipment carefully. This sequence is explained in Table 6.1. Graded exposure therapy tries to eliminate this fear.

Another feature of fear conditioning is avoidance of the CS, such as criticism, and such avoidance prevents the extinction of fear (Knowles & Tolin, 2022). Avoiding such situations is a negative reinforcement because the avoidance of the feared CS reinforces the fear of the CS (Lieberman, 2012b) and it encourages future avoidance (Knowles & Tolin, 2022). Exposure therapy is based on the principles of fear extinction, and it seeks to weaken the association between the CS and the CR. One way to weaken this association is by pairing the CS with a new neutral stimulus (Knowles & Tolin, 2022), such as your partner reassuring you, for example by saying, 'You are really helpful in making me find solutions to my problems.' Alternatively, a way to reduce fear is to expose the person to the fear, allow the fear to elicit the feared memories and allow the person to habituate to it (Foa & Kozak, 1986). Still, this approach does not minimise the likelihood of the fear returning. Another approach is inhibition retrieval, and it aims to further reduce the likelihood of retrieving previously feared associations (Craske et al., 2022; Knowles & Tolin, 2022). Inhibition retrieval involves helping the client to identify unexpected outcomes to the feared CS which is an outcome known as expectancy violation, and it seeks to demonstrate a mismatch between the predicted fear of the CS and the actual fear experienced when encountering the CS (Craske et al., 2022; Knowles & Tolin, 2022). A relevant skill in inhibiting retrieval of fearful memories is perceived control (Healey et al., 2017). The perceived control over threat can determine how anxious individuals expose

Table 6.1 Theory of classical conditioning

1	US (rug catches fire) → UR (you become fearful, lose concentration and become disorganised)
2	US paired with neutral stimulus (Your partner telling you, 'You need to handle electrical equipment carefully') → CS (Your partner telling you, 'You need to handle electrical equipment carefully')
3	CS → CR (you become fearful, lose concentration and become disorganised)

Note: CR: conditioned response; CS: conditioned stimulus; UR: unconditioned response; US: unconditioned stimulus themselves to virtual threat during VR-based exposure therapy (VRET). Indeed, the ability to inhibit behaviours in response to negative situations explained the improvement in social anxiety and public-speaking anxiety in socially anxious individuals following VRET for social anxiety (Premkumar et al., 2024).

Designing a VR-based psychosocial intervention must involve gradual exposure to the sources of threat in order to enable fear extinction. This involves introducing incremental doses of different types of threat, such as the number of people in the environment and the severity of their expressions (Premkumar et al., 2021, 2024). In fact, 'ROOM' is a virtual social meet-up platform that is modelled on a group-based psychological intervention for socially withdrawn individuals (Holt et al., 2025). The goal of ROOM was to help a group of socially withdrawn individuals to reduce their social distance between each other and improve social functioning. Over six one-hour sessions, the group learned about mindfulness, self-compassion and mentalisation, and learned to draw closer to each other virtually. By the end of the intervention, participants reported lower social discomfort (Holt et al., 2025). Regarding sensitivity to criticism, such social relating could help to bridge gaps in understanding the distress felt by the vulnerable person, such as their symptoms and the impact of the criticism from the relative.

7.3 Modelling the digital intervention on family intervention

The design of Depict VR draws on some of the tenets of family intervention (FI). We review a case study where FI was designed for high perceived criticism (PC; Hooley & Miklowitz, 2017). The case study involved JJ, a young boy who was diagnosed with emotional disorders and whose parents expressed high expressed emotion (EE) due to expressing a high level of criticism and emotional over-involvement about JJ during the Five-Minute Speech Sample (Magaña et al., 1986). When JJ and his parents took part in a 10-minute problem-solving discussion around a common topic, namely video games, the parents launched into an elaborate criticism of JJ's engagement in video games. JJ defended himself and projected his temper to objects in the room and eventually recoiled into a placid posture in learned helplessness (Hooley & Miklowitz, 2017). The goals of the FI with the parents then involved the following:

1 Understanding the biological nature of JJ's emotional disorder and recognising JJ's diminished control over his behaviour
2 Recognising JJ's hypersensitivity to criticism and the need to reduce the frequency of criticism
3 Increasing the frequency of positive communication between JJ and his parents
4 Providing positive feedback to JJ without being controlling
5 Help JJ recognise his emotional reactions when the family said things that made him feel rejected and distinguish their emotions from their intensions.

How to observe the goals of family intervention and reduce the impact of criticism:

- Use trusted websites, such as the National Health Service (www.nhs.uk/mentalhealth) in the United Kingdom, to understand the nature of key symptoms of the mental health problem
- Recognise that people with mental health problems are sensitive to criticism
- Reduce the frequency of criticism by practising supportive ways of resolving situations together
- Use positive communication without being controlling
- Understanding the person's emotional reactions to things said that made the person feel rejected and distinguish their emotions from their intensions

The course of 12 sessions of family therapy involved psychoeducation, communication enhancement training and problem-solving skills training (four sessions of each) (Hooley & Miklowitz, 2017). Psychoeducation involved understanding the symptoms of depression and anxiety and recognising and attempting to reduce the impact of stressors. Communication enhancement training involved skills in expressing positive or negative feelings and active listening which proved especially enduring for the father who was highly critical of JJ. Problem-solving skills training involved learning to deconstruct conflict and resolve it using positive communication, and for JJ to label his emotions. The outcome of the intervention was that JJ was able to spend more quality time with his parents engaging in enjoyable activities.

FI was tested more elaborately in a randomised controlled trial (RCT) of adolescents at risk for psychosis and their significant other (Hooley & Miklowitz, 2017). One hundred and twenty-nine adolescents and young adults between 12 and 35 years of age in the United States of America met the criteria for clinical high risk for psychosis. They and their parent(s) or significant other took part of whom 90 dyads of young participants and their significant other completed therapy and the Perceived Criticism Measure. Participants were randomly assigned to either 18 sessions of FI or three sessions of enhanced care (Figure 7.1) and the intervention was delivered over six months. Participants and their mothers perceived less criticism of each other six months after intervention, i.e. 12 months after baseline, but this improvement did not differ between those who received FI and enhanced care. Furthermore, the improvement in positive symptoms at end of treatment (6 months) and follow-up (12 months) was greater in FI than enhanced care (Miklowitz et al., 2014) and the improvement in PC predicted improvement in positive symptoms, although not differently between FI and enhanced care (O'Brien et al., 2015).

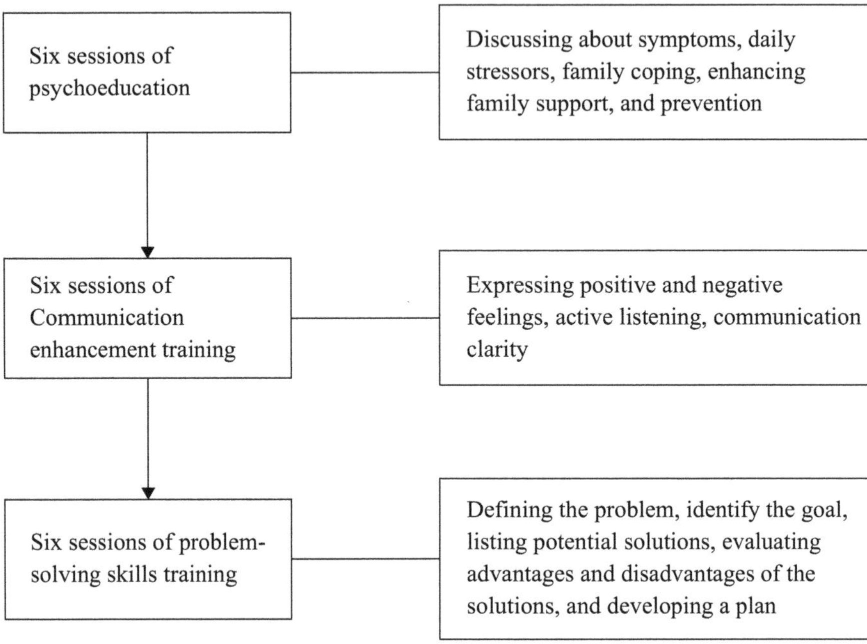

Figure 7.1 Format of family intervention.
Source: Schlosser et al. (2012).

7.3.1 Developing a good VR-based user-experience

There are standards for creating a good VR user-experience (LaRocco, 2020; Ramotion, 2023). The central tenets of best practice in VR design are to create a user-centred design, consider the comfort of the user, have consistency and coherence in the flow of information through the virtual space and create hierarchy in visual texture. Depict VR (see section 7.3.2) employs a virtual narrator to guide the user through the VR space and create a sense of comfort and flow through the experience. In addition, three-dimensional (3D) and four-dimensional (4D) VR environments can foster a sense of flow by helping the user to focus attention on certain visual cues around the virtual space and stimulate interaction between the user and the virtual environment at these junctures (Holt et al., 2025). The fourth dimension refers to listening to sounds and being able to touch objects in the virtual environment, while a 3D environment is limited to seeing things in three-dimensional visual display. Allowing users to rate the stimuli in the environment on arousal and valence at these junctures can also help to validate the emotions that the stimuli seek to elicit (Bradley & Lang, 1999; Marcolin et al., 2021). Creating scenarios and stimuli that reliably elicit valid emotions, such as surprise, happiness and anger, makes the experiences more authentic (Marcolin et al., 2021). In this way, it is possible to create a conducive environment for exposing distressed individuals to aversive social interactions whilst engaging in problem-solving transactions around resolving EE and difficult attachment issues. The virtual environment may bypass the negativity that face-to-face interactions may elicit between the vulnerable individual and the high EE relative (Masland & Hooley, 2015), but also confer the vulnerable individual control over the social interaction (Premkumar et al., 2021). Facilitating a conducive social interaction through the VR experience is particularly pertinent to addressing the goals of conflictual communication in FI.

The key considerations of good VR design are realism, immersion, presence, agency, embodiment and body ownership, multisensory synergetic stimuli, and dynamism and animations (Marcolin et al., 2021). With the advances in 3D and 4D VR technology, the realism of virtual environments is increasingly crucial for determining the effectiveness of VR-based interventions. Immersion refers to the quality of the hardware, software and graphical interface, such as visual resolution when eliciting the sensory experience and the rate at which users' responses are sampled when capturing the experience (Archer et al., 2022). Thus, using state-of-the-art hardware with good audiovisual resolution and rapid access memory, and using approved software, such as Unity and Unreal Engine, can create an immersive virtual environment. Presence refers to the sense of 'being there' in the virtual environment (Archer et al., 2022). It refers to the ability to examine and interact with features of the virtual environment, including the ability to touch objects and listen to sounds, and it refers to the realism of the virtual environment (Witmer & Singer, 1998). These interactive elements can improve the efficacy of the VR-based intervention, since the sense of presence in terms of being able to examine the virtual environment was found to explain improvements in public-speaking anxiety in socially anxious participants after three VRET sessions (Premkumar et al., 2024).

7.3.2 Observing ethical standards in digital mental health interventions

An ethical code of conduct is needed when designing DMHIs to improve access to healthcare services (Wykes et al., 2019). Yet, the proliferation of DMHIs raises concerns for healthcare providers, namely that the interventions are not subjected to extensive and rigorous professional evaluation to test the long-term efficacy and tolerability of the interventions in the same way as traditional clinician-led mental health interventions (Hall et al., 2024; Hollis et al., 2017). Users of DMHIs are not monitored to the same extent as clinician-led interventions (Hall et al., 2024). Secure storage of user data may not meet the standards of data protection regulation. There are also criteria for claiming the efficacy of an intervention. The number of therapy sessions to produce a lasting effect must be predetermined (Hollis et al., 2017). The primary outcome measure and the cut-off point of improvement that represents a clinically significant improvement must be decided beforehand when designing the intervention (Andrade, 2015; Jacobson & Truax, 1991; Premkumar et al., 2024). Another ethical issue relates to exclusion of minoritised groups from the intervention, such as racialised people, disabled people and less educated people (Hall et al., 2024; Zhao et al., 2023). The DMHIs must meet global standards in addressing cultural differences in the experience of mental health problems, such as depression (Hall et al., 2024). For this, diverse groups must be involved in the design of DMHIs to make them more inclusive (Wykes et al., 2019).

7.4 *Designing Depict VR*: a self-guided virtual reality application

In 2023, we received funding from Innovate UK (Mindset XR/Innovate UK, Grant number 10108207) and designed Depict VR. Depict VR is a unique virtual-reality (VR) mental health intervention that involves an interaction between two people in real time and it is designed to encourage young people to share mental health concerns with a trusted confidante (a family member or friend; www.depictvr.com). Here, a trusted confidante can be a close relative, or a close friend in case the young person struggles to discuss their difficulties with their parent or other close relative. Young people often have close friends who they confide in outside the family. This is because young people struggle to disclose mental distress to their parents and healthcare professionals (Ryan et al., 2021). Depict VR operates on MetaQuest (Figure 7.2) where hand-held controllers allow the user to select features and interact with objects. The headset has inbuilt audio to listen to sounds and create a four-dimensional experience.

7.4.1 *User-led development through patient and public involvement*

Co-creating the virtual environment with the target population, e.g. young mental health service users, can create realistic virtual spaces that addresses their needs and minimises harm (Realpe et al., 2020). For instance, young mental health service users like the virtual environment to reflect the real-world therapeutic settings, such as therapy rooms (Realpe et al., 2020). Therefore, before designing Depict VR, the developers (DRR and PP) engaged

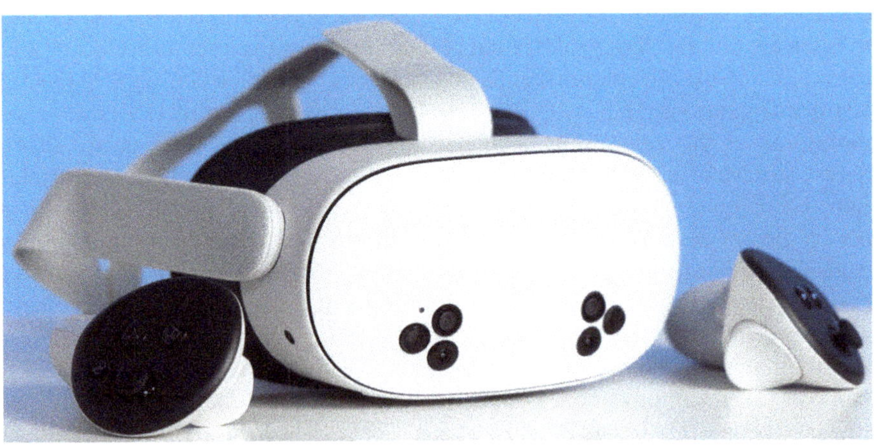

Figure 7.2 A MetaQuest virtual reality headset with two hand controllers.

in patient and public involvement (PPI) research with an adolescent and an adult who heard voices to enquire about how people who hear voices might value a VR experience to help build relationships. The adolescent who had experiences of hearing voices described the voices as demonic, haunting, harassing, possessing and reawakening past trauma. The unprovoked attack of the voices affected the young person's sleep rhythm, alienated them and made them fearful in public spaces which resulted in the voices multiplying. The young person also found it difficult to share their experiences with their family because they were not sure how their family would respond to them and the young person thought their family members might humiliate them. Crucially, the two PPI participants expressed a desire for an easy-to-access VR-based intervention to help relieve the trauma of hearing voices. The adult PPI voice-hearer was willing to confront their fear of public spaces in a VR setting and become resilient and stronger when outdoors. Their desire to address fear of crowds resonates with the evidence that gameChange, a VR intervention to address fear of crowds, helps patients with psychosis (Freeman, et al., 2022). Likewise, the young voice-hearer thought it might be safer and easier to share experiences in a virtual space. The young person suggested that having images of people or pets that the young person feels safe with in the virtual environment might create a sense of safety.

7.4.2 Creating a sense of control and agency in the virtual environment

Shorter waiting times, less reliance on a trained practitioner to deliver the intervention, cost-effectiveness, having a greater sense of active control in their own treatment and balancing the power dynamics between patients and their therapist are some of the benefits of the self-guided format (Premkumar et al., 2021, 2024; Wies et al., 2021). A self-guided format is where the intervention is delivered without input from a therapist (Hall et al., 2024). Perceived control is vital in determining the effectiveness of self-guided therapies (Healey et al., 2017; Premkumar et al., 2024). Therefore, in Depict VR, the young person has control over the appearance of the virtual environment. The young person takes on the role of the 'main participant' and chooses the spoken criticisms and praises that appear in the virtual environment for discussion with their confidante. The young person also chooses the voice of the virtual guide or narrator (male or female) and the voice of the comments (male or female). The main participant can also choose between a realistic living room and a stylised farmyard for the virtual environment that they can navigate (Figure 7.3a and b). We deliberately created a highly animated and surreal outdoor space in case a more realistic outdoor space provoked fear. Once inside this space, the main participant can change the lighting and colour of the environment. Furthermore, spotlights guide the participant from one key station to another (Figure 7.3a). This emphasis on the young person to control the environment can increase their perceived control over the interaction with their confidante and provide a sense of autonomy.

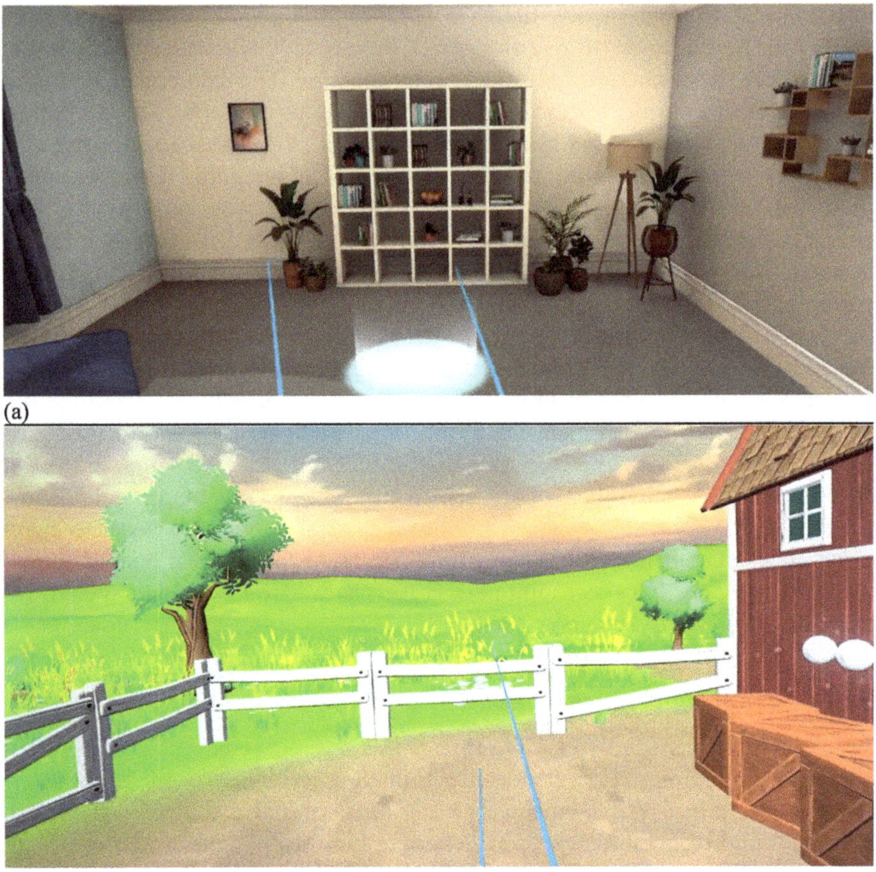

(a)

(b)

Figure 7.3 Choosing between (a) a living room and (b) a stylised farmyard.

Depict VR uses rigorously tested criticisms and praises (Premkumar et al., 2019b, 2020a; Premkumar et al., 2019c; Wang et al., 2021; Zandbagleh et al., 2022). The criticisms and praises build on remarks that might be made by high EE carers (Premkumar et al., 2013) (see Chapter 2). An example of a criticism is, 'You ought to express your feelings and communicate more. I find it hard to understand what you're thinking.' An example of a praise is, 'You are very intuitive when it comes to other people's feelings. You show a deep understanding of people's problems.' Neutral comments served as a non-emotion control audio-clip to help young people to acclimatise to the task. An example of a neutral comment is 'Paul Gauguin was a 19th-century French impressionist artist. His work was influenced by primitive art and Japanese prints.' The neutral comments referred to scientific facts, art, history or the weather.

Four spoken criticisms, four spoken praises and two spoken neutral comments with high fidelity for arousal and relevance to family scenarios were selected out of a larger bank of these phrases (Premkumar et al., 2019a;

Premkumar et al., 2020b). The comments appear as glowing orbs, like a 'lure' in a treasure-hunt VR game, and the orbs were meant to resemble sound bites (Figure 7.4a). The ten glowing orbs appear on a shelf in the VR environment; they begin with neutral comments, then progress to praises and finish with criticism. The main participant is asked to rate each orb in relation to (a) their voices, (b) a problematic relationship, and (c) how they feel about themselves (Figure 7.4b). The orbs turn green if the main participant rates them as

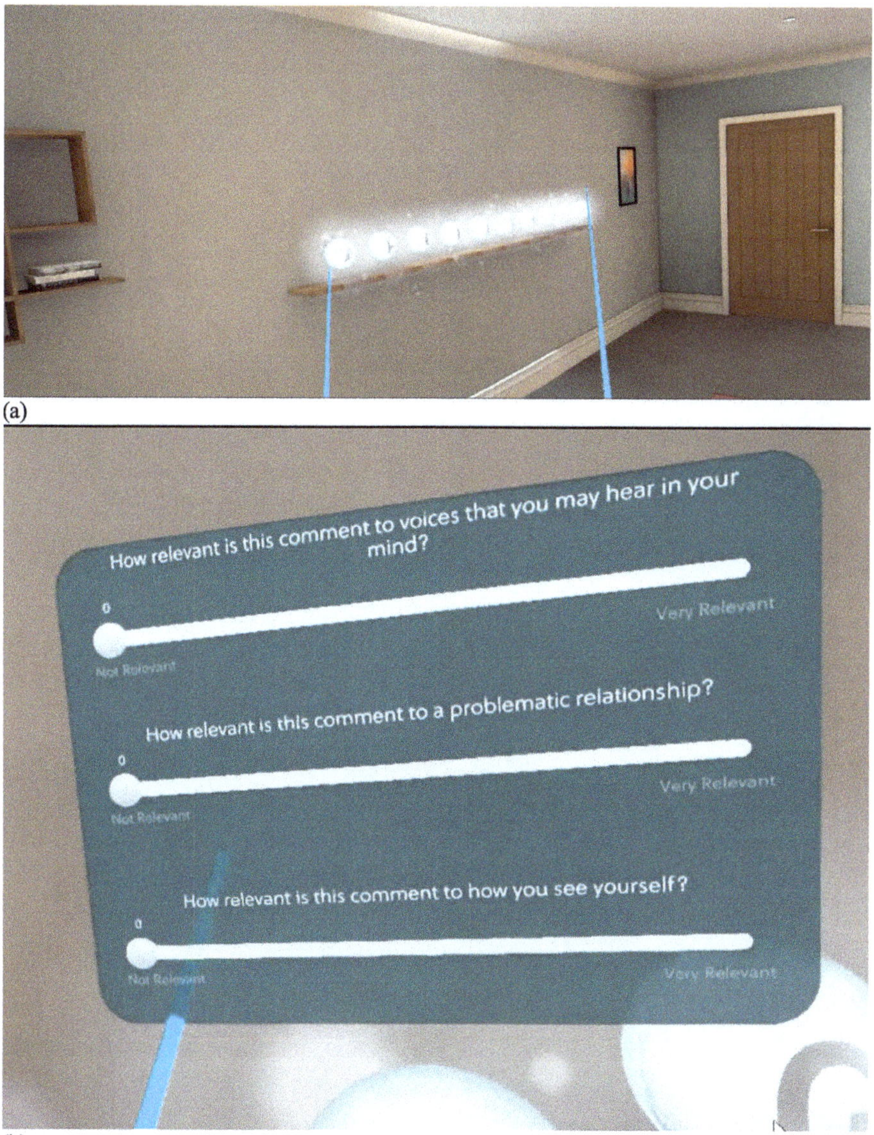

Figure 7.4 Rating the orbs.

relevant to how they see themselves and to red if they do not find the comments relevant.

To get the main participants to engage meaningfully with the orbs, the main participants choose four to five orbs that are relevant to them and places them in a blue box (Figure 7.5a). Next, the virtual narrator tells the main participants to think about a recent situation(s) to which the comments might apply and how those comments might have made them feel in that situation, and if they are criticisms, to think about how they might resolve them. The main participant then sorts the selected comments from least relevant to most relevant on a horizontal platform (Figure 7.5b).

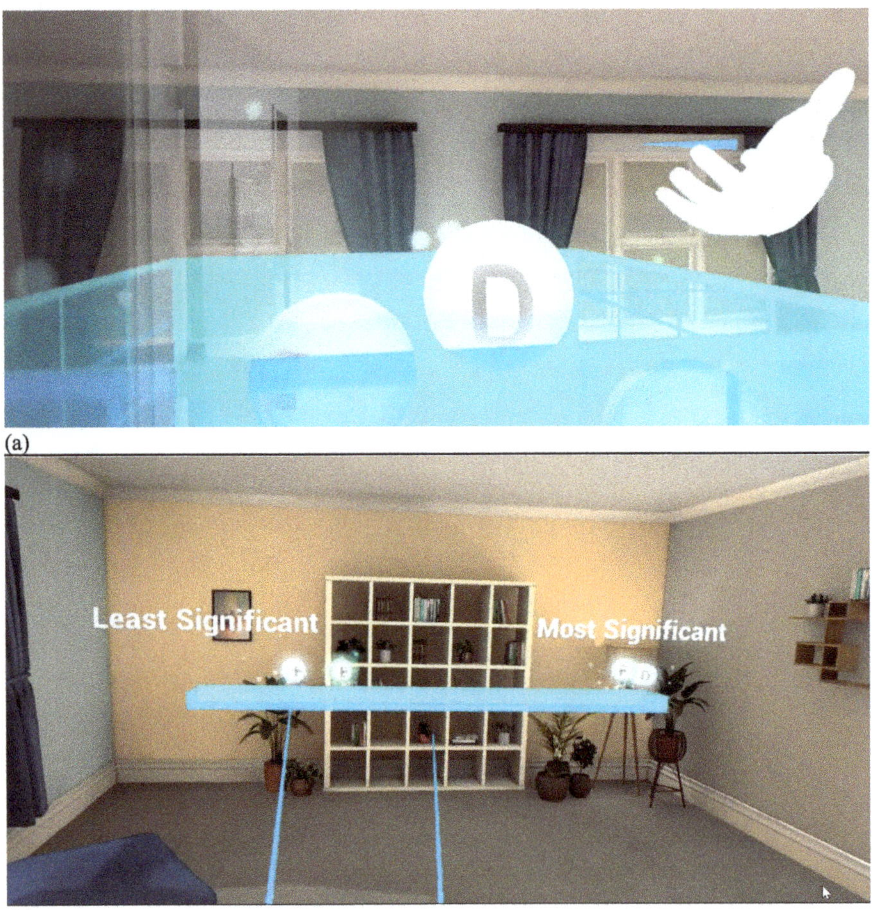

(a)

(b)

Figure 7.5 Selecting the Orbs.

7.4.3 Creating a two-person dialogue

Up to this point, the trusted confidante is asked to wait in a separate physical room so that the main participant can explore the VR environment and interact with the orbs privately. They are then invited to join the main participant in the virtual room by wearing another VR headset and assuming the role of 'the trusted confidante' (Figure 7.6a and b). The virtual narrator asks the main participant to tell the trusted confidante how the comment makes them feel and why it was relevant. Together, the main participant and trusted confidante

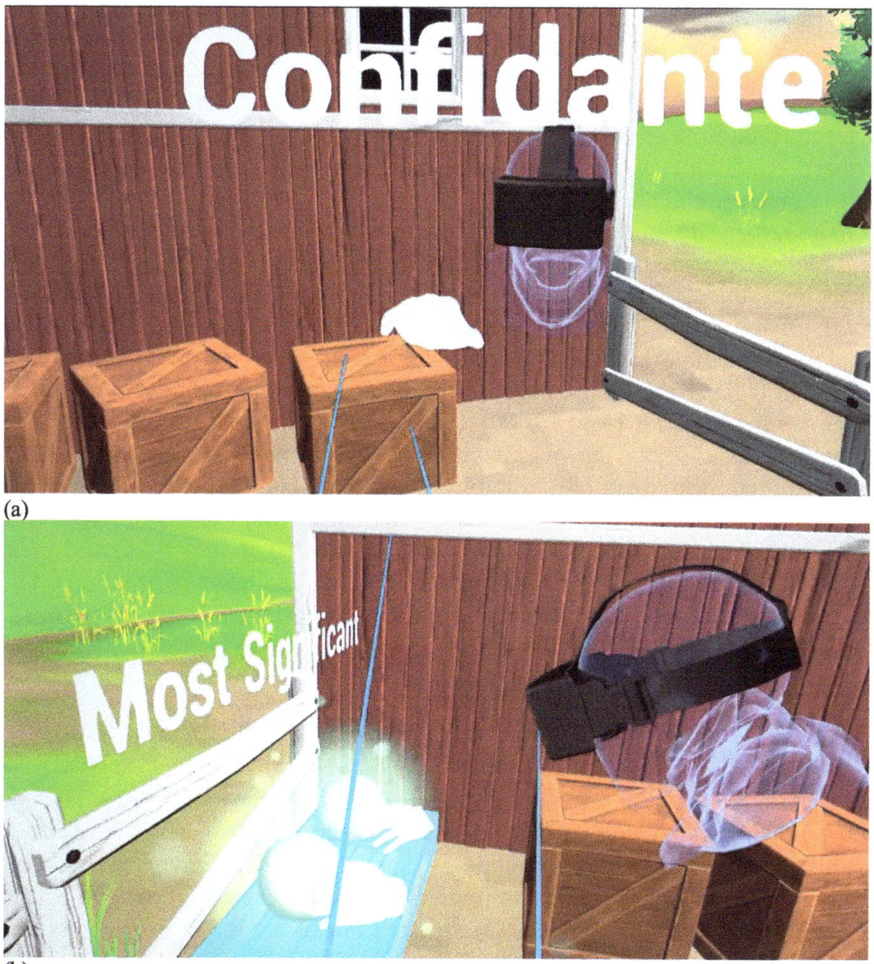

Figure 7.6 Sharing the orbs with a trusted confidante.

discuss which situations they might apply to either in their own relationship with each other or to other situations.

7.5 Study 1: Testing Depict VR in a healthy young population

We tested Depict VR on 17 healthy young people who had a normal propensity for hallucinations (Premkumar et al., in preparation). We selected healthy young people who were aged between 17 and 25 years old and scored in the middle of the range on the Launay-and-Slade Hallucinations – Extended Scale (Larøi & Van Der Linden, 2005; Larøi et al., 2005). That is, we included individuals who scored between 16 and 35, a range that represented one standard deviation above and below the mean score of the scale as reported in the study by Larøi and Van Der Linden (2005). Their confidante who took part was the sibling, friend/peer or partner of the main participant. Although we specified a minimum of 10 hours of contact between the main participant and their trusted confidante per week, we could not always observe this criterion as some trusted confidantes were peers of the main participant on the main participant's undergraduate course.

The researcher guided the main participants through the VR environment initially until the main participant listened to the virtual narrator and followed their instructions. The researcher also interviewed the main participant and their trusted confidante at three stages, first when the main participant was exploring the environment on their own, second when the main participant and their trusted confidante were sharing their views about the orbs, and third after completing the Depict VR session. In the third stage, the researcher enquired further about the meaning of the orbs that they selected, the relationship between the main participant and their trusted confidante, and their wider relationships. The Depict VR exercise took approximately 40 minutes. The relationship between mental distress (Lovibond & Lovibond, 1995) and presence (Witmer & Singer, 1998) in Depict VR was tested using correlations. The researcher (SM) analysed the interviews using thematic analysis (Clarke et al., 2019) to enquire about how Depict VR helped build trusting relationships.

7.5.1 *Preliminary findings of the Depict VR experience in young people*

Correlational analyses revealed that higher positive mood, but lower level of stress corresponded with a greater sense of presence in Depict VR in terms of being able to touch and manipulate objects in the virtual environment. This finding suggests that the ability to immerse oneself and interact with objects in the VR environment corresponds with one's mood at the time. When enquiring about the experience of Depict VR, main participants reported a positive experience, especially when modifying the appearance of the virtual environment to suit their need. They said that the environment had a calming effect.

Listening to the criticism and praise also helped the participants to learn what they liked about themselves and what they did not like about themselves. This finding suggests that exposure to the criticism and praise allows young people to introspect about themselves in a positive way.

7.6 Study 1: Lived experiences of health-care professionals with using Depict VR

In 2024, we were also funded by the British Academy and Leverhulme Trust (Grant number SRG2324\240272) to study how healthcare professionals regarded Depict VR as a tool to facilitate therapeutic engagement and have discussions around hearing voices and building relationships. Fourteen healthcare professionals at the Sussex Partnership NHS Foundation Trust experienced a Depict VR session while the researcher played the role of the trusted confidante. The researcher then interviewed the healthcare professionals about the value of Depict VR as a therapeutic tool to support young people who hear voices.

7.6.1 *Theme 1: emotional safety and personalisation*

A thematic analysis of the clinicians' experiences of Depict VR identified 'emotional safety and personalisation' as a main theme. This theme captures the importance that clinicians placed on personalisation within the Depict VR experience. A consistent finding was that a sense of control, both perceptual and functional, significantly influenced users' comfort and emotional regulation. These features were seen as particularly important for young people who navigate distressing mental health experiences. Two subthemes capture this theme.

Subtheme 1: empowerment through control

A strong sub-theme within this domain was the perceived importance of control and empowerment for young people. Clinicians described how VR might help enhance autonomy and self-direction:

> I felt quite in control of it like if I'd wanted to stop, I could have stopped and yeah, yeah, I didn't feel out of control with it.
>
> (IEGF170)

Control and emotional safety were often linked to personalisation, and clinicians repeatedly expressed a desire for greater interactivity and customisation. Participants noted that they had expected more opportunities to tailor the environment, which could support feelings of ownership and grounding:

> I thought I'd be able to change the colours of the flowers.
>
> (NEBN102)

> It may be nice to interact with it a little bit more...like to be able to pick the plants and put them somewhere else.
>
> (THBN805)

Personalisation also emerged as a major consideration in relation to the orb-based comment system, which is designed to prompt user reflection. While some participants valued this interactive element, many suggested that the orb content should be more tailored to individual voice-hearing experiences, both in content and delivery:

> I think they could be meaner.
>
> (THBN805)

> 10 was a lot...six to eight would probably be a good, decent number.
>
> (INBN299)

> Some of them were just a bit random. Umm I mean, I'm not sure a young person would even know who Paul Cezanne is, umm but I guess maybe the purpose is that it's just neutral, but, yeah, I would say that they probably need to be tailored to like an individual.
>
> (IERH742)

The voice options used to deliver orb content were also a focal point. Participants highlighted the need for broader, more inclusive options to reflect the diversity of clients' experiences and identities:

> Non-binary options or if they more, well, just think about some video games where you can scale the voices from like a really deep male voice to different pitched female voices or higher pitched male voices.
>
> (NYBN000)

Some participants suggested that the most powerful form of personalisation would involve allowing young people to generate their own comments, either by writing or recording them, making the experience more relevant, empowering and potentially liberating for both the young person and the confidante:

> I think a young person's voice in there talking through might be really nice... more young person focused type of language.
>
> (ORBN010)

Subtheme 2: calming environments and familiarity

Several participants described the current VR environments as calming and aesthetically pleasant, particularly the meadow setting.

> It's quite relaxing, to be honest.
>
> (ERBN442)

> Yeah, it was really interesting, I like the environment and um I thought it was quite...it felt like a safe space, yeah.
>
> (IEGF170)

However, many clinicians also commented that the current options felt limited, and that offering more environmental variety could increase comfort, emotional engagement and user agency:

> Maybe like a forest environment...a fireplace...having that one thing you can focus on.
>
> (INBN299)

7.6.2 Theme 2: Sensory and Physical Considerations

This theme reflects participants' experiences of the sensory and physical aspects of using Depict VR. It captures participants' views of Depict VR as an alternative way to communicate with young people when young people struggle to engage, but also to make the experience more enjoyable and informal.

Subtheme 1: eye contact and social anxiety

Both clinicians and clinicians reporting from the perspective of young clients discussed the benefit from the reduction in direct eye contact required in VR, which could ease social anxiety and facilitate more open communication:

> (I) Hate making eye contact...(VR) helps reduce social anxiety.
>
> (ENBN413)

> I think for some young people that really struggle with the face-to-face interactions, it could be brilliant.
>
> (DYTN466)

Subtheme 2: immersion, realism, and visual design

Some clinicians saw value in the gamified elements of the experience, which they felt could help reduce the perceived seriousness or clinical pressure often associated with more traditional interventions:

> That element of play and being in that virtual world isn't there that makes it somehow a bit lighter touch to explore some difficult subjects.
>
> (IEGF170)

7.6.3 Theme 3: Clinicians' involvement

This theme explores clinicians' views on the relational considerations required for the successful integration of Depict VR into therapeutic practice. While clinicians generally recognised the potential value of the tool, particularly in enhancing engagement with young people, they consistently emphasised that VR cannot be implemented as a standalone intervention. Effective use would require thoughtful clinical integration, attention to risk and safety, adequate training and organisational support.

Subtheme 1: the need for clinical presence and therapeutic framing

Many felt that VR should be introduced after the clinician had established a foundation of trust and shared understanding, ideally several sessions into the therapeutic process:

> So usually, I meet with the young person do like maybe one or two sessions of assessment and we do maybe 2 sessions of formulation, goal setting that type of thing. So, I would say around like session five, session six of usually like 16.
>
> (IERH742)

> So you'd want to do your, your standard assessment, obviously. Then bring them in (to VR).
>
> (NYBN000)

Subtheme 2: VR for assessment or engagement?

Some clinicians saw potential for using Depict VR earlier in the process to ease young people into therapy and facilitate disclosure:

> I think an assessment this way might help again young people to bring up what their difficulties they're having in that moment…get rid of that kind of barrier to therapy.
>
> (ENBN413)

There was also caution about whether VR might feel intrusive or inappropriate depending on the individual and the therapeutic alliance:

> Depends on the patient, it depends on the relationship you build with the patient 'cause this can also be kind of intrusive for them.
>
> (ERBN442)

7.7 Discussion of the findings of young people's and clinicians' user experience of Depict VR

The experiences of young people and clinicians of Depict VR indicated the potential for Depict VR to encourage young people to gain control and autonomy over their interaction with a trusted confidante and clinicians. The interactive elements, specifically the ability to pick and choose the orbs as they seemed relevant, allowed young people to envisage their own lived experiences of social situations and bring them to bear on their interaction with their trusted confidante. In turn, the trusted confidante facilitated the recall of past experiences and the mutual sharing of their relationships. These findings concur with evidence that DMHIs facilitate autonomy of young people in the therapeutic process and an ability to implement coping strategies outside the therapeutic setting (Wies et al., 2021).

Increasing the clients' autonomy through Depict VR in a therapeutic context was felt by clinicians to be important in many ways. Clinicians felt that personalising the virtual environment would support the young person's autonomy and give them a sense of control. And this finding is consistent with evidence that DMHIs give young people a greater sense of active control in their own treatment (Wies et al., 2021). Clinicians suggested that personalising the comments in the orbs would enhance the autonomy of young people, make them relevant to their own experiences and allow for diversity in the voices of the comments.

Clinicians also valued Depict VR as a therapeutic tool to ease young people into the interaction with clinicians when they are socially anxious. Yet, clinicians reinforced the importance of traditional models of building a therapeutic alliance prior to introducing the Depict VR experience. Building a therapeutic alliance involves rapport-building, setting therapeutic goals and collaborating on relevant tasks, and building trust (Bordin, 1979, cited in Bourke et al., 2021; Ovenstad et al., 2020). Some clients are naturally inclined and motivated towards forging a therapeutic alliance, while others are better supported with motivational interviewing where the therapist focuses on providing unconditional positive regard and acceptance regardless of the client's volition towards a therapeutic alliance (Ovenstad et al., 2020). Forming the therapeutic alliance is also contingent on the client's own characteristics, such as their attachment style in other relationships and coping styles (Howard et al., 2022). These considerations of the patient's needs explain the clinicians' need to prioritise the therapeutic alliance in the present study.

How to improve the therapeutic relationship between clinicians and clients:

- Increase independence and control of young people during interactions with their confidante. Empower young people to guide the daily interactions with confidante by consulting with them when making decisions.
- Recognise that exposure to criticism can be a starting point for constructive communication and problem-solving between the client and their trusted confidante.
- Suggest using a neutral space, such as a park, for the client to discuss about past social situations with a trusted confidante, in the absence of a virtual-reality environment.
- Build on your strengths in your relationships, such as the ability to build trust, and in your coping strategies, such as learning to accept situations, and use these strengths to develop a therapeutic relationship with your therapist.

7.8 Translating research on Depict VR into

Depict VR was born out of a desire to help young people who hear voices. What follows is a reflection on our experience of developing Depict VR into a viable product. Whilst this process is ongoing and far from complete, there have been many learnings particularly at the interface between fundamental research and commercialisation.

7.8.1 Defining the market and identifying the opportunity

At the heart of Depict VR is a research hypothesis, namely that an immersive interactive VR experience based on the concept of EE can help young people to engage with their inner feelings, have the confidence to express their concerns to a potentially high EE carer, and ultimately attain good mental health outcomes. This foundational research is a crucial starting point for claiming the proof of concept and broadcasting the knowledge to the wider scientific community within the growing space of digital mental health. Still, it does not immediately result in a viable commercial product that can be brought to a mass market. To achieve this, Depict VR must navigate a complicated process that balances robust research with commercial viability. Along the way, the needs and expectations of research collaborators, stakeholders and financiers must be managed to ensure that everyone is working towards the same goal, and the result delivers value for all involved. In short, academic collaborators need publishable results, while investors expect financial returns. In addition, various stakeholders, such as healthcare service providers, want a product that fundamentally works, provides value and is better than the current gold standard (Zhao et al., 2023).

Turning problems into ideas is the essence of innovation, creating new tangible solutions that make real world impact. Modern scientific research requires the researcher to justify their work, especially when applying for research grants. This process forces the researcher to consider the wider impact of their work which will often reveal both a potential market and a problem to solve. Whilst fundamental research seeks to answer a question and create new knowledge, a commercial product aims to solve a problem and create value. Although these are two distinct goals, they overlap and help to define a potential market. For Depict VR, the primary market is Children and Adolescent Mental Health Services (CAMHS) within the National Health Service (NHS). These services cover the UK and are the main point of treatment for young people with mental health issues. These young people represent the end user, i.e. those individuals for whom the Depict VR application is designed, but there are other users who must be considered. For instance, the clinical staff who might offer the Depict VR application to patients, technical staff who might be expected to maintain the application and associated delivery technology (VR headsets) and departmental managers or procurement officers who will decide whether the application is worth buying for the department. With this in mind, different problems can be identified that a digital mental health application, like Depict VR, could solve for these various users. For young people, Depict VR aims to make the provision of mental health more attractive and accessible, delivering an experience that they will be more accustomed to. For the clinician, Depict VR presents an effective way to engage young people and stimulate valuable dialogue, and for the case manager Depict VR could treat more patients for less money versus traditional methods.

Once a potential market has been identified it can be quantified and categorised. The Total Addressable Market represents the total market demand for a product or service – for example the total number of CAMHS units in the UK. At a level below the Total Addressable Market is the Serviceable Addressable Market which is the fraction of the Total Addressable Market that can be realistically targeted with the current capabilities of the business. For example, a new start-up business may only be able to service CAMHS units in one region of the UK. And further below the Serviceable Addressable Market is the Serviceable Obtainable Market which is the percentage of the Serviceable Addressable Market the business might expect to reach in the short term. From a business standpoint, this hierarchy helps to focus the marketing strategy and the financial potential of the product. If the Serviceable Obtainable Market is too low, then the product might not be commercially viable or it might represent too much risk for investors to back the product from the outset. If, however, the proposed market is large and there is scope for it to grow, for example into international territories, the potential financial returns could justify the risks of further developing the product for commercialisation.

The development of a digital mental health application from an idea to a commercial product can be charted through Technology Readiness Levels (TRL) ranging from 1 which represents the basic concept, to 9 which represents an actual product proven in real world operation. It is a stepwise progression when moving from the initial idea to the proof-of-concept, prototype, technology demonstrator and finally the commercial product (Salvador-Carulla et al., 2025). Within this framework, the development of the software underlying a digital mental health application follows established pathways. For immersive interactive applications, the design process tends to be iterative and agile, involving developer teams undertaking distinct periods of software planning, coding and review, using feedback loops to continually improve the product. During these cycles, key information about user experience emerges as explained above (section 7.3). All end users, such as young people with mental distress, clinicians, technical staff and departmental managers, are considered during this process.

Whilst developing software in this way is efficient, proven and cost-effective, it must be tempered with the stringent requirements of the International Organization for Standardization, a global body that ensures standards of quality and safety are maintained in products and services brought to market. ISO9001 is a quality management system standard that is central to any product development and requires set protocols to document and manage the changes to the software. These processes are needed to ensure safety, effectiveness and cybersecurity of the digital mental health application, whilst also reassuring potential customers that the application can be trusted (Zhao et al., 2023). At the heart of the quality management system is the Intended User Statement, which clearly defines who the product is designed for and what purpose it serves. The Intended User Statement goes back to the point of ideation and underpins how the product is risk assessed, clinically evaluated and refined though its research and development life cycle. The specific requirements of the quality management system might require a specialist team member to oversee and manage this process. Ensuring high-quality and complete documentation is vital for later TRLs as the product gets closer to market.

During development, it is easy to focus on bringing the product to life, yet it is also important to develop the market opportunity in parallel. Once the product exists, new applications might emerge providing inspiration to explore new markets and potential revenue streams. For example, a product intended for the NHS might also find value in private healthcare or offered to health insurance providers. Depict VR was primarily designed to help young people who hear voices. We have subsequently discovered its core functionality can be applied to many situations beyond young people's mental health, for example couples therapy. These offer different routes to market that could be quicker and more cost effective to reach and can be the difference between success and failure of the innovation. During technology transfer from research concept to commercial product, the innovator must navigate a period of negative cash flow, known as the 'valley of death'. From the point of ideation, a product is losing money up until it is launched on the market and generating revenue. Therefore, the innovator must find financing to sustain the research and development costs, and the quicker the product can be brought to market the more likely it will survive the valley of death and reach the end user.

7.8.2 *Challenges for implementation in psychiatric services*

A crucial step to transition a general digital mental health application into a DMHI is certification of safety for the user. We use the term 'DMHI' sparingly because an intervention has passed rigorous testing of efficacy and safety through trials in vulnerable populations. Instead, we use the term 'Digital Mental Health application' to refer to products that are a proof of concept and are still in development. For this safety assurance, it is critical to understand if the product must be classified as a medical device, especially if it is to be administered in clinical settings. For DMHIs, the specific classification is typically a 'software as a medical device'. However, deploying new technologies where the evidence base is small and knowledge of potential adverse reactions is limited is inherently risky, particularly when products are being developed for vulnerable groups, for instance children and young people. Furthermore, healthcare professionals are not trained in using DMHIs and they lack specialised physical spaces in the healthcare services to offer the interventions (Hall et al., 2024). As such, stringent health and safety protocols must be followed and in 2025, the Medical Health Regulation Authority (MHRA) published new guidance for DMHIs (Gov.UK, 2025). The guidance clearly explains how to categorise a DMHI and helps innovators understand if their product should be classified as a medical device. The definition of a medical device varies between countries, and this means that it is easier to deliver the DMHIs in some countries than others (Hall et al., 2024). To reduce these barriers, the regulatory agencies classified some DMHIs as 'low-risk' devices, which has the consequence of luring developers of DMHIs into promoting their products as wellbeing devices rather than treatments (Hall et al., 2024). In short, the intended purpose and functionality of the product is assessed which decides if the product qualifies as a software as a medical device and then the level of classification is further delineated as either Class I, Class IIa, Class IIb or Class III. If a product is classified as a medical device, it must be regulated, and documents, including the quality management system, will be prepared and submitted for review.

The need for regulation poses a dilemma for innovators. On the one hand, the need to ensure product and user safety is paramount. Gaining certification demonstrates product quality and opens the door to the clinical market. On the other hand, the regulatory process is costly and requires a robust evidence base. The innovator might own a fledgling product that shows promise but is unable to progress beyond the necessary regulatory steps to reach the desired clinical market. The foreboding challenges also make it difficult to translate the research to healthcare practice, and it denies people of receiving optimal care (Hall et al., 2024). The best evidence comes from real users, for example patients with a mental health issue. Innovators can apply for a Letter of No Objection (LONO) from the MHRA which gives permission to carry out a clinical study with a medical device for the purpose of data gathering. This clinical evidence will form part of the documentation submitted to the MHRA to gain full certification.

Undertaking these regulatory steps can become expensive and long winded and risk enlarging the precarious valley of death. Specialist team members should be sought to oversee the regulatory process, creating and managing the required documentation. If the product is classified as a Class IIa or above medical device, the documentation will need to be assessed by a Notified Body, for example the Health and Safety Executive in the UK, before being sent to the MHRA for approval. This process can take over 12 months and cost over £100,000. To navigate this process many innovators will require public funding from government grants, such as Innovate UK or the NIHR in the UK. However, these grants are highly competitive and can come with conditions that stifle future commercialisation. Private financiers are less likely to support the regulatory steps required to bring a product to a clinical market due to the long timeline and low certainty of commercial success. In particular, products specifically aimed at the NHS have the additional challenge of being procured by NHS Trusts, who might not have the financial resource or departmental flexibility to acquire new technologies. For a digital product to be used within the NHS it must also meet the Digital Technology Assessment Criteria (DTAC), used to assess the supplier and ensure new products meet the organisation's needs and standards. The NHS in England is made up of over 200 Trusts and an innovator may have to approach each Trust individually, addressing these practicalities on a Trust-by-Trust basis in order to get their product procured. For instance, staff need special training to operate and maintain the technology, making ease of use especially important for wider adoption.

7.8.3 Implementation of DMHIs as an early intervention in the community

Despite the challenges facing innovators, there is growing enthusiasm for the digital mental health sector in the UK. In July 2025, NHS England published a new ten-year plan laying out a strategy for future healthcare. The three central tenets of the plan are a move from analogue to digital technologies, from sickness to prevention and from hospital to community. DMHIs have the potential to satisfy all three aims of the plan, detecting potential issues earlier and operating in settings outside of the clinic. Accordingly, an alternative route to market is to design a digital mental health product that is not classified as a medical device. For clarity, these are products that are not intended for medical use nor do they make medical claims. Whilst this risks devaluing the product from a clinical standpoint, there are still many useful applications that can help support users improve mental health. Ultimately, the innovator can create a refined, evidence-backed product that is more appealing to users and more likely to gain market traction and therefore more attractive to potential investors.

The waiting lists for young people trying to access mental healthcare in the UK can take longer than a month, with many individuals giving up on treatment (Valentine et al., 2024; Young Minds, 2022). DMHIs offer a flexibility to the point of delivery that traditional clinical therapies cannot. For instance, whilst a virtual-reality experience might be difficult to deploy within an NHS clinic, it might be more easily offered in an education setting, especially if the school or college already has VR headsets as part of their teaching provision. In this way, a DMHI can be offered to young people in a familiar setting (Hayward et al., 2025). Whilst the clinic has the benefit of highly trained clinical psychologists, the educational setting can still provide an element of structure and safeguarding oversight if the product or experience is curated by a school councillor.

This highlights another potential benefit of digital mental health applications, facilitating meaningful experiences that can be led by less qualified professionals. One reason for the long waiting times is a lack of capacity within CAMHS units and the availability of highly trained clinical psychologists. Digital tools can be created that help young people with emerging mental health issues that can be managed by specially trained clinical assistants and nurses. This increases capacity at lower cost and brings young people into treatment pathways sooner. Such tools could even deliver early interventions, mitigating the onset of more serious mental health conditions and further reducing the burden on CAMHS.

When positioning a DMHI in a community setting such as a school or college, the same practical considerations as positioning the product in a clinical setting must be taken into account. Where will the product be deployed? Who will maintain and deliver the product? What format will the experience take? How will safeguarding be managed? How will risk and safety be monitored? In many respects schools are no different to clinics, with staff working at full capacity, and limited opportunities to deploy new technology that benefits students. Careful consideration should also be taken on how to adapt the digital product to better meet the setting and specific needs of the various users. Learning techniques based on 'common sense' motivates engagement with DMHIs in community settings (Jackson et al., 2024). DMHIs can also refresh memory of skills learned in therapy in clinical settings (Jackson et al., 2024). Users also value learning new skills and find it easy to embed the skills into daily routines, including social interaction (Jackson et al., 2024). Bringing digital mental health applications into community settings offers certain advantages over clinical settings. The organisational hierarchies can be less striated, and decisions can be made more quickly. The familiar setting is more conducive to young people engagement presenting the opportunity to reach more young people, especially those reluctant to engage with mental health issues.

As the product becomes more established and its therapeutic mechanism better understood, new applications and markets can be explored. For example, with Depict VR, we have found that the application is effective at helping couples have meaningful discussions about their relationship. In this context, Depict VR could be adapted to couples therapy. Depict VR could be further adapted to foster constructive dialogue between employer and employee in the workplace and help work through conflict resolution processes. These offer unique settings, use cases and market opportunities, and demonstrate the broad potential of Depict VR to prospective investors. Furthermore, the theory of EE, which lies at the heart of Depict VR, is universal. It means that Depict VR should work in any community across the globe. Whilst this raises special consideration around how a VR experience can be deployed in different cultures, it further broadens the market potential of the product.

Our current interest in developing Depict VR for non-clinical settings has determined that it is not a software as a medical device and does not require regulation. The product is intended to help young people foster constructive conversations to maintain good mental health. Depict VR is best seen as a product for improving wellbeing at a stage when mental distress would be considered to be at sub-clinical levels, rather than clinical levels as part of a diagnosable mental health condition. Whilst maintaining good mental health is an important preventative step, we do not claim to prevent any specific mental health condition.

We still have a long way to go with Depict VR, but by sharing our experiences so far we hope to inspire and support fellow innovators to continue forging ahead. There is a clear need and a growing desire to use new digital mental health technologies. It requires both the support of major organisations and institutions like the NHS and central government and the determination of innovators and entrepreneurs to stay the course and ensure these vital tools are made available to those who will benefit most.

How to offer digital mental health applications to the wider community:

- Research and understand the market problem and opportunity and clearly define the intended purpose and functionality.
- Use platforms that resonate with the target user, for instance virtual reality and young people.
- Consider how the platform will be delivered – what technology is required, specialist skills to operate it and practical resources to host it.

- Engage with regulators early in the research development and innovation about seeking approval of digital mental health applications as a medically safe device.
- Consider the wider infrastructure of delivering the digital intervention at scale, such as commercial investors, community services and clinical services.
- People in the general community may benefit for lay interventions that are preventative, that build on common sense and are an aide memoire for applying specialist strategies learned in therapeutic settings in daily routines, such as social interaction.

Acknowledgements

We acknowledge Dr Shamea Mia (SM) for her role in collecting the data on the user experience of Depict VR from 17 healthy participants in Study 1, for analysing the data and writing the results. We also acknowledge Jennifer Nicholls for her role in collecting the data on the user experience of Depict VR from 14 healthcare professionals in Study 2 at the Sussex Partnership NHS Foundation Trust and for analysing the data and writing the results.

References

Andrade, C. (2015). The primary outcome measure and its importance in clinical trials. *The Journal of Clinical Psychiatry*, *76*(10), 1320. 10.4088/JCP.15f10377

Archer, N. S., Bluff, A., Eddy, A., Nikhil, C. K., Hazell, N., Frank, D., & Johnston, A. (2022). Odour enhances the sense of presence in a virtual reality environment. *PloS One*, *17*(3), e0265039. 10.1371/journal.pone.0265039

Bordin, E. S. (1979). The generalizability of the psychoanalytic concept of the working alliance. *Psychotherapy: Theory, Research & Practice*, *16*(3), 252–260. 10.1037/h0085885

Bourke, E., Barker, C., & Fornells-Ambrojo, M. (2021). Systematic review and meta-analysis of therapeutic alliance, engagement, and outcome in psychological therapies for psychosis. *Psychology and Psychotherapy*, *94*(3), 822–853. 10.1111/papt.12330

Bradley, M. M., & Lang, P. J. (1999). *Affective Norms for English Words (ANEW): Instruction manual and affective ratings* (Technical Report C-1 ed.). The Center for Research in Psychophysiology.

Clarke, V., Braun, V., Terry, G., & Hayfield, N. (2019). Thematic analysis. In P. Liamputtong (Ed.), *Handbook of research methods in health and social sciences* (pp. 843–860). Springer.

Craske, M. G., Treanor, M., Zbozinek, T. D., & Vervliet, B. (2022). Optimizing exposure therapy with an inhibitory retrieval approach and the OptEx Nexus. *Behaviour Research and Therapy*, *152*, 104069. 10.1016/j.brat.2022.104069

Dare, O., Jidong, D. E., & Premkumar, P. (2023). Conceptualising mental illness among University students of African, Caribbean and similar ethnic heritage in the United Kingdom. *Ethnicity & Health*, *28*(4), 522–543. 10.1080/13557858.2022.2104817

Foa, E. B., & Kozak, M. J. (1986). Emotional processing of fear: Exposure to corrective information. *Psychological Bulletin*, *99*(1), 20–35. 10.1037/0033-2909.99.1.20

Freeman, D., Bradley, J., Antley, A., Bourke, E., DeWeever, N., Evans, N., Černis, E., Sheaves, B., Waite, F., Dunn, G., Slater, M., & Clark, D. M. (2016). Virtual reality in the treatment of persecutory delusions: Randomised controlled experimental study testing how to reduce delusional conviction. *British Journal of Psychiatry*, *209*(1), 62–67. 10.1192/bjp.bp.115.176438

Freeman, D., Lambe, S., Galal, U., Yu, L., Kabir, T., Petit, A., Rosebrock, L., Dudley, R., Chapman, K., Morrison, A., O'Regan, E., Murphy, E., Aynsworth, C., Jones, J., Powling, R., Grabey, J., Rovira, A., Freeman, J., Clark, D. M., & Waite, F. (2022). Agoraphobic avoidance in patients with psychosis: Severity and response to automated VR therapy in a secondary analysis of a randomised controlled clinical trial. *Schizophrenia Research*, *250*, 50–59. 10.1016/j.schres.2022.10.008

Freeman, D., Lambe, S., Kabir, T., Petit, A., Rosebrock, L., Yu, L., Dudley, R., Chapman, K., Morrison, A., O'Regan, E., Aynsworth, C., Jones, J., Murphy, E., Powling, R., Galal, U., Grabey, J., Rovira, A., Martin, J., Hollis, C., … West, J. (2022). Automated virtual reality therapy to treat agoraphobic avoidance and distress in patients with psychosis (gameChange): A multicentre, parallel-group, single-blind, randomised, controlled trial in England with mediation and moderation analyses. *The Lancet Psychiatry*, *9*(5), 375–388. 10.1016/S2215-0366(22)00060-8

Freeman, D., Rosebrock, L., Waite, F., Loe, B. S., Kabir, T., Petit, A., Dudley, R., Chapman, K., Morrison, A., O'Regan, E., Aynsworth, C., Jones, J., Murphy, E., Powling, R., Peel, H., Walker, H., Byrne, R., Freeman, J., Rovira, A., … Lambe, S. (2023). Virtual reality (VR) therapy for patients with psychosis: satisfaction and side effects. *Psychological Medicine*, *53*(10), 4373–4384. 10.1017/S0033291722001167

Gov.UK. (2025). Digital mental health technologies guidance launched to help manufacturers and safeguard users. https://www.gov.uk/government/news/digital-mental-health-technologies-guidance-launched-to-help-manufacturers-and-safeguard-users

Hall, C. L., Gómez Bergin, A.D., & Rennick-Egglestone, S. (2024). Research into Digital health intervention for mental health: 25-year retrospective on the ethical and legal challenges. *Journal of Medical Internet Research*, *26*(11), e58939. 10.2196/58939

Hayward, M., John, M., Parry, S., Bibby-Jones, A., Orchard, F., Malpass, F., Dixon, C., & Naito, A. (2025). Support for young people who are distressed by hearing voices: Protocol for an uncontrolled feasibility evaluation of a psychological intervention package delivered within secondary schools (the ECHOES study). *Pilot and Feasibility Studies*, *11*(1), 39–111. 10.1186/s40814-025-01611-x

Healey, A., Mansell, W., & Tai, S. (2017). An experimental test of the role of control in spider fear. *Journal of Anxiety Disorders*, *49*, 12–20. 10.1016/j.janxdis.2017.03.005

Hollis, C., Falconer, C. J., Martin, J. L., Whittington, C., Stockton, S., Glazebrook, C., & Davies, E. B. (2017). Annual Research Review: Digital health interventions for children and young people with mental health problems – a systematic and meta-review. *Journal of Child Psychology & Psychiatry*, *58*(4), 474–503. 10.1111/jcpp.12663

Holt, D. J., DeTore, N. R., Aideyan, B., Utter, L., Vinke, L., Johnson, D. S., Zimmerman, J., Dokholyan, K. N., & Burke, A. (2025). Enhancing social functioning using multi-user, immersive virtual reality. *Scientific Reports*, *15*(1), 2790–2813. 10.1038/s41598-024-84954-4

Hooley, J. M., & Miklowitz, D. J. (2017). Perceived Criticism in the treatment of a high-risk adolescent. *Journal of Clinical Psychology*, *73*(5), 570–578. 10.1002/jclp.22454

Howard, R., Berry, K., & Haddock, G. (2022). Therapeutic alliance in psychological therapy for posttraumatic stress disorder: A systematic review and meta-analysis. *Clinical Psychology and Psychotherapy*, *29*(2), 373–399. 10.1002/cpp.2642

Jackson, H. M., Batterham, P. J., Ohan, J. L., Calear, A. L., & Farrer, L. M. (2024). Skill enactment and knowledge acquisition among community users of digital mental health interventions: qualitative study with thematic analysis. *BMC Psychiatry*, *24*(1). 10.1186/s12888-024-05953-3

Jacobson, N. S., & Truax, P. (1991). Clinical significance: A statistical approach to defining meaningful change in psychotherapy research. *Journal of Consulting and Clinical Psychology*, *59*(1), 12–19. 10.1037/0022-006X.59.1.12

Knowles, K. A., & Tolin, D. F. (2022). Mechanisms of action in exposure therapy. *Current Psychiatry Reports*, *24*(12), 861–869.

LaRocco, M. (2020). Developing the 'best practices' of virtual reality design: Industry standards at the frontier of emerging media. *Journal of Visual Culture*, *19*(1), 96–111. 10.1177/1470412920906255

Larøi, F., DeFruyt, F., van Os, J., Aleman, A., & Van der Linden, M. (2005). Associations between hallucinations and personality structure in a non-clinical sample: Comparison between young and elderly samples. *Personality and Individual Differences*, *39*(1), 189–200. 10.1016/j.paid.2005.01.001

Larøi, F., & Van Der Linden, M. (2005). Nonclinical participants' reports of hallucinatory experiences. *Canadian Journal of Behavioural Science*, *37*(1), 33–43. 10.1037/h0087243

Leavey, G., Rothi, D., & Paul, R. (2011). Trust, autonomy and relationships: The help-seeking preferences of young people in secondary level schools in London (UK). *Journal of Adolescence (London, England.)*, *34*(4), 685–693. 10.1016/j.adolescence.2010.09.004

Lieberman, D. A. (2012a). Classical conditioning. In D. A. Lieberman (Ed.), *Human learning and memory* (pp. 38–64). Cambridge University Press.

Lieberman, D. A. (2012b). Reinforcement. In D. A. Lieberman (Ed.), *Human learning and memory* (pp. 118–157). Cambridge University Press.

Lovibond, S. H., & Lovibond, P. F. (1995). *Manual for the depression, anxiety and stress scales* (2nd ed.). Psychology Foundation.

Magaña, A. B., Goldstein, M. J., Karno, M., Miklowitz, D. J., Jenkins, J., & Falloon, I. R. H. (1986). A brief method for assessing expressed emotion in relatives of psychiatric patients. *Psychiatry Research*, *17*(3), 203–212. 10.1016/0165-1781(86)90049-1

Marcolin, F., Wally Scurati, G., Ulrich, L., Nonis, F., Vezzetti, E., Dozio, N., Ferrise, F., Stork, A., Basole, R. C., Stork, A., & Rahul, C. B. (2021). Affective virtual reality: How to design artificial experiences impacting human emotions. *IEEE Computer Graphics and Applications*, *41*(6), 171–178. 10.1109/MCG.2021.3115015

Masland, S. R., & Hooley, J. M. (2015). Perceived criticism: A research update for clinical practitioners. *Clinical Psychology (New York, N.Y.)*, *22*(3), 211–222. 10.1111/cpsp.12110

Miklowitz, D. J., O'Brien, M. P., Schlosser, D. A., Addington, J., Candan, K. A., Marshall, C., Domingues, I., Walsh, B. C., Zinberg, J. L., De Silva, S. D., Friedman-Yakoobian, M., & Cannon, T. D. (2014). Family-focused treatment for adolescents and young adults at high risk for psychosis: Results of a randomized trial. *Journal of the American Academy of Child & Adolescent Psychiatry*, *53*(8), 848–858. 10.1016/j.jaac.2014.04.020

O'Brien, M. P., Miklowitz, D. J., & Cannon, T. D. (2015). Decreases in perceived maternal criticism predict improvement in subthreshold psychotic symptoms in a randomized trial of family-focused therapy for individuals at clinical high risk for psychosis. *Journal of Family Psychology*, *29*(6), 945–951. 10.1037/fam0000123

Ovenstad, K. S., Ormhaug, S. M., Shirk, S. R., & Jensen, T. K. (2020). Therapists' behaviors and youths' therapeutic alliance during trauma-focused cognitive behavioral therapy. *Journal of Consulting and Clinical Psychology*, *88*(4), 350–361. 10.1037/ccp0000465

Philippe, T. J., Sikder, N., Jackson, A., Koblanski, M. E., Liow, E., Pilarinos, A., & Vasarhelyi, K. (2022). Digital health interventions for delivery of mental health care: Systematic and comprehensive meta-review. *JMIR Mental Health*, *9*(5), e35159. 10.2196/35159

Premkumar, P., Dunn, A. K., Onwumere, J., & Kuipers, E. (2019a). Sensitivity to criticism and praise predicts schizotypy in the non-clinical population: The role of affect and perceived expressed emotion. *European Psychiatry: The Journal of the Association of European Psychiatrists*, *55*, 109–115. S0924-9338(18)30195-0 [pii]

Premkumar, P., Dunn, A. K., Onwumere, J., & Kuipers, E. (2019b). Sensitivity to criticism and praise predicts schizotypy in the non-clinical population: The role of affect and perceived expressed emotion. *European Psychiatry*, *55*, 109–115. 10.1016/j.eurpsy.2018.10.009

Premkumar, P., Heym, N., Brown, D. J., Battersby, S., Sumich, A., Huntington, B., Daly, R., & Zysk, E. (2021). The effectiveness of self-guided virtual-reality exposure therapy for public-speaking anxiety. *Frontiers in Psychiatry*, *12*, 1–12. https://lsbu.idm.oclc.org/login?url=https://search.ebscohost.com/login.aspx?direct=true&db=edb&AN=152000522&site=eds-live

Premkumar, P., Heym, N., Myers, J. A. C., Formby, P., Battersby, S., Sumich, A. L., & Brown, D. J. (2024). Augmenting self-guided virtual-reality exposure therapy for social anxiety with biofeedback: A randomised controlled trial. *Frontiers in Psychiatry*, *15*, 1467141. 10.3389/fpsyt.2024.1467141

Premkumar, P., Kuipers, E., & Kumari, V. (2020a). The path from schizotypy to depression and aggression and the role of family stress. *European Psychiatry: The Journal of the Association of European Psychiatrists*, *63*(1), e79. 10.1192/j.eurpsy.2020.76 (doi)

Premkumar, P., Kuipers, E., & Kumari, V. (2020b). The path from schizotypy to depression and aggression and the role of family stress. *European Psychiatry*, *63*(1), e79. 10.1192/j.eurpsy.2020.76

Premkumar, P., Santo, M. G. E., Onwumere, J., Schürmann, M., Kumari, V., Blanco, S., Baker, J., & Kuipers, E. (2019c). Neural responses to criticism and praise vary with schizotypy and perceived emotional support. *International Journal of Psychophysiology*, *145*, 109–118. 10.1016/j.ijpsycho.2019.05.008

Premkumar, P., Williams, S. C., Lythgoe, D., Andrew, C., Kuipers, E., & Kumari, V. (2013). Neural processing of criticism and positive comments from relatives in individuals with schizotypal personality traits. *The World Journal of Biological Psychiatry: The Official Journal of the World Federation of Societies of Biological Psychiatry*, *14*(1), 57–70. 10.3109/15622975.2011.604101 [doi]

Ramotion. (2023). VR in UX design: Basic guidelines for a better experience. https://www.ramotion.com/blog/vr-in-ux-design/. Retrieved 08.11.2023, from https://www.ramotion.com/blog/vr-in-ux-design/

Realpe, A., Elahi, F., Bucci, S., Birchwood, M., Vlaev, I., Taylor, D., & Thompson, A. (2020). Co-designing a virtual world with young people to deliver social cognition therapy in early psychosis. *Early Intervention in Psychiatry*, *14*(1), 37–43. 10.1111/eip.12804

Ryan, R., Berry, K., Law, H., & Hartley, S. (2021). Therapeutic relationships in child and adolescent mental health services: A Delphi study with young people, carers and clinicians. *International Journal of Mental Health Nursing*, *30*(4), 1010–1021. 10.1111/inm.12857

Salvador-Carulla, L., Tabatabaei-Jafari, H., Woods, C., & Lukersmith, S. (2025). Proof of concept studies in mental health systems research: strategy and steps. *International Journal of Mental Health Systems*, *19*(1), 25–111. 10.1186/s13033-025-00682-w

Schlosser, D. A., Miklowitz, D. J., O'Brien, M. P., De Silva, S. D., Zinberg, J. L., & Cannon, T. D. (2012). A randomized trial of family focused treatment for adolescents and young adults at risk for psychosis: study rationale, design and methods. *Early Intervention in Psychiatry*, *6*(3), 283–291. 10.1111/j.1751-7893.2011.00317.x

Valentine, A. Z., Hall, S. S., Sayal, K., & Hall, C. L. (2024). Waiting-list interventions for children and young people using child and adolescent mental health services: A systematic review. *BMJ Mental Health, 27*(1), e300844. 10.1136/bmjment-2023-300844

Wang, G. Y., Premkumar, P., Lee, C. Q., & Griffiths, M. (2021). The role of criticism in expressed emotion among psychoactive substance users: An experimental vignette study.

Wies, B., Landers, C., & Ienca, M. (2021). Digital Mental Health for Young People: A Scoping Review of Ethical Promises and Challenges. *Frontiers in Digital Health, 3*, 697072. 10.3389/fdgth.2021.697072

Witmer, B. G., & Singer, M. J. (1998). Measuring presence in virtual environments: A presence questionnaire. *Presence: Teleoperators and Virtual Environment*, *7*(3), 225–240. 10.1162/105474698565686

World Health Organization. (2001). *The world health report: 2001 – mental health: new understanding, new hope*. Geneva: World Health Organization. https://iris.who.int/handle/10665/42390

Wykes, T., Lipshitz, J., & Schueller, S. M. (2019). Towards the design of ethical standards related to digital mental health and all its applications. *Current Treatment Options in Psychiatry*, *6*(3), 232–242. 10.1007/s40501-019-00180-0

Young Minds. (2022). Mental health waiting times harming young people. https://www.youngminds.org.uk/about-us/media-centre/press-releases/mental-health-waiting-times-harming-young-people/

Zandbagleh, A., Mirzakuchaki, S., Daliri, M. R., Premkumar, P., Carretié, L., & Sanei, S. (2022). Tensor factorization approach for ERP-based assessment of schizotypy in a novel auditory oddball task on perceived family stress. *Journal of Neural Engineering*, *19*(6), 66028. 10.1088/1741-2552/aca69f

Zhao, X., Stadnick, N. A., Ceballos-Corro, E., Castro Jr, J., Mallard-Swanson, K., Palomares, K. J., Eikey, E., Schneider, M., Zheng, K., Mukamel, D. B., Schueller, S. M., & Sorkin, D. H. (2023). Facilitators of and barriers to integrating digital mental health into county mental health services: Qualitative interview analyses. *JMIR Formative Research*, *7*, e45718. 10.2196/45718

Chapter 8

Conclusion and future directions for studying criticism and mental health

Preethi Premkumar

8.1 Overview of the book

The book explained how a close relative can be critical towards a patient with a mental disorder when they perceive the caring role as burdensome and when they try to control the patient. Such expressed emotion can increase the risk of relapse of mental disorder. The intensity with which people listen to criticism and praise in the laboratory also relates to how they experience mental distress in daily life, such as psychosis-like experiences, depression, anxiety and anger. Nonetheless, children listening to criticism from their teacher in schools learn to understand others better and put more effort into improving their academic performance. People from different cultures also express and interpret criticism differently, such as when criticism is subtle, rather than direct, and is disguised by a subsequent favourable sentiment. Furthermore, collectivistic societies, such as Thais and Indians, and even African-Americans in Western individualistic societies, perceive criticism as a sign of caring. Cultural tensions around autonomy and harmony can surface among immigrant families, and such tensions can lead to attempts to control the social situation and express criticism.

The brain centres for reward, attention, emotional regulation and experiencing social pain can also determine our responses to these social interactions. Therefore, the brain responds differently for different types of mental disorder, and according to the mood and age of the person listening to criticism. Criticism typically engages centres for sustained attention, emotional reactivity, emotional regulation and salience, and to greater and lesser extents in adults and adolescents, respectively. Family interventions seek to educate families about the nature of symptoms of mental disorder, communicating less critically, having more positive expectations about the outcome of mental disorder and managing their own welfare beyond the caring role. Family intervention is especially effective in reducing carer burden and lowering criticism. Culturally informed family intervention also addresses the acculturation of immigrant families. Lastly, digital mental health is a current avenue for engaging those who might be reluctant to seek help from mental health services.

DOI: 10.4324/9781003388159-9

Depict VR is a virtual-reality intervention that allows young people and their trusted confidante to build constructive dialogue around criticism. Early evidence suggests that clinicians value such digital technology in enhancing their therapeutic relationship with clients.

8.2 Further topics for understanding criticism

Several topics remain unexplored and could form a future edition. For instance, how criticism is expressed by families towards children at early development and how children perceive them. The role of criticism in the development of children was explored in a school setting in Chapter 3. However, parents actively use criticism to guide children throughout childhood to adolescence and the perceived criticism relates to an increase in depression over time in adolescents (Hale et al., 2011). Parents overestimate their praise of children over criticism, but actually observations indicate that parents criticise their child three times as much as praising them during play (Swenson et al., 2016). Parental criticism could be seen as a form of authoritarian parenting and a form of operant conditioning and there are parent–child interventions to address this type of communication (Carr, 2019; Peris et al., 2021; Swenson et al., 2016). Chapter 3 explained how such perceived criticism in school pupils is related to having a theory of mind. But further study could explore how to equip the child to handle such parental criticism through conflict resolution and when observing arguments between parents (Narayan et al., 2015). Maternal self-criticism can also be encountered during child rearing, and such criticism towards oneself and rumination is related to greater parenting stress and less mindful parenting, such as listening with full attention, compassion for the child and non-judgemental acceptance of parental functioning (Moreira & Canavarro, 2018).

Future study could also unpack our ability to perceive criticism in connection with certain mental abilities, such as attention, memory and problem-solving. It has been found that having poor attention and memory explains the relationship between the frequency with which criticism is encountered and having unusual thoughts in patients with schizophrenia (Kéri & Kelemen, 2009). Self-criticism is also related to the ability to evaluate the level of reward associated with an innocuous shape during a gambling task (Duek et al., 2018).

The role of spiritual beliefs and morality in expressing criticism is another untapped avenue of enquiry. Chapter 4 on culture and criticism briefly explored the expression of criticism in the Hindu scriptures. Criticism can emerge from a sense of moral authority, either within a theological context or an atheistic context, and such moral beliefs can be expressed as strong views in social interaction and be a cause of tension, although there is no evidence to support this view. On the other hand, patients with mental health problems who have religious beliefs are more likely to have a positive outlook on their mental health (Oxhandler et al., 2024). Chapter 6 explained how culturally informed therapy for schizophrenia embraces spiritual beliefs and applies mindfulness and acceptance to variation in cultural and spiritual rituals.

Lastly, a key topic for further exploration is handling criticism in the workplace and learning strategies to achieve and be successful in the workplace. This is a subject that is explored limitedly, as engaging with employees and customers harmoniously is essential for satisfaction and successful progression in the workplace. Translating the mental health outcomes of perceived criticism to the workplace can improve productivity. Criticism from people in the community of social welfare workers who were involved in relief work following an earthquake in Japan was associated with more post-traumatic stress of social welfare workers (Ueda et al., 2017). More broadly, poor communication styles explain the link between interpersonal conflict and aggression among workers in the steel industry (Singh et al., 2024). Thus, supportive communication between colleagues at different ranks can have far-reaching benefits.

References

Carr, A. (2019). Family therapy and systemic interventions for child-focused problems: The current evidence base. *Journal of Family Therapy*, *41*(2), 153–213. 10.1111/1467-6427.12226

Duek, O., Shahar, G., Osher, Y., & Kofman, O. (2018). Role of self-criticism in reward and punishment probabilistic learning. *Personality and Individual Differences*, *134*, 155–163. 10.1016/j.paid.2018.06.007

Hale, W. W., Raaijmakers, Q. A. W., van Hoof, A., & Meeus, W. H. J. (2011). The predictive capacity of perceived expressed emotion as a dynamic entity of adolescents from the general community. *Social Psychiatry and Psychiatric Epidemiology*, *46*(6), 507–515. 10.1007/s00127-010-0218-y

Kéri, S., & Kelemen, O. (2009). The role of attention and immediate memory in vulnerability to interpersonal criticism during family transactions in schizophrenia. *British Journal of Clinical Psychology*, *48*(1), 21–29. 10.1348/014466508X342926

Moreira, H., & Canavarro, M. C. (2018). The association between self-critical rumination and parenting stress: The mediating role of mindful parenting. *Journal of Child and Family Studies*, *27*(7), 2265–2275. 10.1007/s10826-018-1072-x

Narayan, A., Cicchetti, D., Rogosch, F. A., & Toth, S. L. (2015). Interrelations of maternal expressed emotion, maltreatment, and separation/divorce and links to family conflict and children's externalizing behavior. *Journal of Abnormal Child Psychology*, *43*(2), 217–228. 10.1007/s10802-014-9911-8

Oxhandler, H. K., Polson, E. C., Pearce, M., Vieten, C., & Pargament, K. I. (2024). Current mental health clients' religious/spiritual beliefs and practices: A national survey. *Social Work Research*, *48*(3), 163–175. 10.1093/swr/svae014

Peris, T. S., Thamrin, H., & Rozenman, M. S. (2021). Family intervention for child and adolescent anxiety: A meta-analytic review of therapy targets, techniques, and outcomes. *Journal of Affective Disorders*, *286*, 282–295. 10.1016/j.jad.2021.02.053

Singh, S., Rai, S., Thakur, G., & Singh, A. (2024). The communicative buffer: How organizational communication tempers the impact of interpersonal conflict on workplace Aggression. *Academy of Marketing Studies Journal*, *28*.

Swenson, S., Ho, G. W. K., Budhathoki, C., & Belcher, H., Tucker, S., & Miller, K., & Gross, D. (2016). Parents' use of praise and criticism in a sample of young children seeking mental health services. *Journal of Pediatric Health Care, 30*(1), 49–56. 10.1016/j.pedhc.2015.09.010
Ueda, I., Sakuma, A., Takahashi, Y., Shoji, W., Nagao, A., Abe, M., Suzuki, Y., Matsuoka, H., & Matsumoto, K. (2017). Criticism by community people and poor workplace communication as risk factors for the mental health of local welfare workers after the Great East Japan Earthquake: A cross-sectional study. *Plos One*, *12*(11), e0. 10.1371/journal.pone.0185930

Index

For Product Safety Concerns and Information please contact our EU
representative GPSR@taylorandfrancis.com
Taylor & Francis Verlag GmbH, Kaufingerstraße 24, 80331 München, Germany

www.ingramcontent.com/pod-product-compliance
Ingram Content Group UK Ltd.
Pitfield, Milton Keynes, MK11 3LW, UK
UKHW022359190926
475702UK00015B/2385

* 9 7 8 1 0 3 2 4 8 2 5 8 3 *